Windows 10 for Seniors and Beginners

Keith Johnson, MBA, MS Education

Senior Technical Writer, CSPO

www.techwriterguy.com

ISBN-13: 978-1532844454

ISBN-10: 153284445X

Table of Contents

About "Windows 10 for Seniors and Beginners" 6
The Windows Saga: Windows 1 to Windows 10 7
Section 01: Windows 10 Welcomes You 13
Section 02: Windows 10 Best New Features 14
Section 03: Windows 10 Editions Released by Microsoft 16
Section 04: Windows 10 Installation & Activation 17
Section 05: Windows 10 Logging On Steps 22
Section 06: Windows 10 User Interface 25
Section 07: Windows 10 User Navigation 30
Section 08: Windows 10 "Cortana" 36
Section 09: Windows 10 File Search 43
Section 10: Windows 10 "Edge" Web Browser 45
Section 11: Windows 10 Skype App 49
Section 12: Windows 10 Entertainment & OneDrive 50
Section 13: Windows 10 Accessing Apps 54
Section 14: Windows 10 Accessories 60
Section 15: Windows 10 Administration 80
Section 16: Windows 10 Ease of Access 96
Section 17: Windows 10 Powershell 101
Section 18: Windows 10 System Apps 103
Section 19: Windows 10 Total Apps – Listing 136
Section 20: Windows 10 Settings – Overview 146
Section 21: Windows 10 Settings for System – Overview 147
Section 22: Windows 10 System Display 148
Section 23: Windows 10 System Notification 149
Section 24: Windows 10 System Apps and Features 150
Section 25: Windows 10 System Multitasking 152

Section 26: Windows 10 System Tablet Mode 153
Section 27: Windows 10 System Battery Saver 154
Section 28: Windows 10 Power and Sleep 155
Section 29: Windows 10 Storage 156
Section 30: Windows 10 Offline Maps 157
Section 31: Windows 10 Default Apps 158
Section 32: Windows 10 "About" 159
Section 33: Windows 10 Settings for Devices – Overview 160
Section 34: Windows 10 Settings for Printing/Scanning 161
Section 35: Windows 10 Settings for Connected Devices 163
Section 36: Windows 10 Settings for Bluetooth 164
Section 37: Windows 10 Settings for Mouse/Touchpad 165
Section 38: Windows 10 Settings for Typing 166
Section 39: Windows 10 Settings for Autoplay 167
Section 40: Windows 10 Settings for Network and Internet 168
Section 41: Windows 10 Settings for WiFi (Sense) 169
Section 42: Windows 10 Settings for Airplane Mode 171
Section 43: Windows 10 Settings for Data Usage 172
Section 44: Windows 10 Settings for VPN 173
Section 45: Windows 10 Settings for Dialup 174
Section 46: Windows 10 Settings for Ethernet 175
Section 47: Windows 10 Settings for Proxy 176
Section 48: Windows 10 Settings for Personalization – Overview 177
Section 49: Windows 10 Settings for Background 178
Section 50: Windows 10 Settings for Colors 180
Section 51: Windows 10 Settings for Lock Screen 181
Section 52: Windows 10 Settings for Themes 182
Section 53: Windows 10 Settings for Start 183
Section 54: Windows 10 Settings for Accounts – Overview 184

Section 55: Windows 10 Settings for Your Account 185

Section 56: Windows 10 Settings for Sign-In Options 186

Section 57: Windows 10 Settings for Work Access 187

Section 58: Windows 10 Settings for Family 188

Section 59: Windows 10 Settings to Sync Devices 189

Section 60: Windows 10 Settings for Time/Language – Overview 190

Section 61: Windows 10 Settings for Date/Time 191

Section 62: Windows 10 Settings for Region/Language 192

Section 63: Windows 10 Settings for Speech 193

Section 64: Windows 10 Settings for Ease of Access 194

Section 65: Windows 10 Settings for Narrator 195

Section 66: Windows 10 Settings for Magnifier 196

Section 67: Windows 10 Settings for High Contrast 197

Section 68: Windows 10 Settings for Closed Captions 198

Section 69: Windows 10 Settings for Keyboard 200

Section 70: Windows 10 Settings for Mouse 201

Section 71: Windows 10 Settings for Other Devices 202

Section 72: Windows 10 Settings for Privacy 203

Section 73: Windows 10 Settings for General Privacy 204

Section 74: Windows 10 Settings for Location 205

Section 75: Windows 10 Settings for Camera 206

Section 76: Windows 10 Settings for Microphone 207

Section 77: Windows 10 Settings for Speech/Inking/Typing 208

Section 78: Windows 10 Settings for Account Information 209

Section 79: Windows 10 Settings for Contacts 210

Section 80: Windows 10 Settings for Calendar 211

Section 81: Windows 10 Settings for Messaging 212

Section 82: Windows 10 Settings for Radios 213

Section 83: Windows 10 Settings for Other Devices 214

Section 84: Windows 10 Settings for Feedback & Diagnostics 215
Section 85: Windows 10 Settings for Background Apps 216
Section 86: Windows 10 Settings for Updates/Security 217
Section 87: Windows 10 Settings for Windows Update 218
Section 88: Windows 10 Settings for Windows Defender 222
Section 89: Windows 10 Settings for Computer Backup 229
Section 90: Windows 10 Settings for Recovery 231
Section 91: Windows 10 Settings for License Activation 232
Section 92: Windows 10 Action Center 233
Section 93: Thank You for Reading 235
Section 94: References (by Section) 236

About "Windows 10 for Seniors and Beginners"

Welcome to "**Windows 10 for Seniors and Beginners**"! I am grateful for your time and sincerely hope you enjoy this book. This book has been written, essentially, for all Windows 10 users, with the exception of System Administrators and Windows Developers. This is not an advanced book that dives into sophisticated configuration concepts. Rather, this book presents a very generous cross-sectional analysis of navigational tools, apps, and features that 99% of Windows 10 users will eventually use. So, whether you are a student, a working professional, a teacher, a retiree, a veteran, a government employee, a white collar worker, a blue collar worker, a business executive, a sales professional, or a single parent with a small business, then this book is for you. I have done my best to keep this book as cheap as possible given the constraints of the self-publishing platform I have used. To keep it under 250 pages, I have had to focus on the most *important aspects* of Windows 10. After I finish the paperback version, I will get to work immediately on the ePub version for those of you who prefer eBooks. This book features four major sections: *Installation and Access, Navigation, Apps, and Settings*.

Happy Reading and Best Regards, Keith Johnson, Author

Disclaimer

Microsoft ® Windows 10 is a registered trademark, brand name, system platform name, and product name of Microsoft ® Corporation.

This book comes with absolutely no warranties or guarantees of any kind. This book is neither personal nor professional advice in any way. This book is exclusively for reading enjoyment only. By reading ahead, you therefore accept the reading terms of this book.

The author is not affiliated with Microsoft ® Corporation in any way. If you have any questions about Microsoft ® Windows 10, the author encourages you to contact the official Microsoft ® Windows 10 Help Website and direct your questions to its Technical Support Department. Caveat Emptor (buyer beware); Caveat Lector (reader beware). Thank you.

The Windows Saga: Windows 1 to Windows 10

Since its first release in 1985 as a simple graphical shell for Microsoft's Disk Operating System (DOS), Windows has come a long way. The following table shows how Windows has evolved over the past thirty-one years.

Windows 1 (1985) – was released as a 16 bit multi-tasking shell for MS-DOS (the underlying Microsoft "prompt" or "command driven" OS at the time). Windows 1 was used to create IBM OS/2.	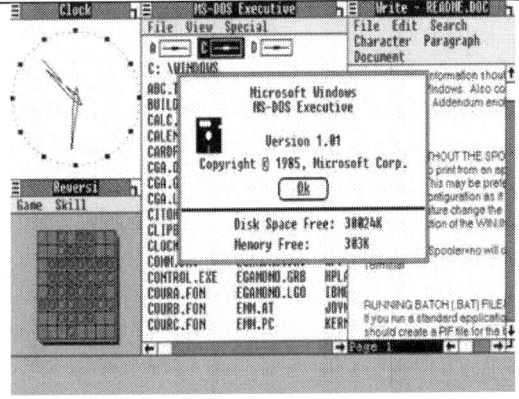
Windows 2 (1987) – this version enabled windows to overlap as opposed to be shown in tile format only. Here, 16 color VGA graphics were introduced.	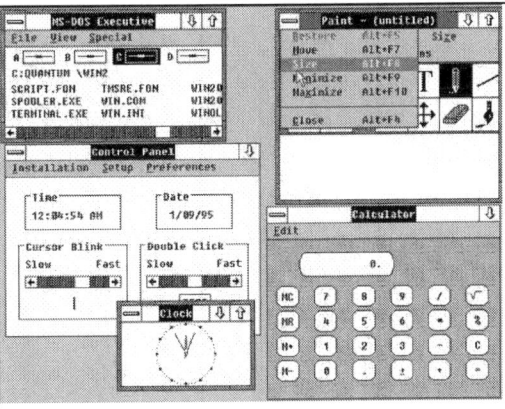
Windows 3 (1990) – was released to rival the Apple Macintosh computer. Windows 3 featured better memory management and DOS commands could be run within a specific DOS window.	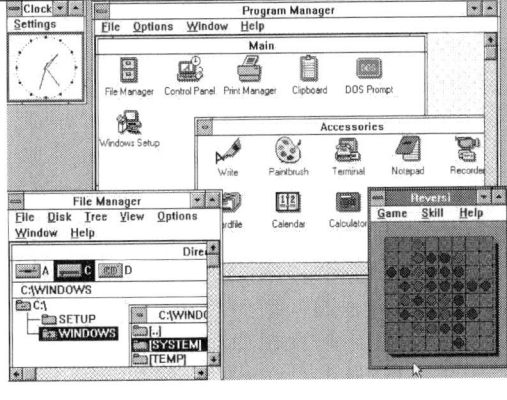

<u>Windows for Workgroups 3.1</u> (1992) – this was an extended version of Windows 3.1 but now with support for Local Area Networks (LANs). Also, this version of Windows supported, for the first time, a Winsock program enabling TCP/IP communications.	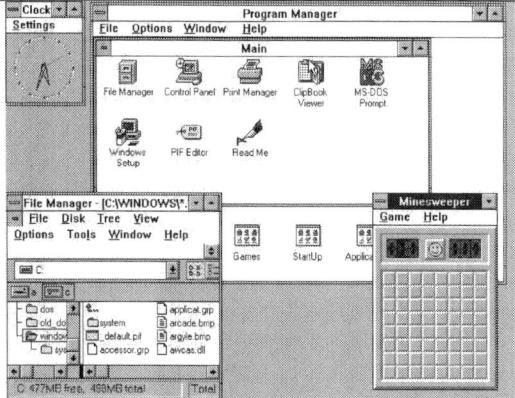
<u>Windows NT 3.5</u> (1994) – this was the second release of Windows NT, codename Daytona, because Microsoft created unique versions - one for the client machine and one for the server machine.	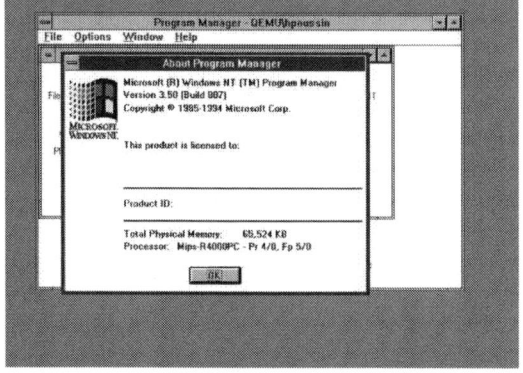
<u>Windows 95</u> (1995) – this was released as a major Windows improvement for all Windows users. For the first time, Windows was no longer a DOS shell. Rather, Windows and DOS became one OS. Also, 16 bit architecture was expanded to include 32 bit architecture and a better overall GUI experience.	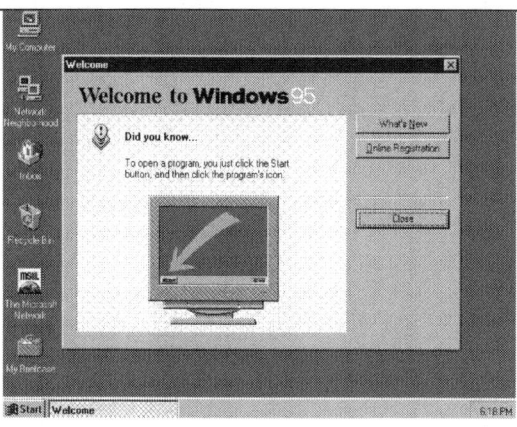

Windows 98 (1998) – this was a second major release of Windows 9.x – this is when Microsoft started to include Internet Explorer (IE) as part of the OS – and this led to the infamous dogfight with Netscape (Navigator) over the emerging Internet market and issues of antitrust.	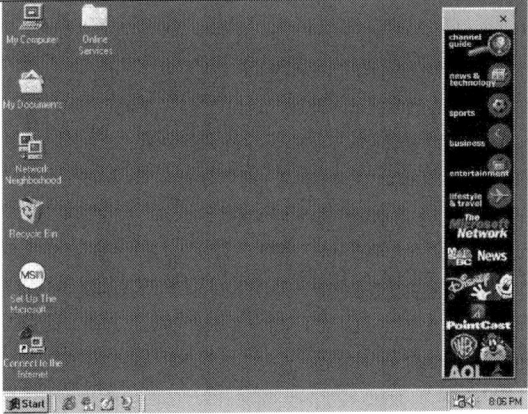
Windows 2000 – this was a true 32 bit system and this OS could serve on both client and server machines. 2000 featured an encrypted file system as well as dynamic data storage.	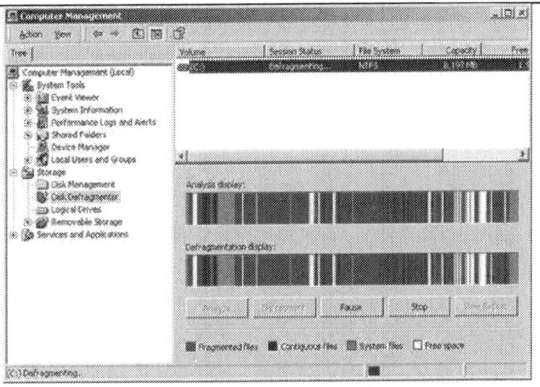
Windows ME (2000) – this release was a revision of Windows 98 and featured Windows Movie Maker, Windows Media Player 7, and Internet Explorer 5.5. This was the last release of Windows version 9.x.	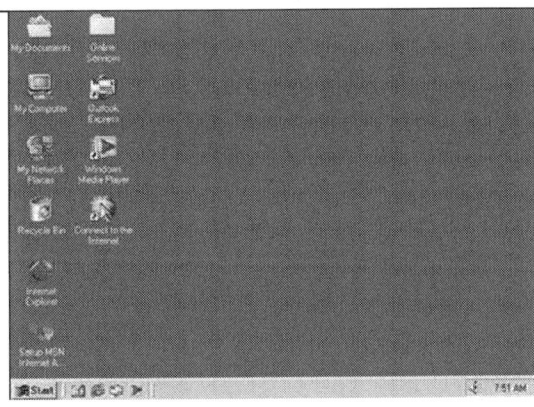

Windows XP (2001) – this Windows release was based on the Windows NT kernel and it is with XP that Microsoft really started to enforce legitimate use via online product activation. XP was a great release in terms of OS security and stability.	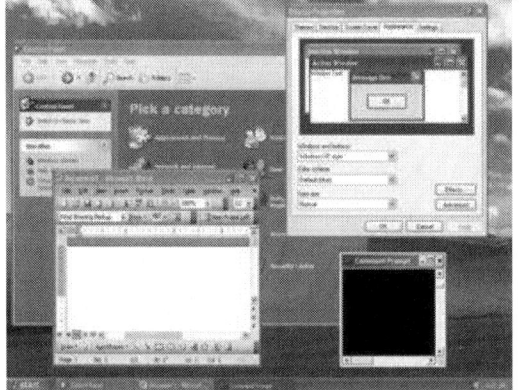
Windows Server 2003 – this release was an upgrade from Windows Server 2000 plus some features of XP. Internet Information Services (IIS) had its debut with WS 2003.	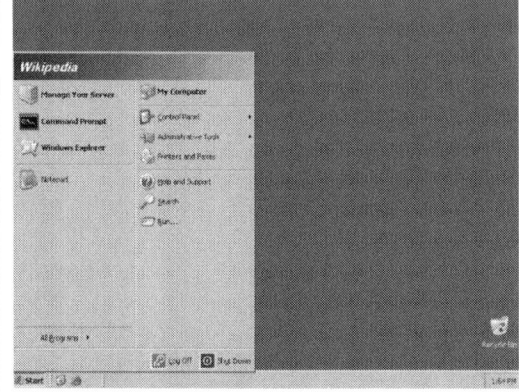
Windows Vista (2006) – this release was designed for not just corporate computers but also home computers. Vista was highly criticized because it featured restrictive licensing terms and new DRM (digital rights management) technologies.	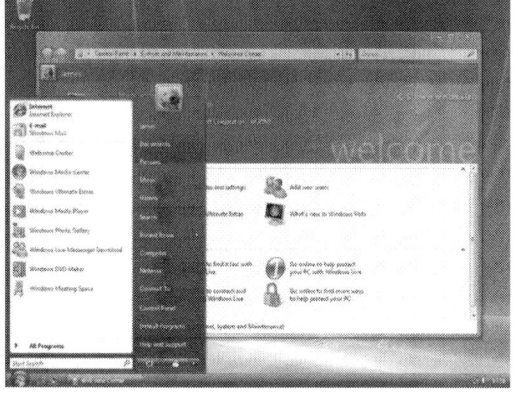

Windows Server 2008 – this release was a follow-up to Windows Server 2003 and featured cutting-edge diagnostics, monitoring, logging, and reporting tools.	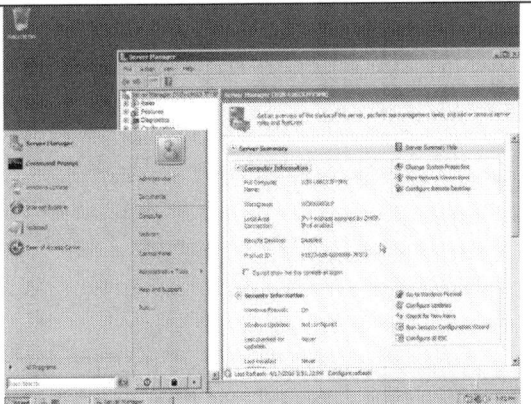
Windows 7 (2009) – among the top features of this new Windows OS release were Windows Power Shell, Windows Media Center, Control Panel, Windows Security Center, Windows Photo Viewer, Handwriting recognition, better Taskbar and better Start Menu.	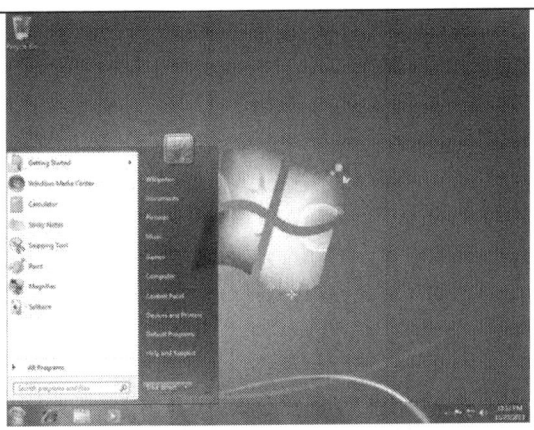
Windows Server 2012 – this was the sixth release of Windows server. New features included IP address management, improved Task Manager, and a new File System.	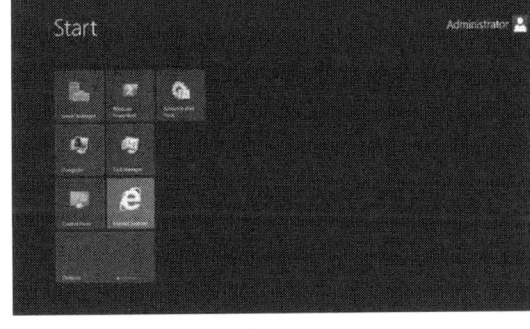

Windows 8 (2012) – Microsoft anticipated a massive shift to tablets and therefore changed the Home Screen on Windows 8 to tiles. This was called a "metro" design.	
Windows 10 (2015) – this release re-implemented the Start Menu and incorporated tiles as a part of the Start Menu. There are many amazing features in Windows 10 – keep on reading this book and you will learn about just how dynamic this Windows OS really is.	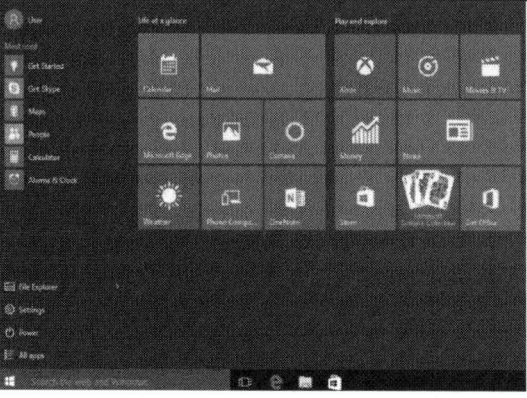

Section 01: Windows 10 Welcomes You

Make sure you have a Microsoft Account.

About nine months ago, Microsoft released, officially, its latest Operating System (OS) called Windows 10. This is the next major release after Windows 8. Before you do anything, you need to make sure you have a basic Microsoft Account. This essentially means you need to have either a Hotmail or Outlook e-mail account. Hotmail is now being integrated into the Microsoft Outlook e-mail portal, but either way is fine. What matters is that Microsoft knows who you are before you upgrade or install Windows 10. If you already have a Microsoft Account and hence e-mail, well, then, you are all set. If not, then you can accomplish this through either one of these two major Microsoft e-mail portals…

http://www.hotmail.com

http://www.outlook.com

Click on the "Sign up now" link (as shown below) and this will prompt you with a screen that says "Create an account". Complete the fields that are required and then at the bottom click on the large blue button that says "Create account". You will then need to log into your new Microsoft e-mail account and open the e-mail Microsoft has sent you and click on the confirmation link. At this point, you should be all set and ready to go as a legitimate Microsoft user.

Section 02: Windows 10 Best New Features

Get ready to work with a great Operating System (OS)!

I am really excited about Windows 10. For the first time since Windows 7, in my humble professional opinion, Microsoft has succeeded in improving many critical aspects of its Windows Operating System (OS) that users have discussed intensely since Windows 8 was released in 2012. Windows 10 now features many tremendous OS capabilities and resources. However, due to the limited time I have to write, publish, and release this book, I am going to try to focus on the very best features so that you, the reader and Windows 10 user, can also optimize your time and user experience. The following new features in Windows 10 are reason enough to upgrade your Windows OS (to Windows 10). I will be discussing each one of these features in more detail in the following chapters of this book.

New Feature	Description
	Fast, Comprehensive and Versatile *Start Menu*
	Microsoft SkyDrive is now *Microsoft OneDrive*
	Groove Music – awesome media streaming
	Wi-Fi Sense keeps you well-connected to the web
	New *Microsoft Edge* web browser … this rocks!
	Settings that keep your machine optimized
	Hello – secure biometric login to Windows 10
	Cortana – your new Personal Digital Assistant
	Windows Explorer is now *File Explorer*

Section 03: Windows 10 Editions Released by Microsoft

There are two major editions of the Windows 10 Operating System that were released on July 29, 2015 for the general public – Home and Pro.

Microsoft has also released Windows 10 Education (for *schools* to be managed via a System Administrator) and Windows 10 Enterprise (for *businesses* to be managed via a System Administrator).

This book features Windows Home since all the features of Windows Home are found on all other versions of Windows 10.

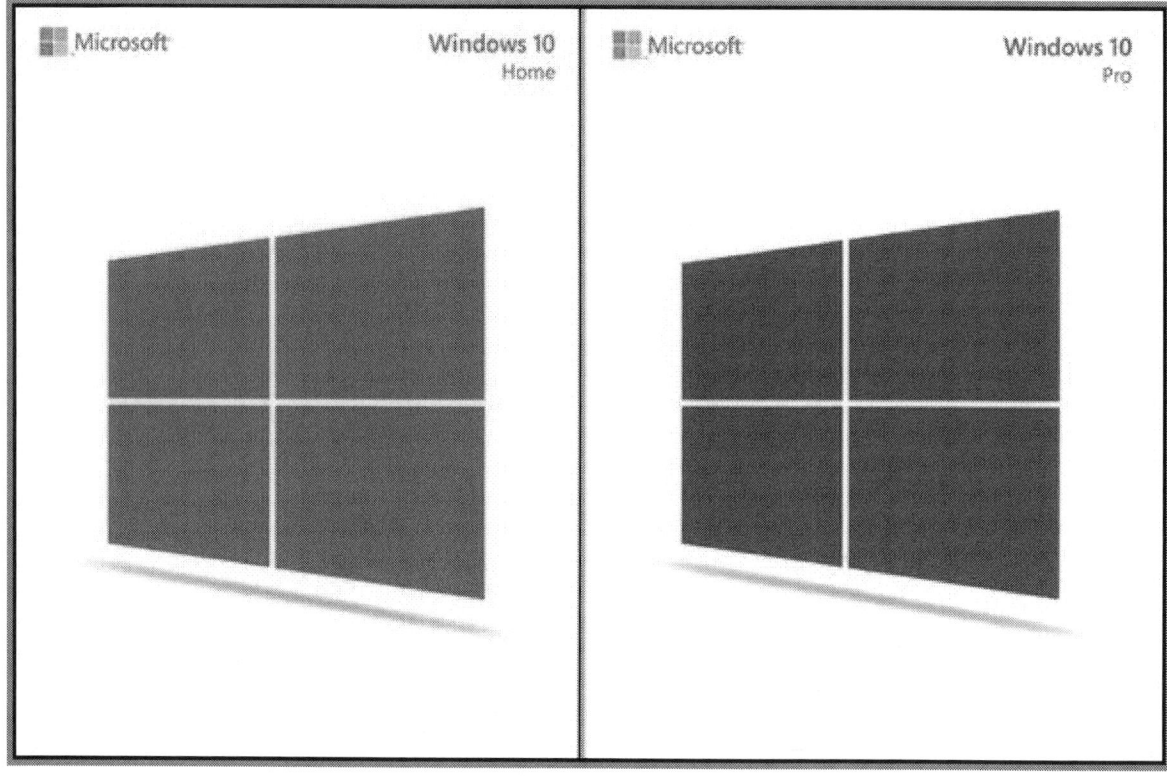

Section 04: Windows 10 Installation & Activation

Verify your computer's hardware configuration.

Before you *either* upgrade to Windows 10 from Windows 7 or Windows 8 *or* perform a clean install of Windows 10 onto your computer, make sure that your hardware meets the following basic requirements.

CPU (Central Processing Unit):

1 gigahertz (GHz) or faster processor or SoC (System on a Chip)

RAM (Random Access Memory):

1 gigabyte (GB) for 32-bit or 2 GB for 64-bit

Hard Disk (Space):

16 GB for 32-bit OS 20 GB for 64-bit OS

Graphics (Card):

DirectX 9 or later with WDDM 1.0 driver

Display (Monitor):

800x600

There are FIVE ways to get Windows 10:

1. Purchase a computer with Windows 10 preloaded and preinstalled.

2. Upgrade directly from Windows 7 or 8 to Windows 10 through updates.

3. Upgrade from Windows XP or Vista to Windows 7 then to Windows 10.

4. Clean install of Windows 10 from a CD/DVD.

5. Clean install of Windows 10 from a Windows Insider ISO file.

PATH #1: Purchasing a computer with Windows 10 preinstalled is easy.

The only caveat (warning) I would offer here is to make sure that the hardware requirements for Windows 10 on the preceding page are all met by the computer you are getting. Remember to check the CPU, RAM, Hard Disk Capacity, Graphics Card, and finally your display – for not only laptops but also desktops, tablets and Surface Pros. Also, make sure that when you get the computer, the vendor has not already registered Windows 10! That is for you to do as the rightful owner of the computer. You can first check on this through the manufacturer's website – you can actually locate the product ID code and verify that it HAS Windows 10 but that the installed copy is not yet registered. At that point, you are good to go. What is the best hardware/ machinery for Windows 10? I have a Dell Inspiron laptop but there are many great computers out there ranging from Acer to Lenovo to Toshiba, brand-wise. Here is an article from a website I trust called CNET that always gives accurate and timely computer hardware advice. However, feel free to read whatever tech articles you trust like those from PC Magazine and PC World both are awesome too.

http://www.cnet.com/news/the-best-pcs-for-windows-10/

Microsoft of course is pushing its Surface Pro, and from what I have seen and heard it is a great computer/tablet for Windows 10.

PATH #2: Upgrading directly from Windows 7 or 8 to Windows 10 is easy. Follow Microsoft Update instructions to upgrade to Windows 10 successfully.

Upgrading to Windows 10 (from Windows 7 and/or Windows 8) is easy. Microsoft will prompt you with a message (like this one) recommending that you upgrade to Windows 10.

If you choose "GET YOUR FREE UPGRADE", then Microsoft will walk you through each and every step of the process. This will involve the machine being turned on and off several times during the process. Make sure you have a dependable Internet connection and that you first back up any important data files and/or application files. This way, you eliminate the possibility of losing important data should something not go well. If you click on the "Learn more" link, then you will get this web browser information (or something similar ...

Click "Upgrade now" if you want to upgrade to Windows 10 or if you need a computer already with Windows 10 preinstalled, then click "Shop now" to see what is available through this link. Both of these are *optional* – you can of course decline both invitations by simply closing down your browser.

Install Windows 10 before using OneDrive and/or Office 365.

Microsoft is going to "push" two resources during the installation/upgrade experience of Windows 10. First, it is going to ask you to start using "OneDrive" which is essentially a cloud-service where files can be stored centrally so you can access them from different devices. Also, Microsoft is going to "push" Office 365 – which is essentially Microsoft Office as a Cloud-Based Service (also called SaaS –

Software as a Service). I did not choose either of these in my installation/upgrade process. I chose to assess my storage and productivity needs first. At a future date, however, I will surely use OneDrive for data storage and Office 365 for my business productivity needs.

You can directly request the specific Microsoft Windows Update that prompts you to update to Windows 10.

From Windows 7 and Windows 8, you should not have to seek out Windows 10 as an upgrade. Microsoft should be sending you an OS update (e.g. Windows Update) that invites you to upgrade. However, if for some reason you do not get this invitation, here is the web page to request a Windows 10 upgrade directly from Microsoft.

http://goo.gl/3BZupc

PATH #3: If you have an older version of Windows like XP or Vista, I recommend that you first upgrade to Windows 7.

There are many super cheap (or even free if you look hard enough) Windows 7 CDs/DVDs out there. Once you gotten hold of your Windows 7 CD/DVD, then make sure that your *hardware* meets the specs outlined at the beginning of this section. When all lights are green hardware-wise, do a clean install of Windows 7 onto the computer and from there you can upgrade to Windows 10. If you are not prompted with an invite from Microsoft to update to Windows 10, here is the URL for the Microsoft webpage where you can directly request Windows 10.

http://goo.gl/3BZupc

PATH #4: Installing Windows 10 from a CD/DVD.

There are times where you are going to have problems with Windows updates or with the Windows Insider program (which I discuss next). So, in these cases, to save time and grief, just go out and get the CD/DVD for Windows 10. It has on the box the key you will need to register the Operating System and it should take you just minutes to install as opposed to several hours because you are not doing this over the web but locally on your machine through your CD/DVD drive.

PATH #5: For those of you who want to do a clean install of the latest and greatest Windows 10 that might be considered a beta release (e.g. still in testing), you are going to have to join the Windows Insider program.

Here is the URL for Windows Insider. https://insider.windows.com/

Please note that this tip/path is for super geeks and super nerds only...

In order to join Windows Insider, you will need a Microsoft account.

Once this is done, you can choose the version of Windows 10 you want. Be prepared to mount the Windows 10 ISO image. There are many high-quality programs out there that work with ISOs. However, if you are tight on cash and need to look to a free open-source alternative, I personally recommend "WINCDEMU".

http://wincdemu.sysprogs.org/

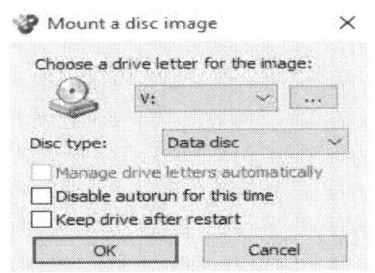

Follow the steps that Windows Insider puts you through ... exactly.

Then, you will have, in the end, the ISO image file needed to install Windows 10 as a full OS onto your machine. After Windows 10 is working fully, Microsoft will e-mail you the key you need to register your copy of Windows 10. You can also get it sent to you via text message. Just follow the instructions Microsoft sends you as part of the Insider program.

Section 05: Windows 10 Logging On Steps

Customize your login process to Windows 10 in the Settings section.

I will be covering most Settings topic later in this book, but for right now, we need to go to the Settings section to setup a login process that is right for you.

Go to Start Menu > Settings > Accounts and you will see your options.

They are: Your Account, Sign-In Options, Work Access, Family and Other Users, and Sync Your Settings. For right now, let us only worry about Sign-in options.

You can establish and update your Password here.

Click on the Change button in the Password section. A pop-up window called Change Your Microsoft Account Password displays. Enter the old password once and new password twice.

Click Next. You will then see a message saying "You've successfully changed your password! Please lock your machine then use your new password to get back in. (We find that using your password right away helps you remember it later). Click Finish. Congrats – your password is now updated.

You can change your PIN which grants you device access.

Click on the Change button in the PIN section and in the same way Password prompts you through the change process, so will the PIN update process.

You can setup, change, and/or remove a Picture Password.

In this option, you select an image, draw three easy designs like a circle or line or square on the image, and then Windows authenticates this image as your profile base. When you access your machine, the image will show up and from there the options you are allowed per your previous setups will be there. For me, I have set up both PIN and password access. Hence, those two options show below the image I have selected.

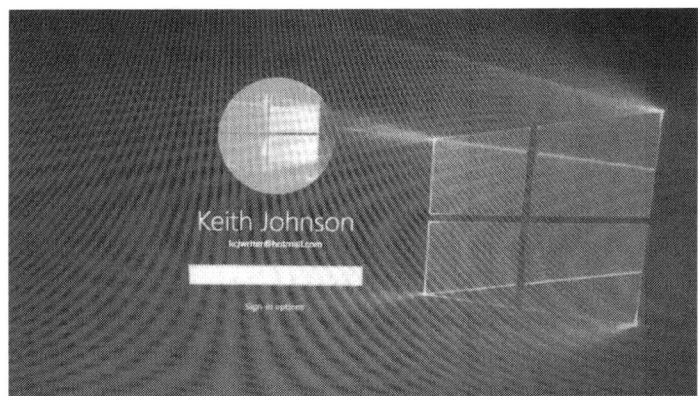

Secure Access to your Computer with Windows Hello has finally arrived.

This is a very new option for Windows 10. You will need a computer that comes with technology *that is ready to work with Windows 10*. There are specific *microphones* that enable you to setup audio-only access to your machine. There are *cameras* that enable you to setup retina-scan only access to your machine.

Several great tech blogs on the web reveal that this new technology is 999% accurate meaning that there is only a one in one-thousand chance for error from Microsoft's side. In other words, the technology is awesome.

So, this prevents others from accessing your machine without your permission; Hello will be explained in greater detail in the Settings section of this manual.

There are two other login setup processes in Settings > Accounts > Sign-In Options. They are Require Sign-In and Related Settings.

Require Sign-In asks you the following question: "If you have been away, when should Windows require you to sign in again?" There is a drop-down menu and you must choose from the options there. As for the Related Settings option, the only one that is shown on my screen here is Lock Screen. If you click on this, then you can setup Preview, App(s) to show detailed Status, App(s) to show quick status, Screen timeout settings, and finally screen saver settings.

Preview

Background

Windows spotlight

Choose an app to show detailed status

Choose apps to show quick status

Screen timeout settings

Screen saver settings

Section 06: Windows 10 User Interface

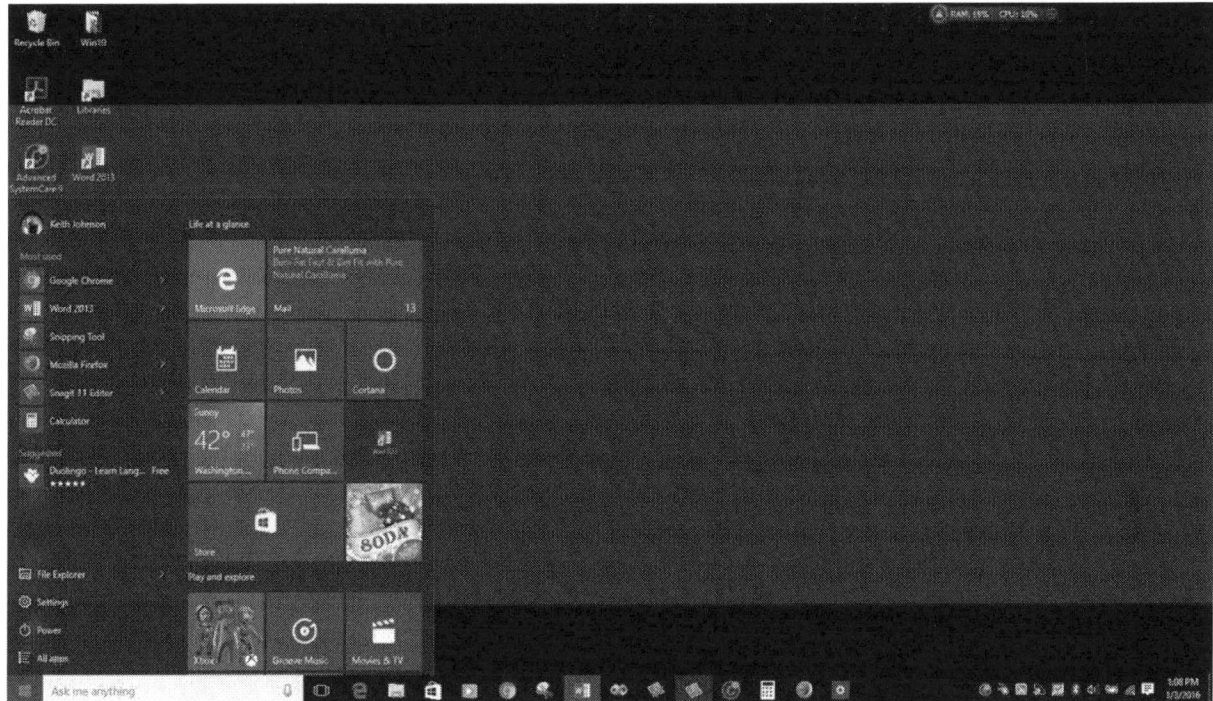

This book focuses on Windows 10 Home for personal computers.

This book is about Windows 10 as your Operating System (OS) for personal computers (desktops, laptops, etc.). Even though Windows 10 runs the Windows phone, Xbox and tablets, that is not the focus of this particular book. In any case, the name of the technology that enables for Windows 10 to span all possible Windows devices is "continuum". You can read more about Continuum at this Microsoft web page, if interested in learning more.

http://www.windowscentral.com/continuum

Note: Windows 10 for personal computers can be managed and driven by both keyboard and mouse commands. From your mousepad or USB-connected mouse, remember that when I say "click" that means clicking the left mouse button, unless otherwise instructed. Usually right-button clicks on the mouse are done to open pop-up menus that provide you with navigational and operational options and choices.

The following Windows 10 keyboard *shortcuts* enable you to *bypass* many frequent mouse-driven commands.

What You Must Press	What This Accomplishes
Popular Keyboard Shortcuts	
Ctrl+C (or Ctrl+Insert)	Copies the selected item
Ctrl+X	Cuts the selected item
Ctrl+V (or Shift+Insert)	Pastes the selected item
Ctrl+Z	Undoes an action
Alt+Tab	Switches between open apps
Alt+F4	Closes active item or exits active app
New W10 Keyboard Shortcuts	
Windows key ⊞+L	Locks your PC or switch accounts
Windows key ⊞+D	Displays and hide the desktop
Windows key ⊞+A	Opens Action center
Windows key ⊞+S	Opens Search
Windows key ⊞+C	Opens Cortana in listening mode
Windows key ⊞+Tab	Opens Task view
Windows key ⊞+Ctrl+D	Adds a Virtual Desktop
Windows key ⊞+Ctrl+Rt arrow	Switches between virtual desktops you've created on the right
Windows key ⊞+Ctrl+Lft arrow	Switches between virtual desktops you've created on the left
Windows key ⊞+Ctrl+F4	Closes the virtual desktop you're using
General Keyboard Shortcuts	
F2	Renames the selected item
F3	Searches for a file or folder in File Explorer
F4	Displays the address bar list in File Explorer
F5	Refreshes the active window
F6	Cycles through screen elements in a window or on the desktop
F10	Activates the Menu bar in the active app
Alt+Esc	Cycles through items in the order in which they were opened

What You Must Press (cont'd)	What This Accomplishes (cont'd)
Alt+Enter	Displays properties for the selected item
Alt+Spacebar	Opens the shortcut menu for the active window
Alt+Left arrow	Goes back
Alt+Right arrow	Goes forward
Alt+Page Up	Moves up one screen
Alt+Page Down	Moves down one screen
Alt+Tab	Switches between open apps
Ctrl+F4	Closes the active document (in apps that are full-screen and allow you to have multiple documents open simultaneously)
Ctrl+A	Selects all items in a doc or window
Ctrl+D (or Delete)	Deletes selected item and moves it to the Recycle Bin
Ctrl+R (or F5)	Refreshes the active window
Ctrl+Y	Redoes an action
Ctrl+Right arrow	Moves the cursor to the beginning of the next word
Ctrl+Left arrow	Moves the cursor to the beginning of the previous word
Ctrl+Down arrow	Moves the cursor to the beginning of the next paragraph
Ctrl+Up arrow	Moves the cursor to the beginning of the previous paragraph
Ctrl+Alt+Tab	Uses the arrow keys to switch between all open apps
Ctrl+arrow key (to move to an item)+Spacebar	Selects multiple individual items in a window or on the desktop
Ctrl+Shift with an arrow key	Select a block of text
Ctrl+Esc	Opens the Start Menu
Ctrl+Shift+Esc	Opens the Task Manager
Ctrl+Shift	Switches the keyboard layout when multiple keyboard layouts are available
Ctrl+Spacebar	Turns the Chinese input method editor (IME) on or off
Shift+F10	Displays the shortcut menu for the selected item

What You Must Press (cont'd)	What This Accomplishes (cont'd)
Shift+Delete	Deletes the selected item without moving it to the Recycle Bin first
Right arrow	Opens the next menu to the right, or open a submenu
Left arrow	Opens the next menu to the left, or close a submenu
Esc	Stops or leave the current task

The following Microsoft Windows Keyboard Shortcuts Help Page will help you to learn and master additional keyboard shortcuts according to how you want to approach the keyboard during your Windows 10 experience.

http://windows.microsoft.com/en-us/windows-10/keyboard-shortcuts

* Windows Logo Keyboard Shortcuts
* Command Prompt Keyboard Shortcuts
* Dialog Box Keyboard Shortcuts
* File Explorer Keyboard Shortcuts
* Virtual Desktop Keyboard Shortcuts
* Taskbar Keyboard Shortcuts
* Settings Keyboard Shortcuts
* Ease of Access Keyboard Shortcuts
* Magnifier Keyboard Shortcuts
* Narrator Keyboard Shortcuts
* Narrator Touch Keyboard Shortcuts
* Keyboard Shortcuts for Apps

As a Technical Writer, I prefer to navigate via the mouse over the keyboard, usually, but do appreciate easy-to-remember keyboard shortcuts.

I have created this section for those of you who are keyboard shortcut "aficionados". However, I do recommend these commands as a backup set of commands should your mouse or touchpad fail. Unless you are absolutely sure about the keyboard shortcut command, there is a chance you could user the wrong keys and therefore give Windows 10 a wrong command/instruction. So, sure, use these shortcuts, but be mindful of what you are doing so that you do not derail yourself from whatever it is you are trying to accomplish.

As a former IT Instructor and Software Developer, I recommend that you exercise caution regarding "Command Prompt" keyboard shortcuts.

Unless you really know your MS-DOS commands well, I advise you *not* to approach system tasks through this venue. Stick with the well-tested Windows 10 keyboard shortcuts. I will be explaining Powershell, Command Line, and Run options in this book that are available via Windows 10. However, you really need to know your commands in order to work with them successfully.

Keyboard Privacy: The default setting for Microsoft Windows 10 is to allow your user data to be reported back to Microsoft. So, to disable this (e.g. disable the "logger" which records your keyboard activity), go to Settings > Privacy > General. You will see the option of "Send Microsoft info about how I write to help us improve typing in the future" Turn this OFF. Also, go to Settings > Privacy > Speech > click on the STOP GETTING TO KNOW ME button. Between these two options, you are effectively disabling the key logger from both audio and text input and keeping your privacy as you work with Windows 10.

Section 07: Windows 10 User Navigation

Accessing the Windows 10 Start Menu is easy.

Microsoft has taken the very best from its Windows 7 Start Menu and made it even better now for Windows 10. Click on the Start Menu icon ⊞ at the lower left-hand corner of your screen or select Control-Esc on your keyboard to access and open your Start Menu on your Home Screen.

It is easy to select a program or featured tile.

Not only does the Start Menu give you a vertical listing of all major programs on your machine, but it also features *tiles* that were the original home screen of Windows 8. Microsoft has kept this functionality, but now it is a supporting feature of the Start Menu as opposed to the entire screen.

To show absolutely everything on your machine, click on "All apps".

The Start Menu will refresh and show a complete alphanumerical listing of each and every "app" (application) Windows 10 can locate on your machine.

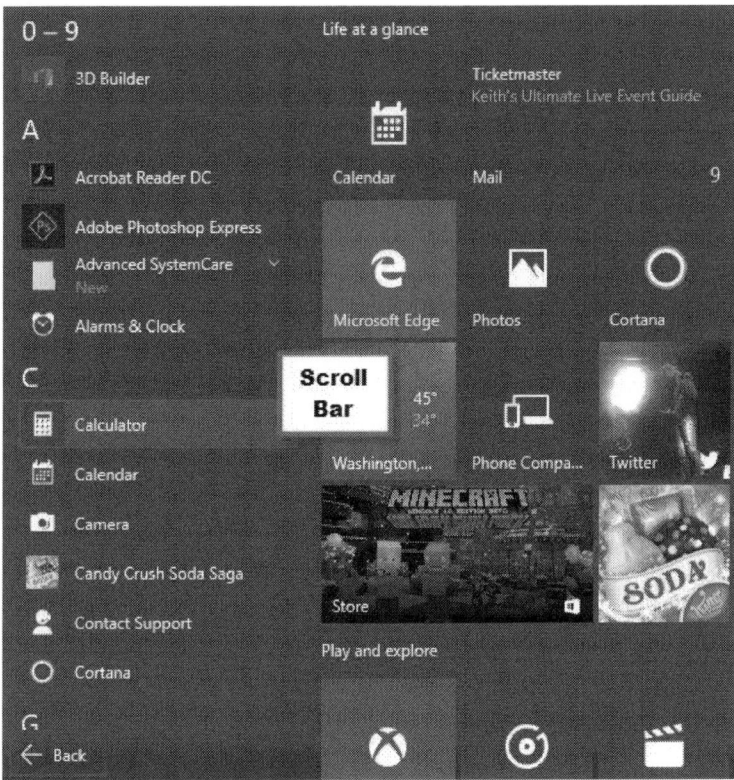

To add a program to the Start Menu, if it has not already been added via its installation program, then all you need to do is right click on the program icon and select "Pin to Start" from the pop-up menu.

The next time you access the Start Menu, the program will be shown in the new listing.

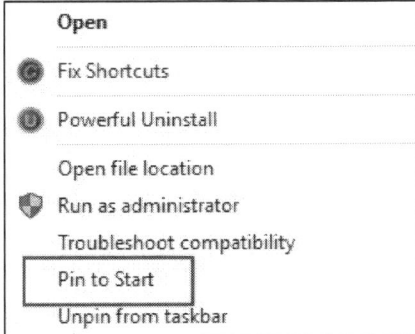

To pin a program to the Taskbar that is already listed in the Start Menu, then right click over the program icon and in the pop-up menu, select "Pin to Taskbar".

The program will then also be shown at the bottom of your screen in the Taskbar, in addition to its current listing in the Start Menu. Here is what a typical Taskbar in Windows 10 looks like...

Windows 10 also features Tiles as part of the Start Menu. Tiles are shown to the right of the vertical apps listing and you can easily drag and drop tiles as you wish to re-structure their appearance.

In the example below, I have selected the Calendar tile, held the mouse's left-button down, and moved the mouse down on my mousepad ... bringing this tile under the Microsoft Edge tile. Notice how they switch places on the screen. Windows 10 automatically moves the Microsoft Edge tile above Calendar. I can now release the left button on my mouse. There...all set now.

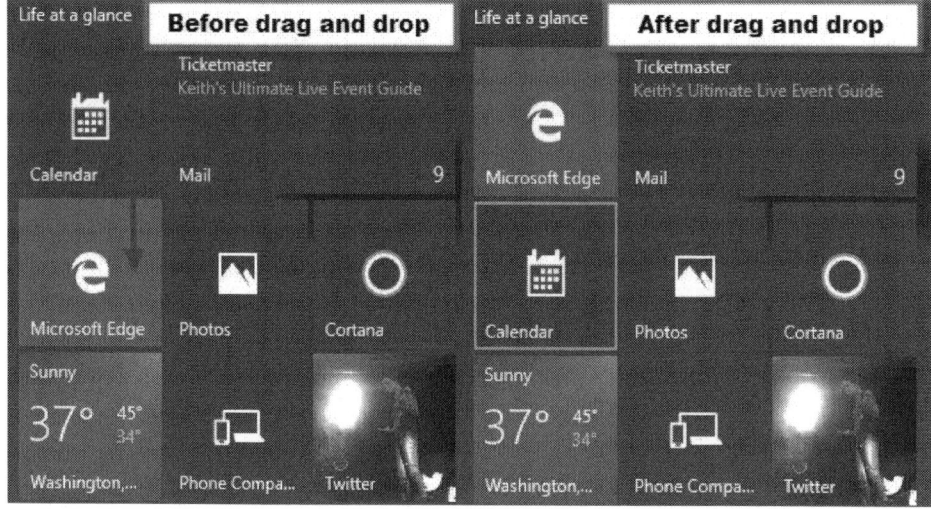

You can resize a tile by first right-clicking on it.

Then, in the pop-up menu, select the size you want for the tile – small, medium, wide or large.

You can remove a specific tile from the Start Menu by first right-clicking on it.

Then, in the pop-up menu, select "Unpin from Start".

You can disable a tile quickly and easily.

All you have to do is right click on the specific tile you want disabled. Then, in the pop-up menu, select "Turn live tile off". Now, the tile is shown but its hyperlink does not work. So, if this is a program, it will not run and if this is a webpage you cannot get to it. To reverse this process, follow the very same steps and then select (in the pop-up menu) "Turn live tile on". The active link is now restored.

You can easily pin a tile (e.g. program or hyperlink) to the Taskbar.

Right click on the tile and when the pop-up menu is displayed, select "Pin to Taskbar". If the program is already on the Taskbar, then you can also reverse this by selecting "Unpin from Taskbar". If you are in Microsoft Edge (we will get to this later in the book), there is an icon with three dots. If you select this icon, a drop-down menu is shown where you can choose "Pin to start". The hyperlink to the present webpage is then featured in one of the Start Menu tiles for quick access.

Programs (Apps) listed in the Start Menu can be run in Admin mode, if need be.

All you have to do is right click on the App and in the pop-up menu select "Run as Administrator". This option is great if you are having problems accessing certain functionalities in the program that require Admin access.

Programs (Apps) listed in the Start Menu can be easily uninstalled from the Start Menu.

By right-clicking on the App and selecting "Uninstall" in the pop-up menu, you can remove the App from your machine. Windows 10 will prompt you with a pop-up warning dialog box that requires you to confirm by clicking "Uninstall". Click on this button to remove the app from your PC.

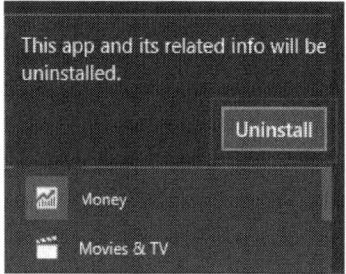

Note: In this screenshot, the "Money" app that comes with Microsoft Windows 10 is being uninstalled.

Customizing what can show in your Start Menu is easy.

First, go to the Start Menu icon and choose Settings.

Select Personalization.

Then, select Start.

A window is shown where you can choose (on or off) exactly what you are going to allow to show in the Start Menu listing. They are as follows:

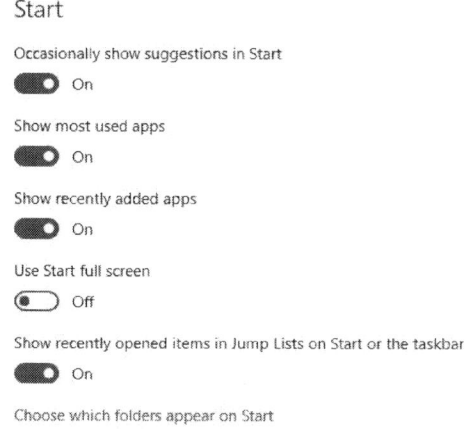

Here, you can click on the "choose which folders appear on Start" link and then select from the following listing that is presented.

What is nice about Windows 10 is the auto-save feature – so that when you make modifications especially in the Settings section, there is no need to click a Save button. Windows 10 immediately adjusts the OS to meet your new specification, request, and/or configuration.

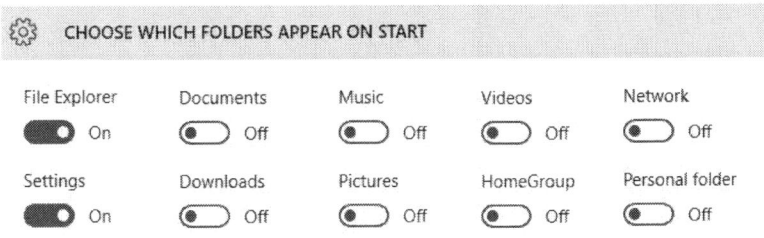

You will love the new Windows 10 Personal Assistant called "Cortana".

I currently have Cortana on not only Windows 10 on my Dell laptop but also on my iPhone (smartphone). Cortana works very well on both platforms.

To access Cortana in Windows 10, click on the "Search the web and Windows" text box at the bottom left-hand corner of your screen. Cortana pops-up ready to assist you. You will see a Greeting pop-up window followed by "Here are some of the things I can do for you". Click "Next" and then select "Use Cortana" at the bottom of the displayed window.

Section 08: Windows 10 "Cortana"

Cortana - your new *Windows 10 Personal Digital Assistant* - is one of the hottest new features in Microsoft Windows 10. Cortana comes from the Windows Phone and can now be found on your Windows 10 desktop. Cortana is able to work with voice input as well as traditional user inputs that are typed in – such as requests and questions.

Setting up Cortana is easy.

Cortana prompts you with a message saying "Great! Now what would you like me to call you?" Enter your name or alias in the given text box as shown below and then click the Next button to continue.

Cortana will tell you when it is ready to be used.

Cortana has now finalized its setup to work with you as a recognized user of Windows 10. The following window is displayed where you can test out Cortana, via either text or voice input.

You will most likely need to set up the microphone on your computer or that is part of your headset (if you use one like I do) so that Cortana can hear your voice-driven requests. Cortana does this all by itself because it is able to work with natural language.

Click on the tiny microphone icon you see at the right side of the text field saying "Ask me anything". Then speak clearly something like "what is the time" to start Cortana with an easy question.

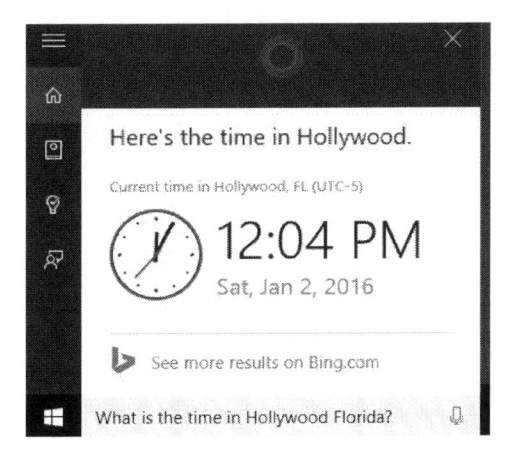

Cortana can field complex questions.

Let us ask Cortana a more challenging question now. Click on the Cortana icon (the Circle icon) and then then click on the microphone icon to ready it for voice input. In this example, I am going to ask Cortana how the Miami Dolphins did in their most recent football game. Here is what I got.

Note: This is fantastic! Cortana is able to work with my current location (South Florida, USA) as well as other web data to know who the Dolphins are (e.g. Miami Dolphins) as well as the sport-type (U.S. football) and league (NFL) and hence games related. Then, Cortana was able to index the latest game per the Dolphins schedule, retrieve the data, and present it nicely here.

You can ask Cortana questions via text input.

Let us type in, as an example, the question "what is the square root of 10?" This is what I received back from Cortana...

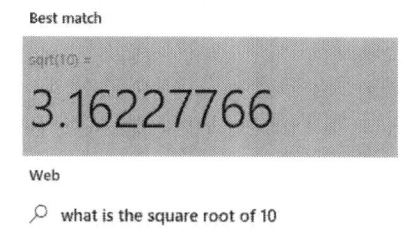

Best match

sqrt(10) =

3.16227766

Web

🔍 what is the square root of 10

To enable Cortana to respond to you saying "Hey Cortana", you need to select "Notebook" from within Cortana's utility window, then go to Settings and turn "on" the "Hey, Cortana" option.

To disable this option, just turn "Hey Cortana" off using the same button (displayed in the image below).

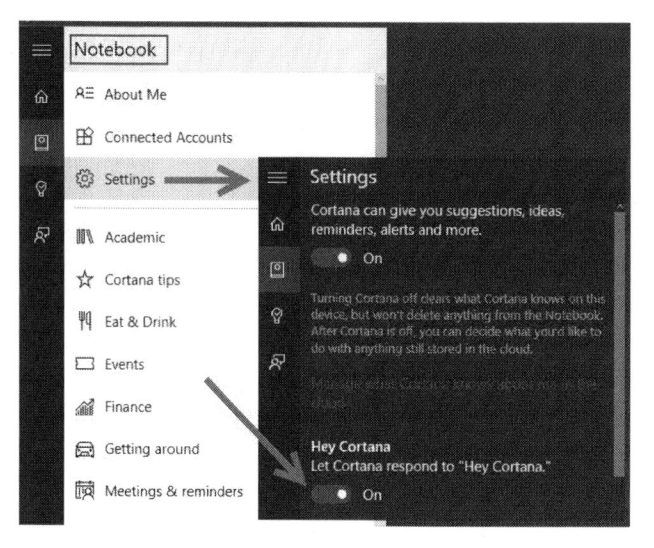

To enable Cortana to work successfully with your voice, choose the same path: Cortana > Notebook > Settings but this time choose "My Voice" underneath the "Hey, Cortana" option.

Click on the "Me" option and also the button where Cortana can study your voice called "Learn my voice". You will be asked about six questions. Respond in the way that you would to any other person. Cortana will then adjust its settings to be able to better understand your voice requests and commands.

Cortana can help you as a "Virtual Reminder Assistant".

Click on the Light Bulb icon beneath the Notebook icon, click on the Plus (+) icon at the bottom of the displayed window, and Cortana will prompt you with the details needed to create the reminder. Next, click "Remind" ... Cortana confirms this action by showing the following window and text: "I'll remind you. You can also see it in your Reminders list any time."

Cortana can help you discover the name of a song.

Other virtual assistants like Google Now (for Android devices) and Siri (for Apple iOS devices) are able to work with a huge number of songs out there on the web and can help you to identify the song's name, if you cannot. What happens is Cortana uses your machine's microphone to get the input it needs. But first, of course, you must say or type something like "Hey Cortana, what is the name of this song?" If it is able to make this determination, it will ...

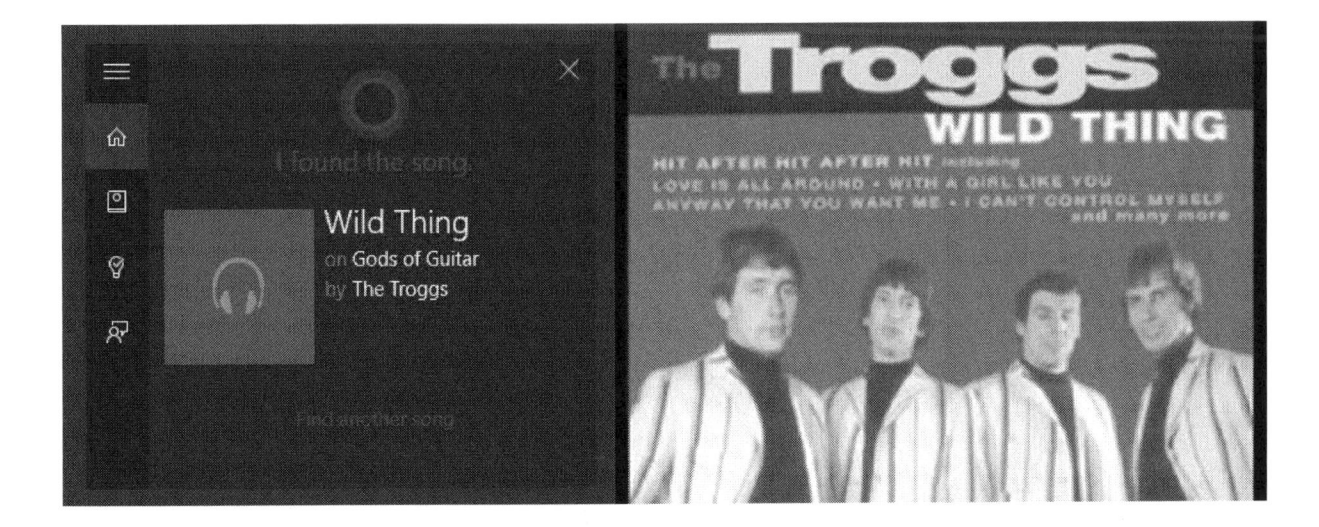

Cortana can help you with your travel itinerary.

Let us ask Cortana to help us find the best driving route between Chicago and Miami. I said "Hey Cortana ... what is the best way to drive from Miami to Chicago?" Here is what Cortana returned for me ... via Bing:

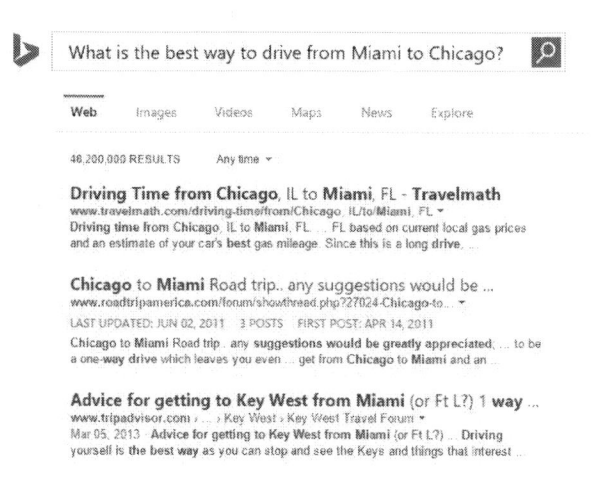

> **What is the best way to drive from Miami to Chicago?**
>
> Web   Images   Videos   Maps   News   Explore
>
> 46,200,000 RESULTS   Any time
>
> **Driving Time from Chicago**, IL to **Miami**, FL - **Travelmath**
> www.travelmath.com/driving-time/from/Chicago,IL/to/Miami,FL
> Driving time from Chicago, IL to Miami, FL ... FL based on current local gas prices and an estimate of your car's best gas mileage. Since this is a long drive, ...
>
> **Chicago** to **Miami** Road trip.. any suggestions would be ...
> www.roadtripamerica.com/forum/showthread.php?27024-Chicago-to-...
> LAST UPDATED: JUN 02, 2011   3 POSTS   FIRST POST: APR 14, 2011
> Chicago to Miami Road trip.. any suggestions would be greatly appreciated, ... to be a one-way drive which leaves you even ... get from Chicago to Miami and an ...
>
> **Advice for getting to Key West from Miami** (or Ft L?) 1 way ...
> www.tripadvisor.com › ... › Key West › Key West Travel Forum
> Mar 05, 2013 · Advice for getting to Key West from Miami (or Ft L?) ... Driving yourself is the best way as you can stop and see the Keys and things that interest ...

Cortana can help you with monetary conversions.

Let us ask Cortana to help us convert 100 US Dollars to Euros. I said "Hey Cortana ... how many euros are 100 US dollars?" Here is what Cortana returned for me:

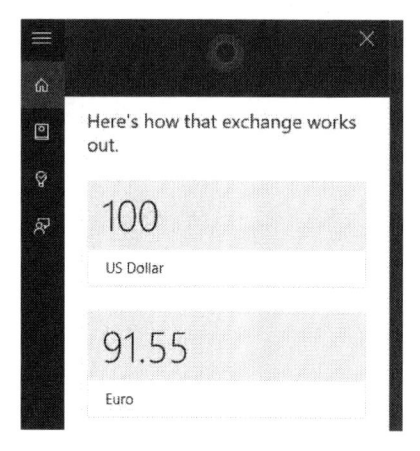

> Here's how that exchange works out.
>
> **100**
> US Dollar
>
> **91.55**
> Euro

Cortana can help you track a package that has a tracking code.

Type into the Home Screen Search box (at the bottom left-hand corner of your screen) or say "Hey Cortana" and then enter the tracking number; Cortana will plug it into your default web browser and you will see where the package is.

Cortana can help you launch apps on your computer.

Let us ask Cortana to open the Microsoft Windows 10 app called "Paint". I simply said "Hey Cortana open Paint" …. Successful!

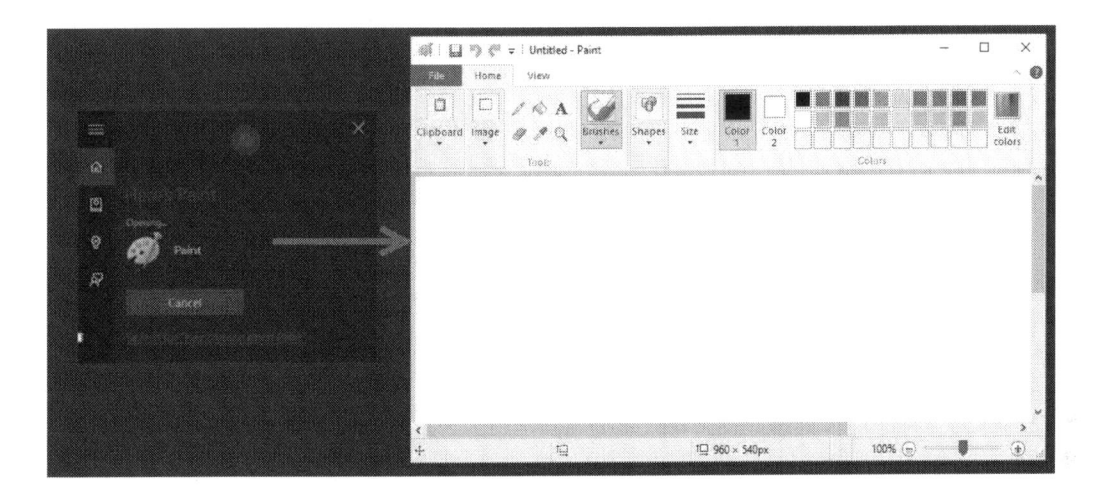

Cortana can help you set an alarm clock to wake you.

Cortana can help you know the time anywhere, anytime …

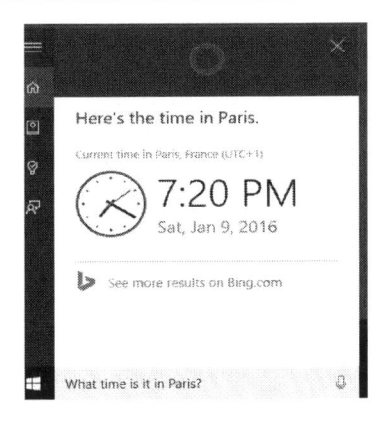

Cortana can help you undo something you have already set up (via Cortana), like the alarm clock setting we set up in the previous tip.

Cortana can help you to e-mail someone in your Microsoft Outlook Contacts List.
Please note that you must have a version of Microsoft Windows 10 that supports a legitimate installation of Microsoft Outlook. Otherwise, you can ask Cortana to open/access an e-mail program on the web like Gmail.

Cortana has a "Notebook" icon in the left pane of its window.

Each section of "Notebook" enables you to enter personal information that Cortana can use to further its ability to personalize service to you as a Windows 10 user.

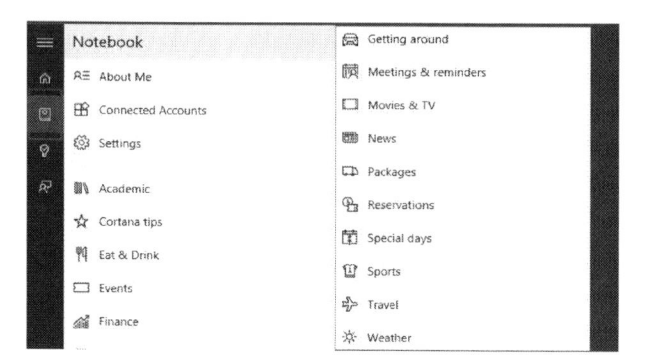

You can help Microsoft to make Cortana better.

In the left pane of the Cortana interface locate the icon of a generic user. Click on this icon to open the feedback window, where you can give Microsoft direct feedback regarding your Cortana experience. You can feature Ideas, Likes and Dislikes along with explanations. Finally, click the Send button and Microsoft will immediately get your feedback.

Section 09: Windows 10 File Search

Searching for files and/or folders in Windows 10 is easy.

Windows 10 features a great and powerful Search Engine. Whether you use Cortana (or not), the text box at the bottom left of your Windows 10 Taskbar is where you enter the Search criterion. If using Cortana, simply state the file or folder or resource you want to locate. If using just straight-up Search, type in what you seek and then press Enter. Here is a sample Search.

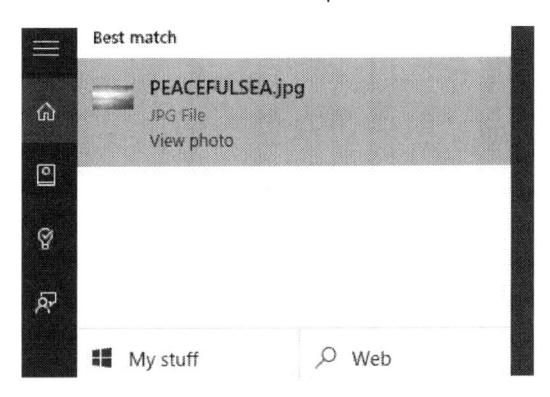

Windows 10 not only retrieves what you seek, but also gives you a chance to further your Search on your local machine (e.g. the My Stuff option as shown in the screen shot above), or on the Web (e.g. the Web option as shown in the screen shot above).

Click on the appropriate icon to enable this continuance of your Search process. Let us choose Web (because we know Windows 10 Search has succeeded with locating a local file already). Windows 10 now successfully accesses Bing and shows query results, in this case, for "peacefulsea.jpg". So, we now know that Windows 10 Search works perfectly for not only a local drive but also with the World Wide Web via Bing.com.

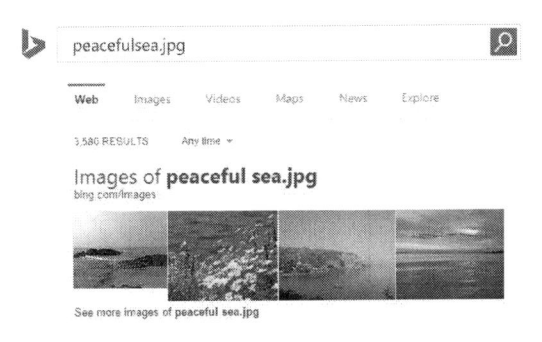

Windows 10 Search can help you generate a listing of files.

For example, if you type in *.doc in your Taskbar Search box or tell Cortana "Hey Cortana list all Word files" then Windows 10 Search will generate a listing of all Microsoft Word files it finds locally on your machine but of course will give you a chance to also continue this Search on the web if you choose.

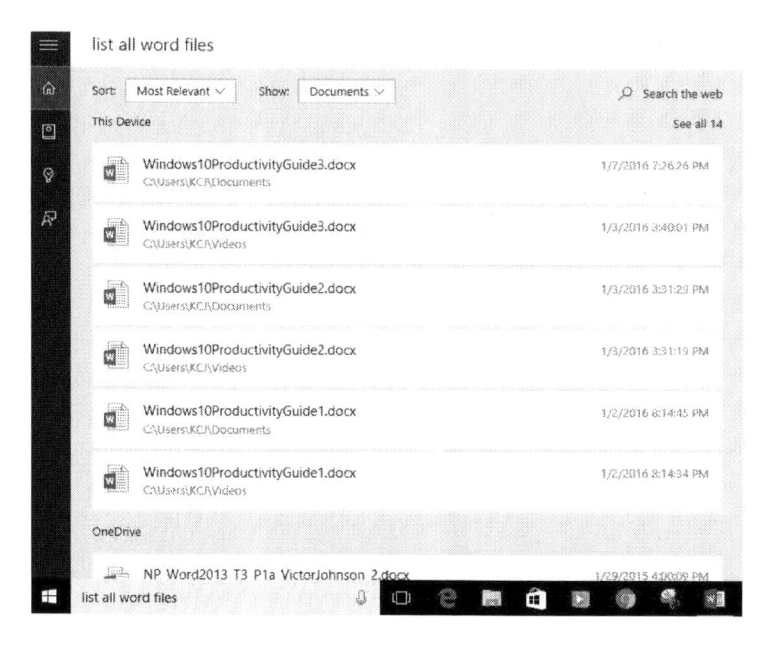

Windows Search (and Cortana) both can help you find local food.

I simply said "Hey Cortana, find me a local pizza place". This is what I got from this Search request. If I typed in this text, I would have gotten the same ...

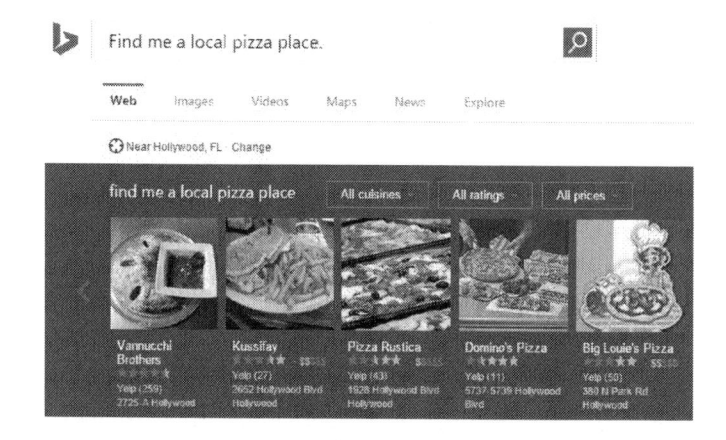

Section 10: Windows 10 "Edge" Web Browser

You will love the new Microsoft Windows 10 Edge web browser.

Welcome to the Windows 10 "Edge" web browser! For the longest time, Microsoft's former browser, Internet Explorer (IE), was called "the browser you use to download a better web browser". Well, Microsoft has finally stepped up to the plate, if you will, and re-engineered and improved IE to bring us all Microsoft Edge. To open Edge, you can single click on its icon in the Start Menu or Taskbar as well as double click on its icon on the desktop.

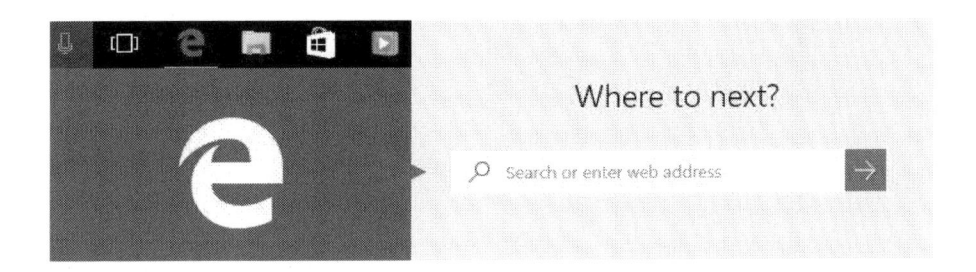

Use the arrow icons at the top left-hand corner of your browser window to navigate Edge.

The left arrow takes you to a previous webpage. The right arrow takes you to the next webpage that is cached (e.g. in Edge's browser history section). The almost-circle icon is the one you use to refresh the current page.

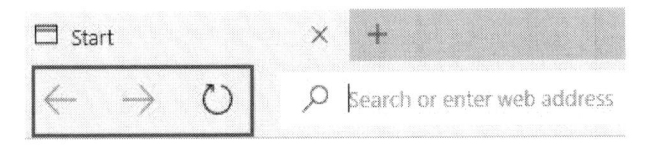

Use the text box (that you see in the image above) to enter your Search criterion (while using Edge).

Press Enter on your keyboard or if the browser gives you an option to select the Search Criterion as a Bing search, click on that option. As an example, I entered "Google Productivity Guide", a book I wrote about a year ago about the Google Platform, to see what Bing would list per the Microsoft Edge search. It found the book at its home page on CreateSpace. Well done, Microsoft Edge.

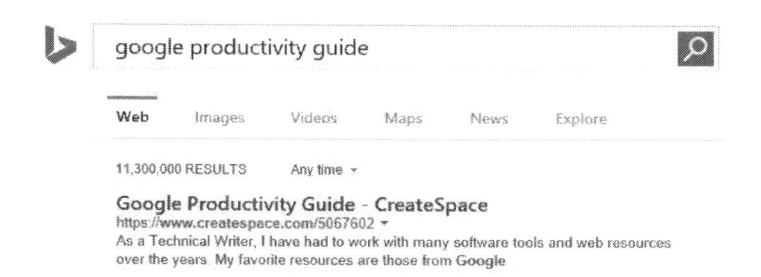

You can customize the homepage for Microsoft Edge, if you do not want to use the default page of Microsoft Bing.

Follow this path ... Edge > More Actions (...) > Settings > Open with a Specific Page. Then, enter the URL of the new page (for the Edge's Home Page). Click on the Refresh button.

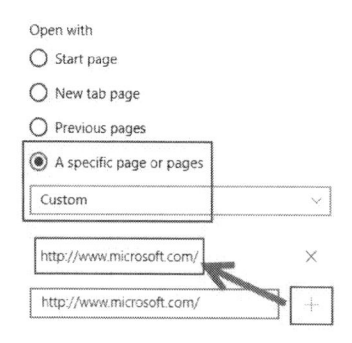

As an example let us enter www.microsoft.com. Then, click the + icon to establish this as our new sample Home Page. Refresh your Edge browser and it should show the Microsoft General web site.

Adding to Favorites is easy.

You can add a specific webpage to your favorites listing in Edge simply by clicking on the Star icon at the top right hand corner of the browser.

The Three Horizontal Lines menu is called the Hub Menu.

You can select the Hub menu option to then access Favorites, Reading List, History, and Downloads sub-options).

You can create a Web Note on a selected page by clicking on the icon that looks like a piece of paper with a pen.

This alters the screen "mode" into one where you can write something onto the screen, as a note. You can also, through this option, highlight, select and copy, and erase your notes.

You can share a web page by clicking on the icon that looks like circle with three tiny mini-circles.

This opens a side-panel window where you can share the web page via Email, One Note and sites like Twitter.

In the More Options (final) option at the top right-hand corner of Edge, there are several choices here.

They are as follows: New Window, New InPrivate Window, Zoom, Find (something on the current webpage), Print, Pin to Start, F12 Developer Tools, Open (webpage) with Internet Explorer (aha, so we see that IE is still here even from within Edge), Send Feedback, and Settings.

At the bottom of Edge Settings, you can select the "Choose what to clear" button if you wish to clear part or all of your browsing history.

The following window lets you define this process; then click "Clear" to wipe as per your guidelines.

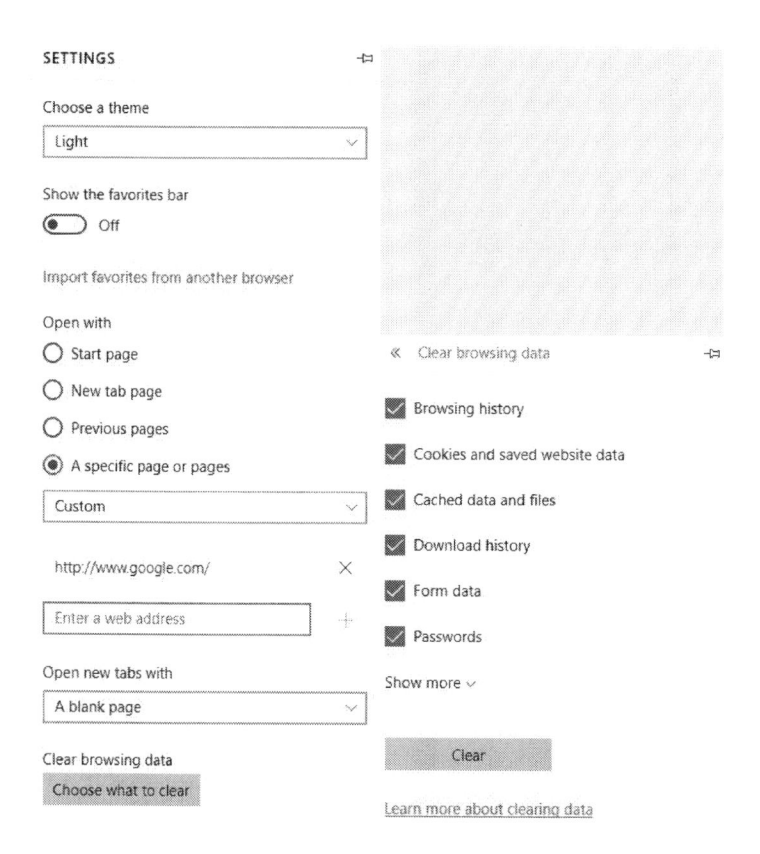

To close the Microsoft Edge browser, click on the X icon located at the top right-hand corner of the browser window.

Note: To create a tile on the Start Menu based on a website URL, go to that site (in Edge) and click on the three dots you see above. Select "Pin to Start". Done!

Section 11: Windows 10 Skype App

Skype (for both the Microsoft Windows 10 Desktop and Microsoft Edge browser) is tremendous. You can accomplish great things with Skype.

Microsoft acquired Skype in 2011 and has worked tirelessly to improve this app designed to run on its Windows OS and also Edge browser. When you first install or upgrade to Windows 10, you will notice a listing in the Apps section of the Start Menu saying "Get Skype". This is for the desktop app. Skype is easily downloaded from the Microsoft Store and after just a few clicks, it should install quickly and seamlessly for you.

Here are five great things you can do via Skype.

1. Calling:
Skype to Skype calls, Calls to mobiles and landlines, Group calls, Personalized Skype Number, Call Forwarding, Caller ID, Skype to go, and Skype Click to Call.

2. Video:
One-to-one video calls and Group video calls.

3. Messaging:
Mojis and emoticons, video messaging, instant messaging, SMS, voice messages, and GroupMe.

4. Sharing:
File sending/transmission, Screen sharing, Group screen sharing, Contact information sending.

5. Other:
Skype WiFi, Skype Manager, Skype Connect, Skype for Outlook.com, Contact Me button, Share button, Skype translator, and Skype browser extension.

Section 12: Windows 10 Entertainment & OneDrive

If there is one aspect of Windows 10 that is controversial – it is Entertainment. So, that is why I am covering it now – right up front - to share my honest opinion and insights. It is usually issues regarding Entertainment and Data Storage that cause Information Technology (IT) professionals to have opposing reviews of this OS.

Please note that the Windows 10 upgrade will most likely remove your Windows Media Player (from your current Windows 7 or 8 OS). So, what you can do is download and install a program that many Microsoft MVPs actually recommend – the VideoLAN VLC Media Player. Here is its free download page.

http://download.cnet.com/VLC-Media-Player/3000-13632_4-10267151.html

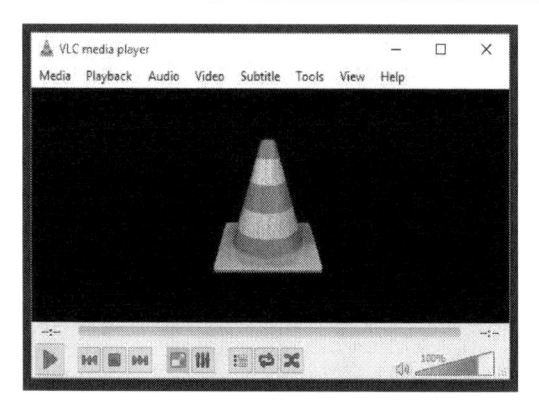

You can use the new Groove Music app to stream music via the web.
This can be done on your computer and on a Windows phone or tablet.

You can use the Windows DVD Player to play a movie or DVD if your computer has a CD/DVD drive. You can access this app via the Windows Start Menu and also the Taskbar if you have it pinned there.

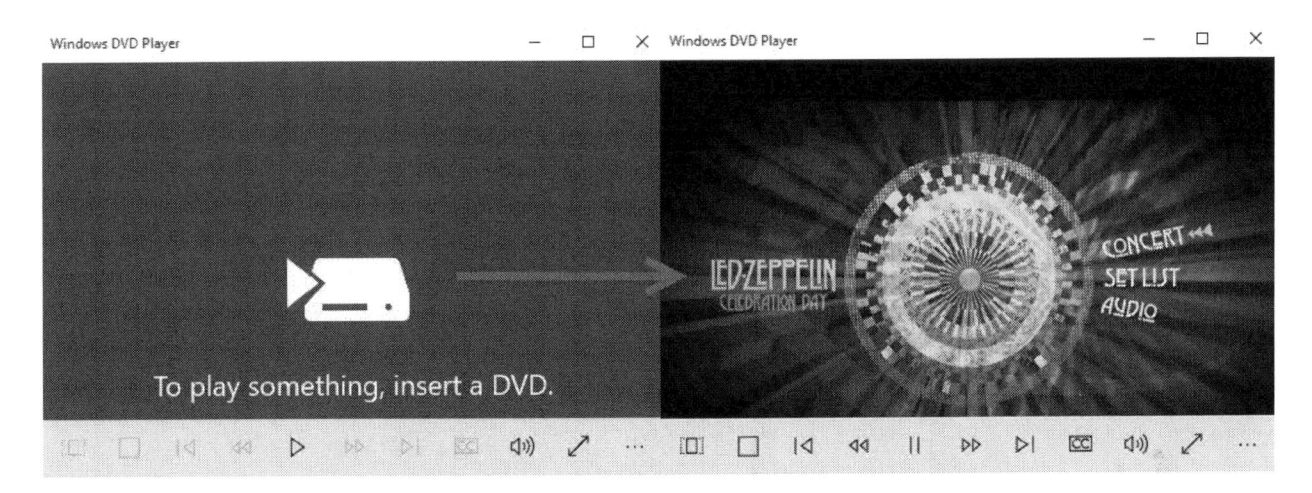

For those of you into creating movies, you can still download the Windows Live Movie Maker program from the web and use it with Windows 10. The following download link is originally for Windows 7 but because Windows 10 is technically an upgrade from both Windows 7 and 8 – this program will run just fine on the Windows 10 OS. Here is the download link – this program is one I have used for many years now and is a great way to present video footage taken with your phone or tablet as well as photos, lives performances and more.

http://download.cnet.com/Windows-Live-Movie-Maker/3000-13631_4-10965753.html

You can now use Microsoft Edge (to be covered soon in this guide) to successfully cast media – video, pictures, and audio content – from within the browser to any device on your network that is Miracast and DLNA enabled. All you have to do is open to the web page you want to cast. Then, select the three dot menu button. You will then see "cast media to device". Select this. You will be prompted with a list of devices which can be used to show/cast the selected content.

You can store data files, music, and much more on Microsoft OneDrive. Microsoft SkyDrive is now called *Microsoft OneDrive*. Microsoft is finally making its move to provide a high-quality cloud data storage platform. You can create your OneDrive account when installing Windows 10 or you can create it anytime as you need, for example, when starting to use Groove Music (where you can then save your music files).

Setting up and using OneDrive is really easy. From your Windows 10 setup, you will be prompted (e.g. asked) if you want to setup OneDrive and save, for example, music files onto OneDrive.

If you select "Yes", then this is like clicking the Setup button at the www.onedrive.com website. If you already have an account, then click Sign in and start using OneDrive.

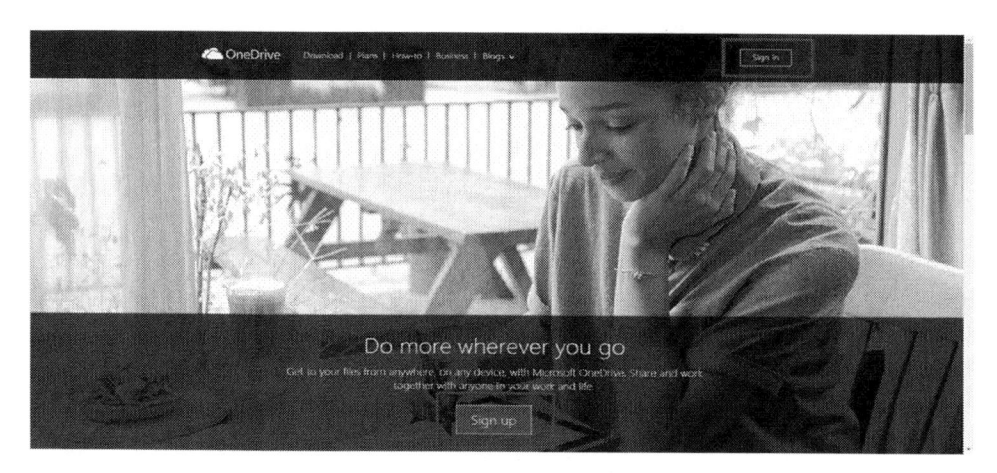

The Signup process is for someone who does not yet have a Microsoft account. You will be prompted to create a Microsoft account which then will let you access the basic free OneDrive account that Microsoft gives all of its Outlook.com e-mail users.

As you can see in the sample screenshot below, there is also a chance to try out a premium (e.g. paid) OneDrive account that gives you more data storage space (this is OneDrive for Business).

To Sign In to OneDrive, click on this button at the top right hand corner of your browser window and you will be prompted to enter your Microsoft e-mail (myemail@outlook.com) twice.

When you enter OneDrive, this is what you will see.

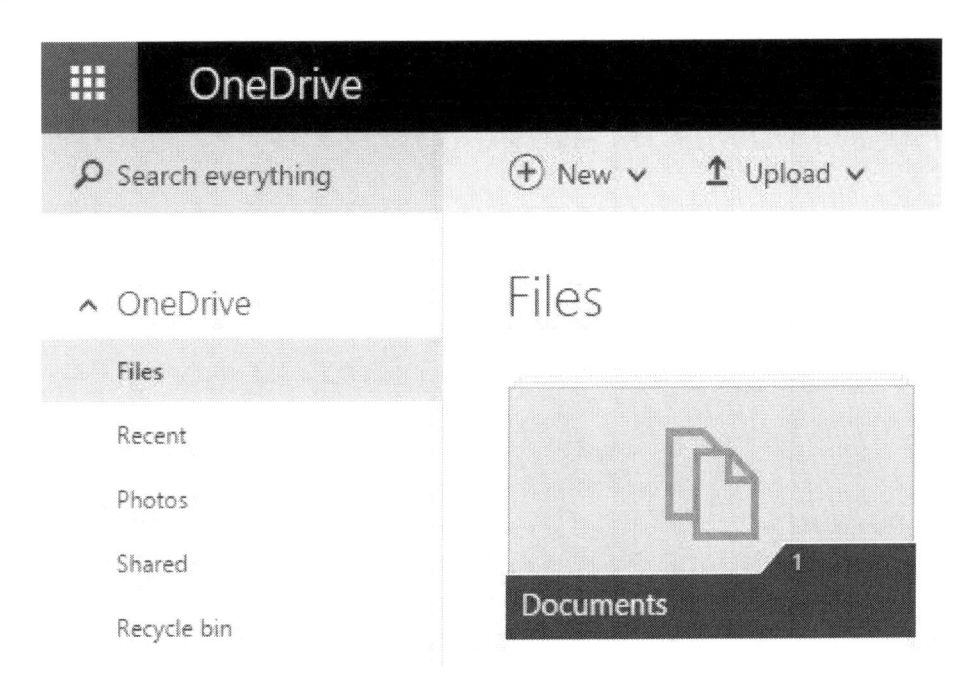

At OneDrive, you can safely store files like word processing files, text files, graphic files music files, and more. As shown in the sample screenshot above, there are tools that enable you to upload, save, and download files as you need, and more.

At the time of the writing of this book, Microsoft allows its Outlook.com e-mail users to store 15 Gigabytes (GB) of data free of charge. If you need more space, you will have to inquire about premium storage plans. But for starters, that is definitely enough space to store essential files.

Section 13: Windows 10 Accessing Apps

There are four major ways to access Applications on your personal computer using Windows 10: Start Menu, Taskbar, Icons on your Desktop, and Windows Explorer 10 File Manager. Let us access an App, here, via the Start Menu.

If you do not see the App you want to access in the immediate Start Menu listing or Tile Presentation, do not fret. All you need to do is click on the "All Apps" option and then Windows 10 refreshes the Start Menu listing absolutely every single App on the machine in alpha-numerical order. Let us do this now and let us scroll down to open the Windows 10 Calculator.

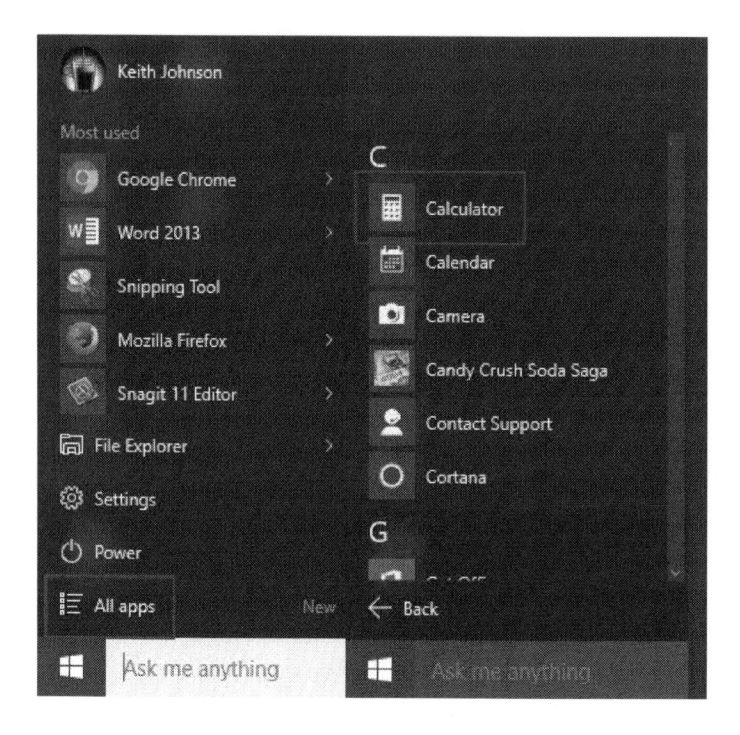

A single click with the left button of your mouse will open Calculator from within the Start Menu.

Let us open the Calculator App from the Taskbar...

Because I do not currently have the Calculator in my Taskbar, let's put it there before accessing it from the Taskbar. Right click on the Calculator App listing in the Start Menu.

From the pop-up menu that is displayed, select "Pin to Taskbar". A single-click on the new Calculator icon in the Taskbar (at the bottom of your screen) will enable you to access this Windows program.

You can open a Microsoft Windows 10 App from your desktop by double-clicking on its displayed icon (also called a shortcut).

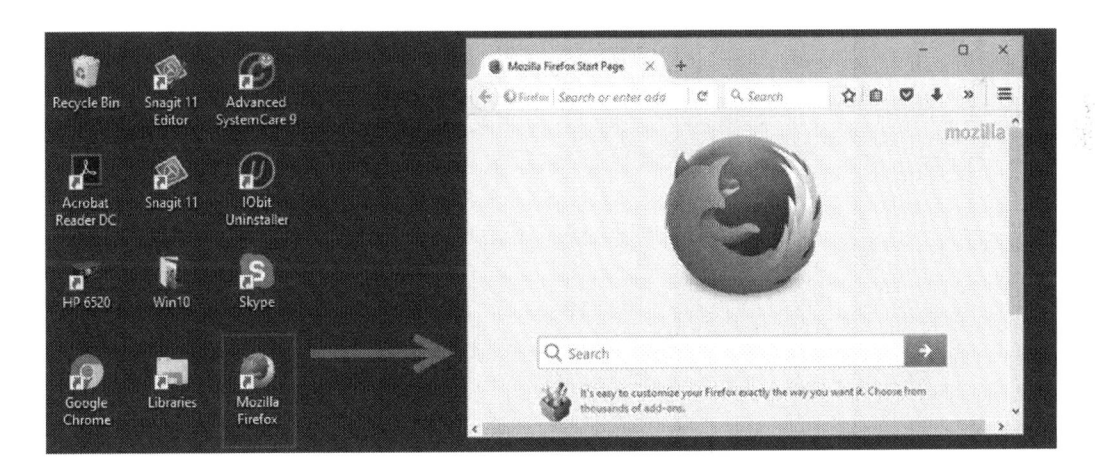

Note: To create a shortcut on your desktop, right click on the desktop's empty space and you will see a pop-up window. Go to New > Shortcut >Browse. Find the executable (.exe) file for the program. Click OK, Next, Finish, in that order.

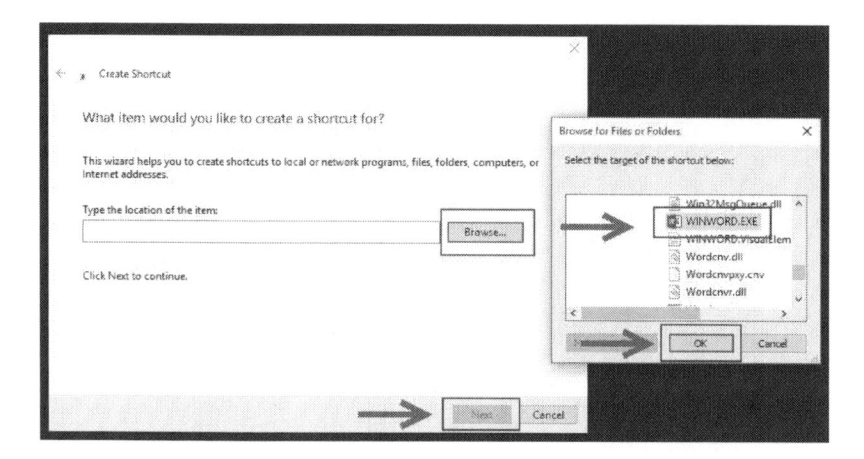

You can modify the display name for the shortcut, if you wish.

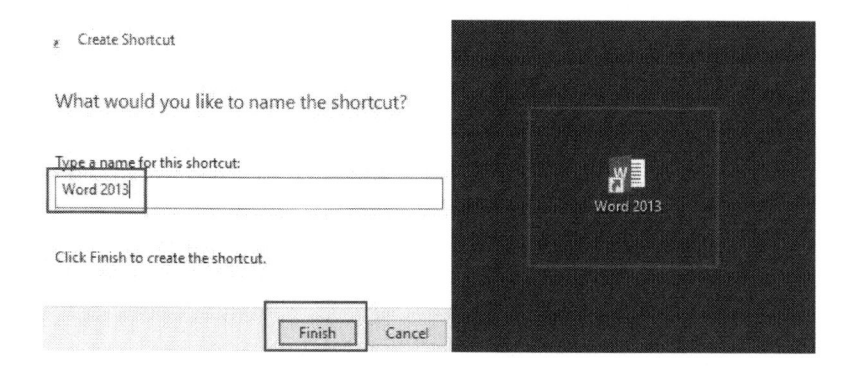

Finally, you can open your App via the Windows 10 File Explorer.

"Windows Explorer" now is called "File Explorer".

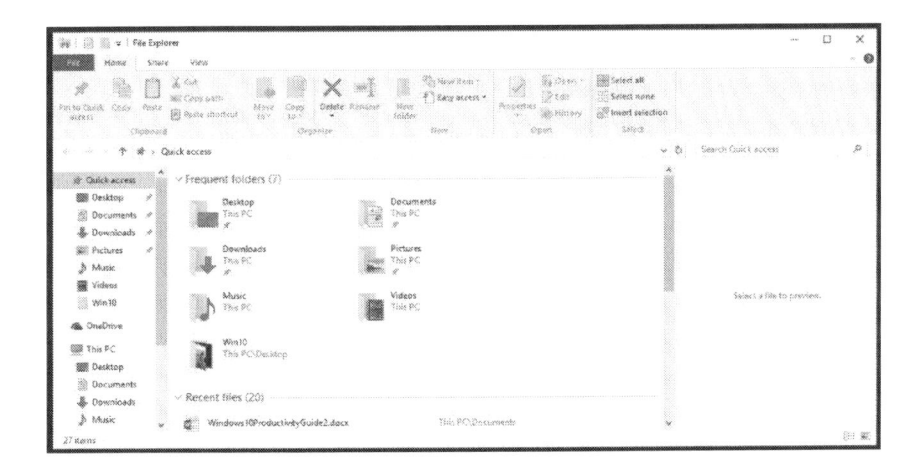

Microsoft Windows 10, like previous versions (as far back as I can remember), requires you to locate the executable (.exe) or dynamic link library (.dll) file that is the true *enabling file* for the app. Let us try to open Microsoft PowerPoint via the Windows 10 File Explorer. We must first find the executable file and then double-click on it to open it up. The next two screenshots illustrate this path.

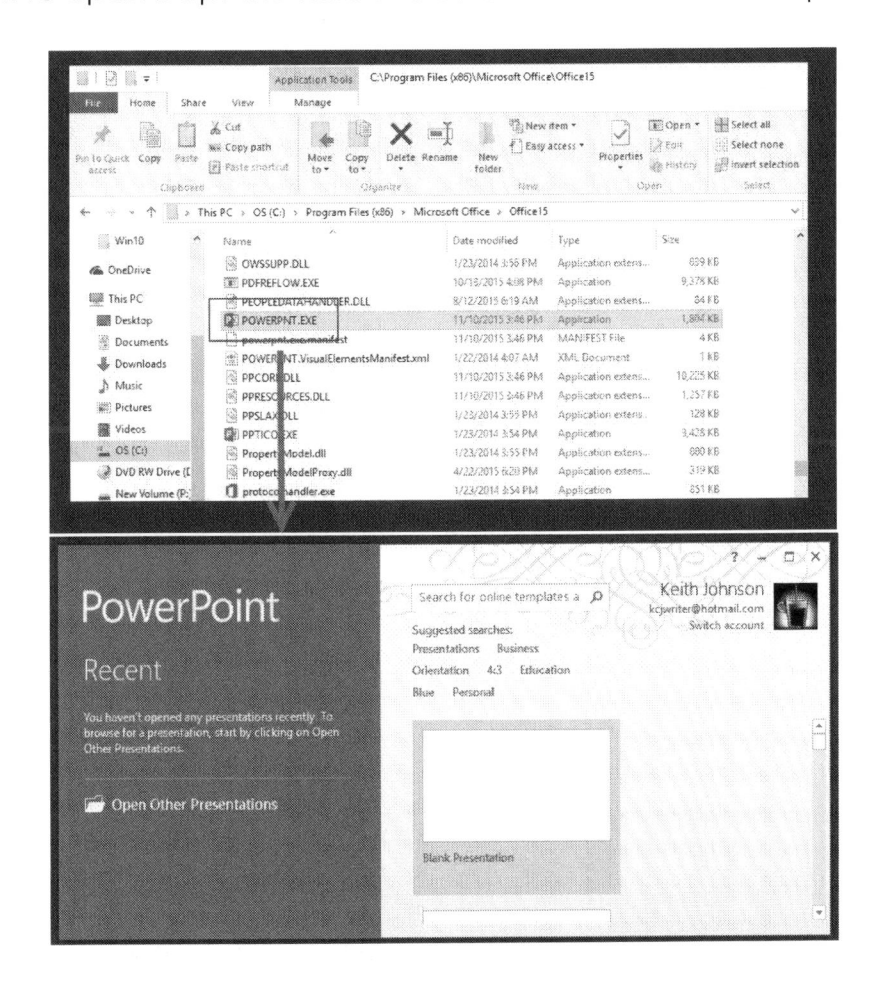

If you cannot open an App via Start, Taskbar, Desktop, Windows Explorer or the enabling program file itself, then perhaps you need to find the App itself via Search.

This is a last-resort option because the others should work fine if the App is truly there in your system. Let us imagine for a second that we cannot find Microsoft Excel – via the Start Menu, Taskbar, Windows 10 Explorer File Manager, or enabling program. Thus, we must search. Go to the text box for either Cortana or direct Search at the bottom of your screen. Type in "excel.exe" and see what Windows 10 shows for you. It should be something like this ...

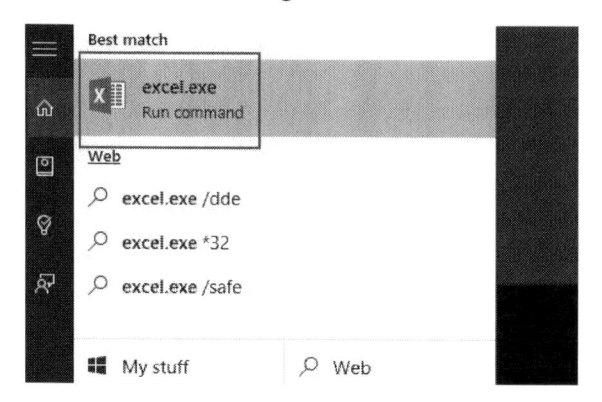

Of course Windows 10 has found "excel.exe" which is the enabling program file for the entire Microsoft Excel program, because I have installed on my machine Microsoft Office 2013 – which includes Word, Excel, and PowerPoint.

You can drag and drop icons in the Start Menu to reorder them.

You can drag and drop icons in the Taskbar to reorder them.

You can drag and drop icons on your Desktop to reorder them.

For the three instructions listed above, click on the icon you want to move, hold the left (or whichever primary) button of your mouse down while moving and then and only then let up on the mouse button after you have dragged it (the icon) to the new location at which you want it to show.

If you want Microsoft Windows 10 to organize your Desktop icons, then simply right click in the desktop empty space and then select View > Auto arrange icons.

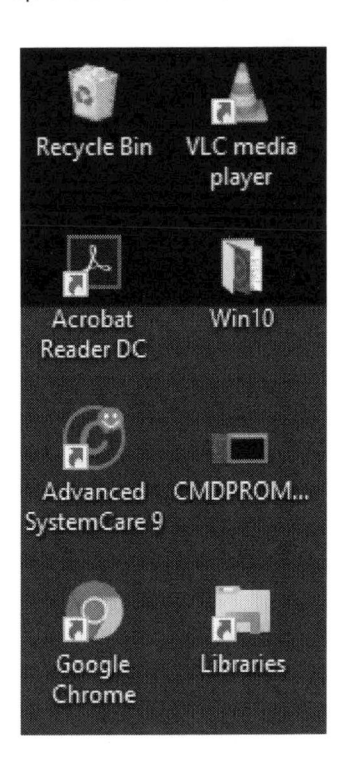

If you want Microsoft Windows 10 to resize your Desktop icons, then simply right click in the desktop empty space and then select View > Large Icons or Medium Icons or Small icons according to your needs.

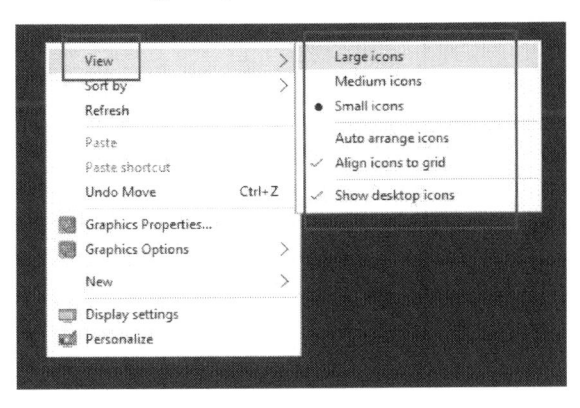

Section 14: Windows 10 Accessories

All of the Accessories listed in this section can be accessed *easily* by going to your Windows 10 Start Menu > All Apps > Scroll down to Windows Accessories > Open the Program Listing > Make your individual selection.

Using Windows 10 Character Map

This program from the Windows 10 Accessories listing is easy to use and is very helpful. All you need to do is open the Character Map program and also open your word processing editor. Perhaps you are creating a document that requires strange characters that you cannot seem to find. Well, within all the options of Character Map, you should be able to find the symbol because just Windows 10 has over 200 fonts that show from within this program and there are different "modes" of displaying the individual font which gives you a chance to produce character or symbol variations. Once you locate what you need, click on the "Select" button and then the "Copy" button in Character Map. From there, in your word processing editor, position the cursor to where you want to insert the selected character or characters. Then either go to File – Paste or press Ctrl-V. Your characters should now show up in your word processing editor.

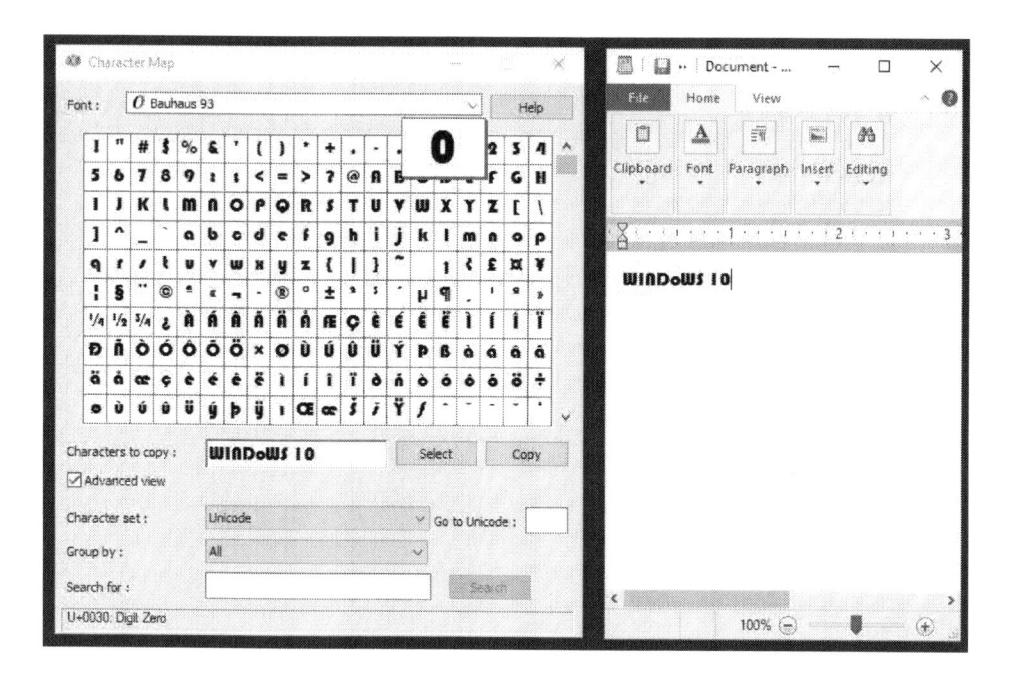

Using Windows 10 Internet Explorer

Even though Microsoft has spent millions of dollars to improve its web browser and now features Edge as its primary browser for Windows 10, it has still decided to include Internet Explorer as a secondary browsing resource via the Windows Accessories menu. The version I have here (January, 2016) is v11; and upon first use, IE asks you to set it up ... recommended settings are best.

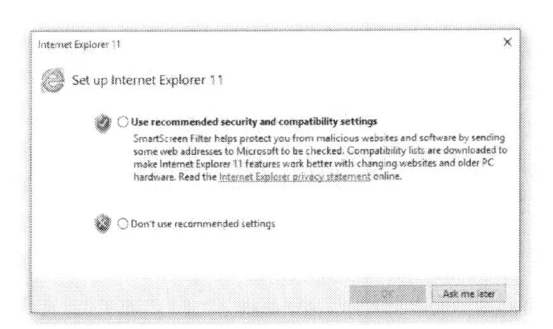

After clicking OK, IE will open normally, as it has for many previous versions of Microsoft Windows, since IE is always part of the OS. Notice that you are encouraged to use Edge; still, Microsoft knows there are users who prefer to work with tools with which they are already familiar. Hence, IE is still in Windows.

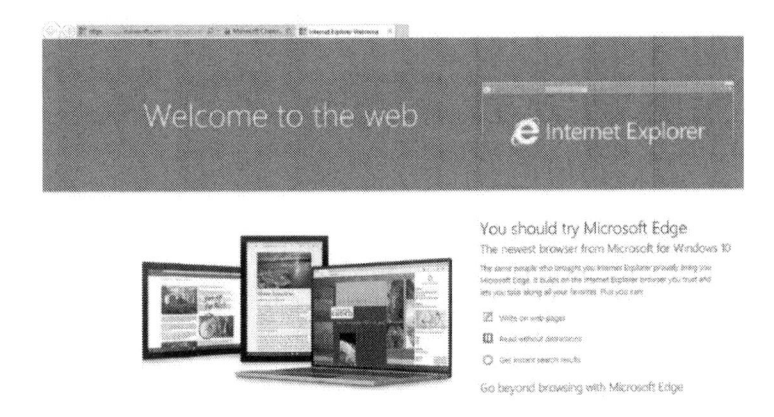

At the time of the writing of this book, Microsoft has already discontinued support for Internet Explorer v8, v9, and v10. Even though you can still use v11, I recommend that you start using Edge in case Microsoft also decides to discontinue support for v11 of Internet Explorer.

Using Windows 10 Math Input Panel

The Math Input Panel is an editor where you can practice typing in sophisticated mathematical formulas. Math Input is the third app listed in Windows Accessories, as follows.

Sample input and use of an inputted math formula using this app.

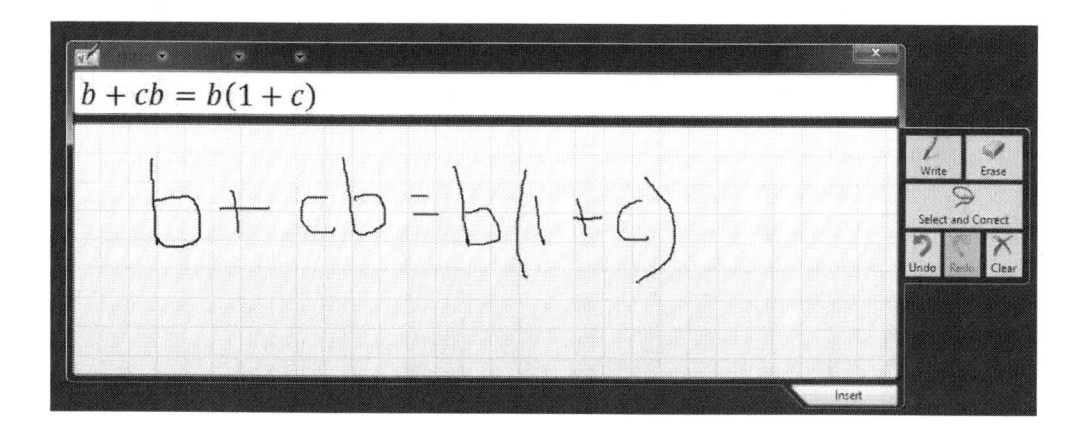

You can use the insert button to create a clean slate for input; you can use the other buttons for tasks equivalent to their label – write, erase, select and correct, undo, and clear, as you need.

Using Windows 10 Mobility Center

The Windows Mobility Center is a Windows 10 Accessory app that enables you to see your display settings – that is – the most important ones in one summarized pop-up window. You must access this program via Windows Accessories > Mobility Center in your Start Menu, as follows.

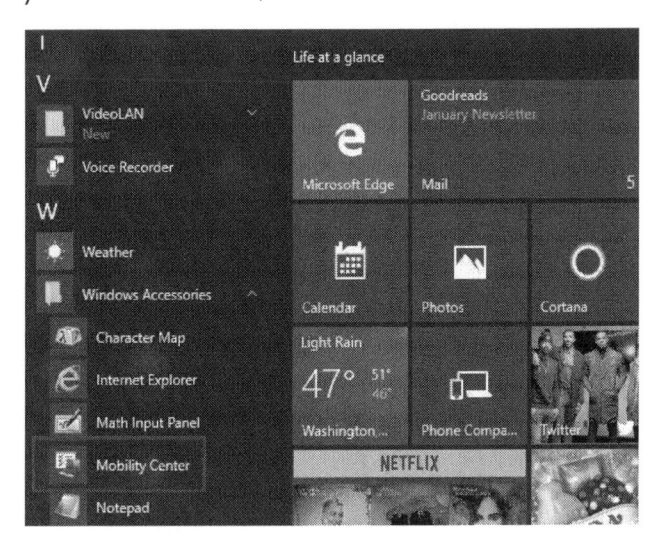

This is how the Windows 10 Mobility Center app should display for you.

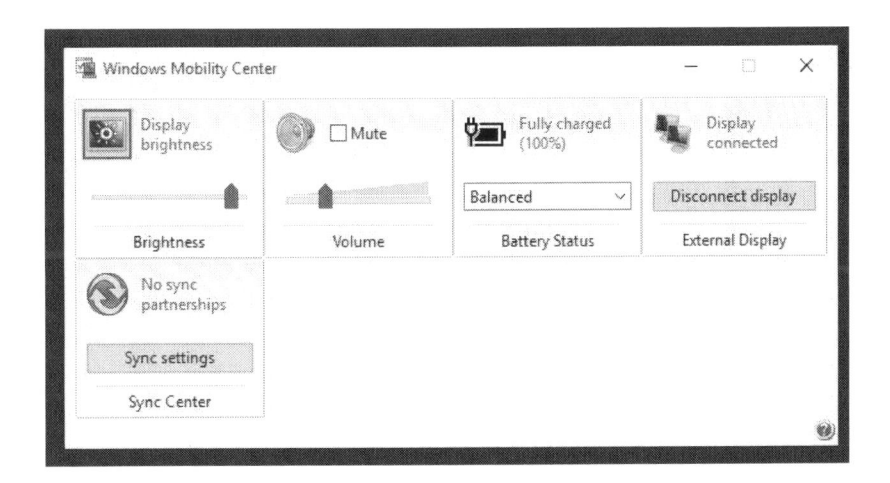

There are five sections of this pop-up window-like app. You can modify them as you need to optimize your Windows 10 experience and interface – Display Brightness, Mute, Battery Status, Display Connected, and Sync Settings.

Using Windows 10 Notepad

The Windows Notepad accessory is a Windows 10 app that enables you to work essentially with a text-only editor. This is a great resource for notes or other simple files that are exclusively text. Go to Windows Accessories > Notepad:

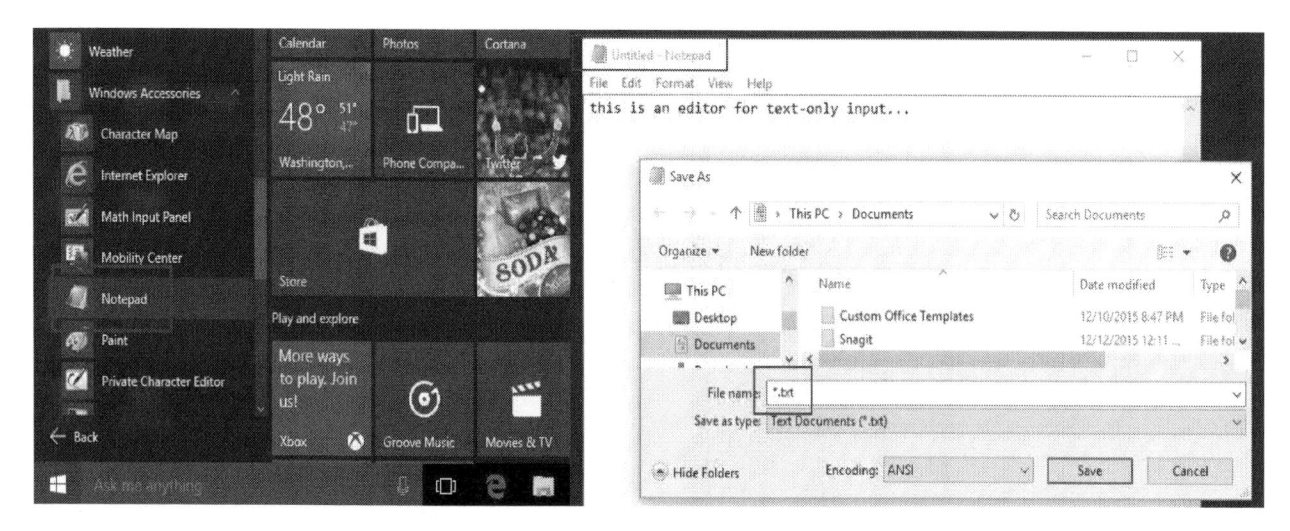

Notepad works like any other text-only word processing software but here you are encouraged to save specifically in the .txt file format so that when you open the file in this app or another program – it will *render* correctly as a *text file*.

Here are three reasons to use Notepad, and hence text-only files:

1. Text files are truly simple files; they can be used for secure data storage.

2. Text files are a good choice to bypass some problems that can otherwise affect more sophisticated file formats: like unnecessary padding (data bloats) and differences in the actual number of bytes in a machine word.

3. Should there be any kind of data trauma or corruption, then a text file has a far greater chance of being saved and recovered than a file with a more sophisticated format.

Using Windows 10 Paint

For those of you who enjoy both creative design as well as creating images for your documents (at work) and/or projects at school, Paint is a fantastic Windows 10 Accessory app.

As a Technical Writer, I use a program called Snag-It, but this program will cost you almost fifty US dollars ($50.00 USD). Paint, however, is *totally free* with your Windows 10 Operating System and can do many tasks that you can do in an advanced Graphics editor like Snag-It.

Access to Paint is through the following path: Windows Start Menu > All Apps > Windows Accessories > Paint.

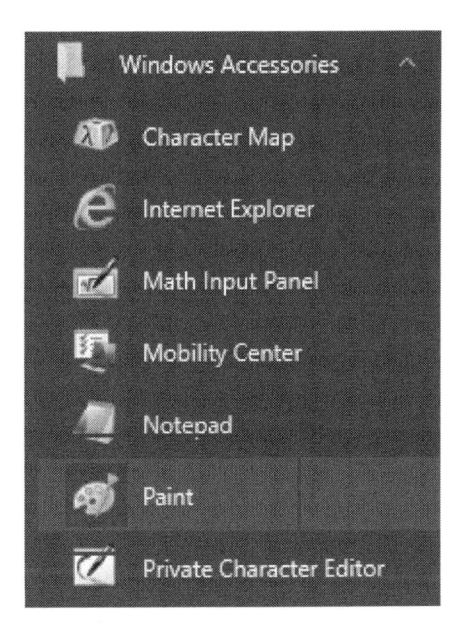

Note: If you have already pinned Paint to your Taskbar (as many users do), you can also open it with a single click to the Paint icon at the bottom of your screen.

The Paint app is opened as follows:

Paint Menu	Options Available
File	New, Open, Save, Save As, Print, From Scanner or Camera, Send in Email, Set as Desktop Background, Properties, About Paint, Exit.
Home	Cut, Copy, Paste, Select, Crop, Resize, Rotate, Pencil, Color Fill, Text, Eraser, Color Picker, Magnifier, Brushes, Shapes, Outline, Fill, Size, Color Palette.
View	Zoom In, Zoom Out, 100%, Grid Lines, Rulers, Status Bar, Full Screen, and Thumbnail.

Using Windows 10 Private Character Editor

The Microsoft Windows 10 accessory app that enables you to create your very own characters is called the Private Character Editor. You can locate this Windows resource via the following path: Start Menu > All Apps > Windows Accessories > Private Character Editor.

In this program you can easily and intuitively create new characters as well as edit existing characters. From within this program, you can save your work as well as visit any folder or library you create and see what you have done.

The major menu options for the Private Character Editor are as follows: File, Edit, View, Tools, Window, and Help.

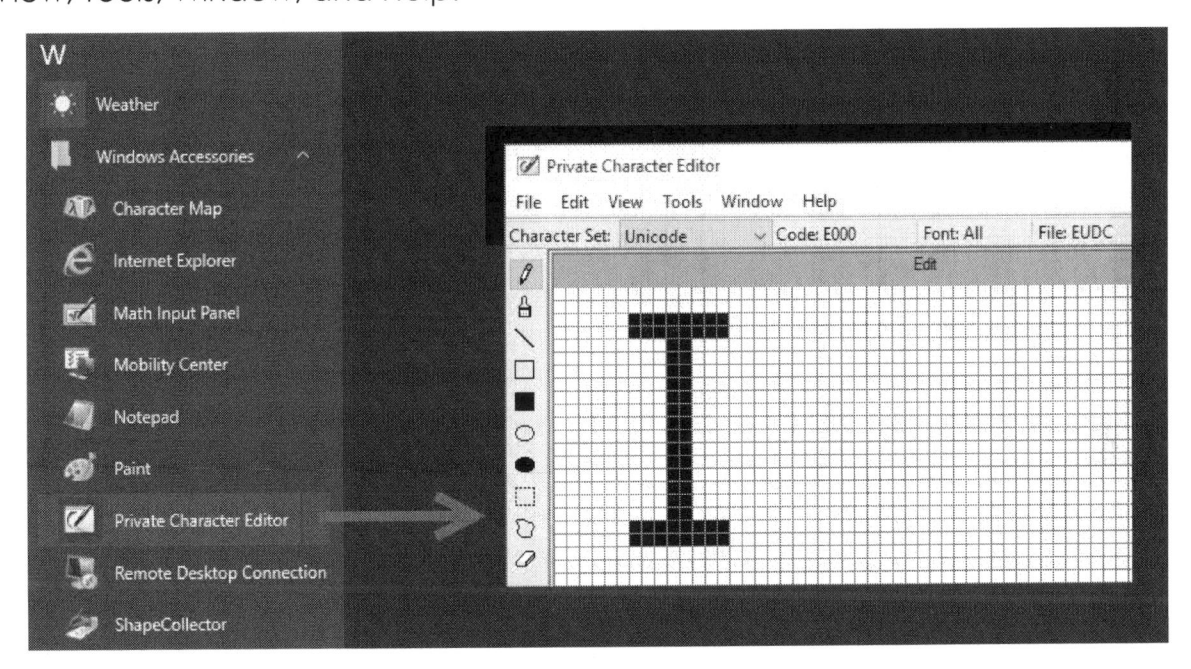

Using Windows 10 Remote Desktop Connection

Let us say I am at work and I need to check on a web article I read last night. The page is bookmarked in my Microsoft Edge web browser, but for some reason I cannot find it during my Search at work. So, with the permission of my supervisor remote in to my home computer to find the web page's URL. This is a situation that requires this Windows resource: Remote Desktop Connection.

The path to this resource is as follows: Start Menu > All Apps > Windows Accessories > Remote Desktop Connection.

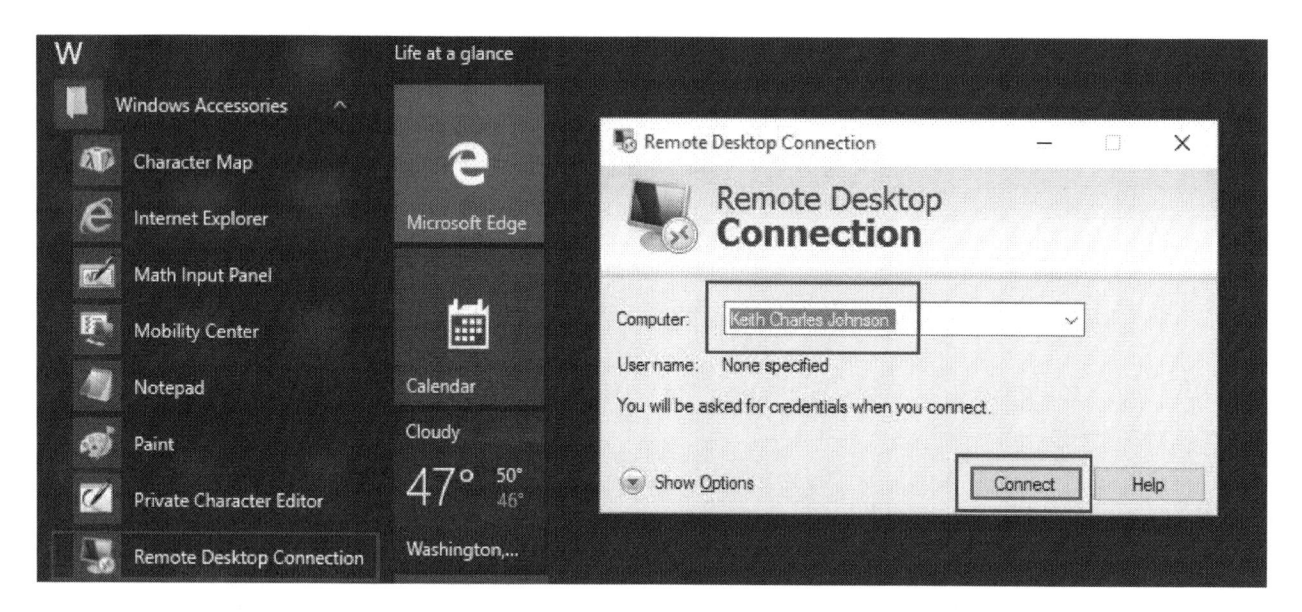

In the Remote Desktop Connection window, enter the correct computer name for the machine into which you want to remote. The click on the Connect button. As you are connecting, you will have to provide legitimate login credentials to gain access. Please note that if you click on the Show Options button, new tabs will be displayed. The Advanced tab has a Settings button that needs to be properly configured for this Windows resource to work correctly and completely

Using Windows 10 ShapeCollector

ShapeCollector is a new accessory program that enables Windows 10 to be able to recognize and work with handwriting – your signature and more. The path to this program is Start Menu > All Apps > Windows Accessories > ShapeCollector.

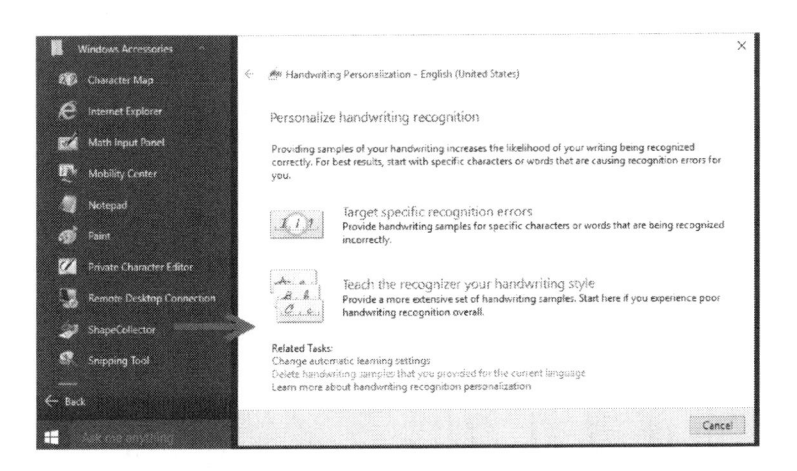

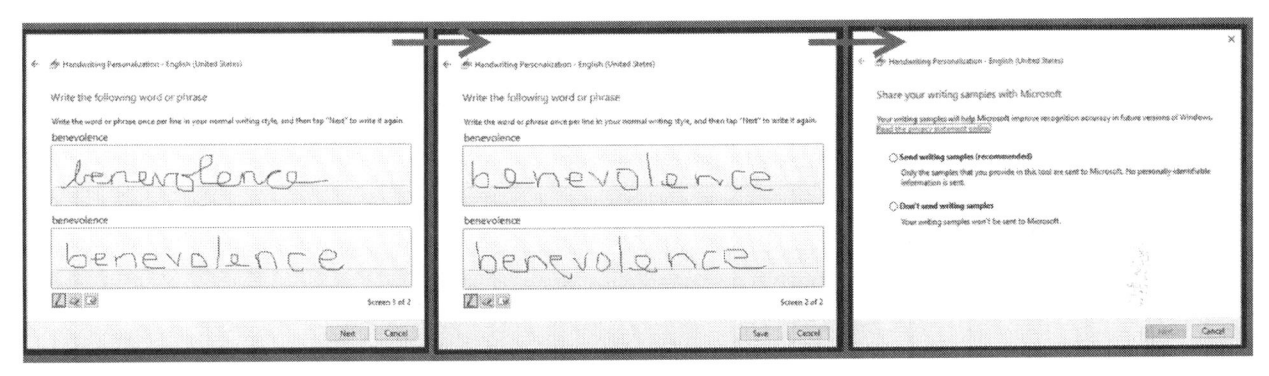

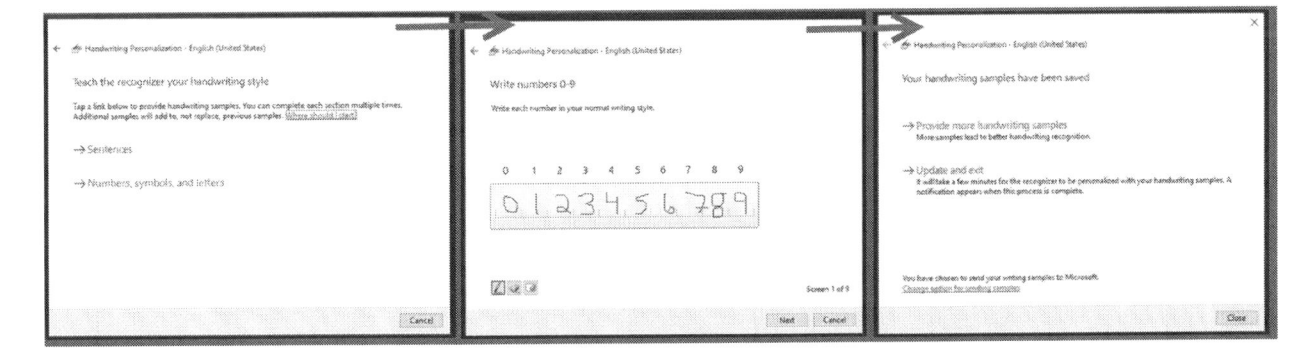

The first option "Target specific recognition errors" enables you to submit writing samples to Microsoft so it can recognize you as the writer. The second option "Teach the recognizer your handwriting style" is similar to the first but requires much more – numbers, characters, and many different writing notations.

I highly recommend you complete both options and then send these samples to Microsoft so that it can work with you better if you are using an input device that is geared toward actual writing as opposed to keyboard or menu-driven inputs, like a tablet or Microsoft Surface Pro.

After submitting each one to Microsoft, Windows 10 will give you a physical confirmation via an Updates message in the lower right hand corner of your screen, as follows.

Recognizer updated
The handwriting recognizer has been updated for English (United States).

Using Windows 10 Snipping Tool

The Windows 10 Snipping Tool is an Accessory app that is easy to use and enables you to make a copy of something on the screen in a snap. Go to Start Menu > All Apps > Windows Accessories > Snipping Tool. I personally feel it is a good idea to pin this app to your Taskbar, as follows:

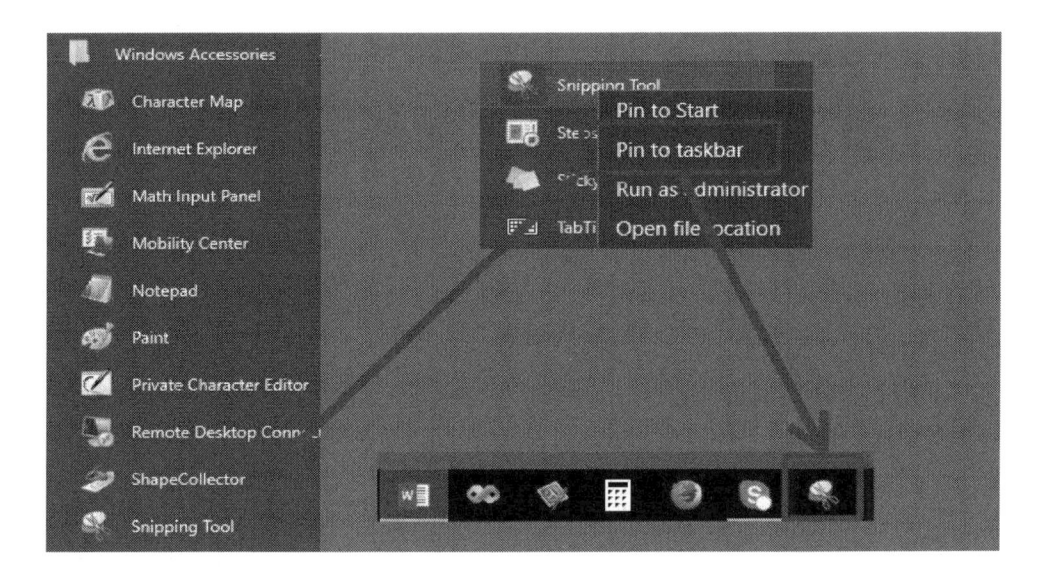

So, if you are using a program or are on the web and you need to take a fast screen shot, use the Snipping Tool. Select it from Start or the Taskbar. A small pop-up menu for the app is shown in the top right-hand corner of your computer screen. Click "New"; the screen turns into a hazy gray – this means you can now grab what you need.

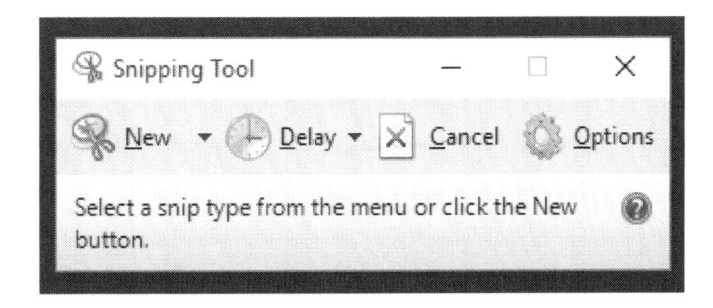

Step One: Go to the part of the screen you want to copy.

Step Two: Go to the top left hand corner of the square region you want to grab and press your mouse down and hold it down as you drag it to the lower right hand corner of the selection. Release the mouse. What you have selected appears now in the Snipping Tool window.

Step Three: Use the Save button to save this "grab" in the desired location and using the desired file format. Now you can use the saved file, for example, in a word processing document or in a presentation.

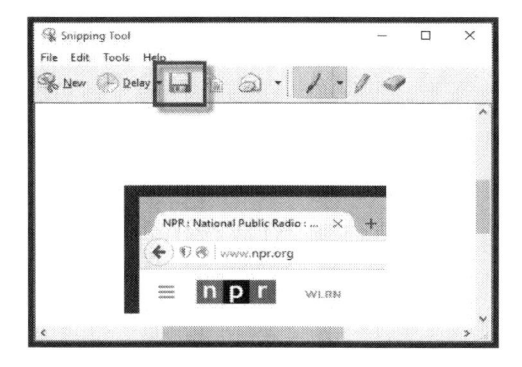

Using Windows 10 Steps Recorder

The Windows 10 Steps Recorder is an Accessory app that is easy to use and enables you to record process steps in an easy and intuitive manner. Go to Start Menu > All Apps > Windows Accessories > Steps Recorder.

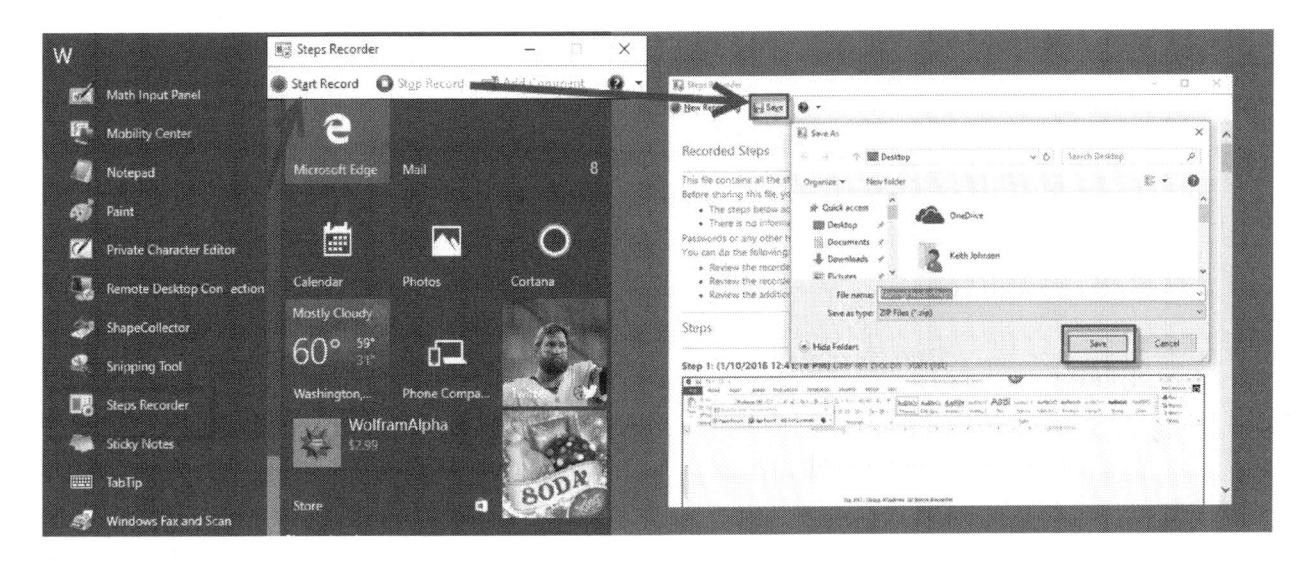

Using this app is very simple. A tiny pop-up window is shown where you can click "Start Record". Next, use your mousepad, keyboard, etc. to carry out actual steps that you want to document and record using this program. When finished, click on the "Stop Record' button.

Another window will be shown where you can save the recorded steps by entering a meaningful file name, saving to a meaningful file location, and ensuring the right file format to be saved.

This program is very useful if you are documenting a process and perhaps there are intricate details that are hard to explain – but through an actual recorded process, this becomes easier to revisit and communicate to others.

Using Windows 10 Sticky Notes

Since I was a college student in the late 1980s, "post-its" have been a way of life for me as a student and more recently as a working professional. I know many people who still do brainstorming, note down call-back numbers (on the telephone), take a message for others, and more – all via something called the "post-it" – which is essentially an earlier version of the Sticky Note.

This piece of paper is great because the back-side has a light strip of glue so that you can put the paper on a computer monitor or chair or desk or keyboard or door – and the person for whom the information applies – will see it and get the information it has. Sticky Notes – albeit in a virtual form now via Windows 10 – is the same general idea and approach to noting down and working with information "bits". The notes are not intended to last, but just to provide a temporary reminder – you can create them, drag and drop and display as needed…The path to this Windows 10 Accessory app is as follows: Start Menu > All Apps > Windows Accessories > Sticky Notes.

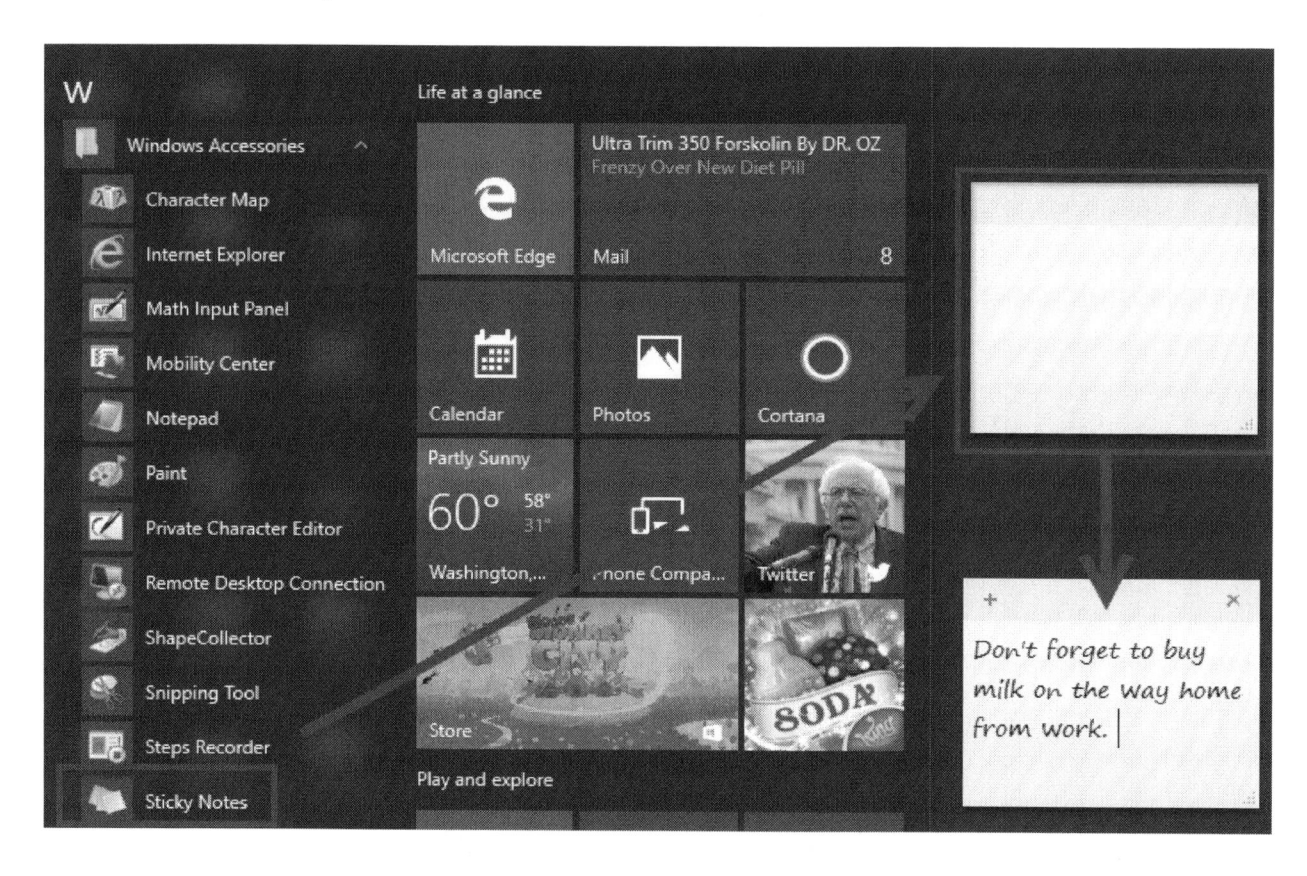

Using Windows 10 TabTip

The "TabTip" app is an abbreviation for "Tablet Tip". This Windows 10 Accessory app works as a type of "input panel" for when the computer (e.g. like a Microsoft Surface Pro) is functioning in tablet mode. The app opens a virtual keyboard that you see at the bottom of the screen and you can use this virtual keyboard to input information for whatever you are doing. What happens, essentially, is this app, via the virtual keyboard, enables you to enter text and other icons and symbols in a sort of free hand form because you are not using a physical keyboard right now but rather a virtual one. The path to this app is as follows:

Start Menu > All Apps > Windows Accessories > TabTip

Here are several virtual keyboards that are shown on the Windows 10 Home Screen based up what you have chosen to display as your input range …

Using Windows 10 Fax and Scan

Windows 10 Fax and Scan is an app that enables you to scan photos and/or documents right from your Windows 10 OS screen. You must, of course, attach a scanner to your computer (for scans) and attach a fax to your computer (for faxes) to gain full app functionality.

The path for this app is Start Menu > All Apps > Windows Accessories > Windows Fax and Scan. Essentially, this program works as a front-end and user interface to fax and/or scanning hardware that you connect to your computer running Microsoft Windows 10.

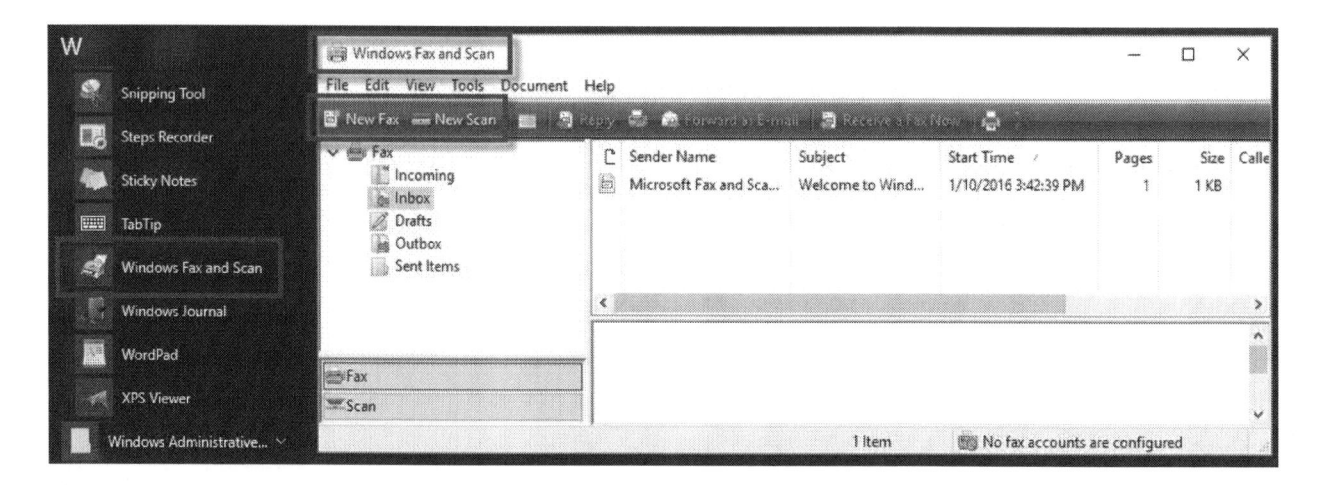

This app is very user friendly. Just look for the command you need at each step of the processes involving faxes and/or scans. Either you will see the option in one of the displayed menus or you will be prompted with pop-up windows which will provide you with the necessary input and connection information and steps needed to complete the faxes and/or scans.

Using Windows 10 Journal

Windows 10 Journal is an app that enables you to create "manual" (e.g. via your handwriting) notes like you would do on a physical notepad of lined paper. The path to this app is Start Menu > All Apps > Windows Accessories > Windows Journal. Please note that upon first use of this app you will be prompted with a pop-up window asking you if you want to install the Journal Note Writer printer driver. Unless you know for certain that you will not be printing out your journal notes, I would most definitely click the Install button here. When you finally enter the app, to get more info on this resource you can click the "About" option.

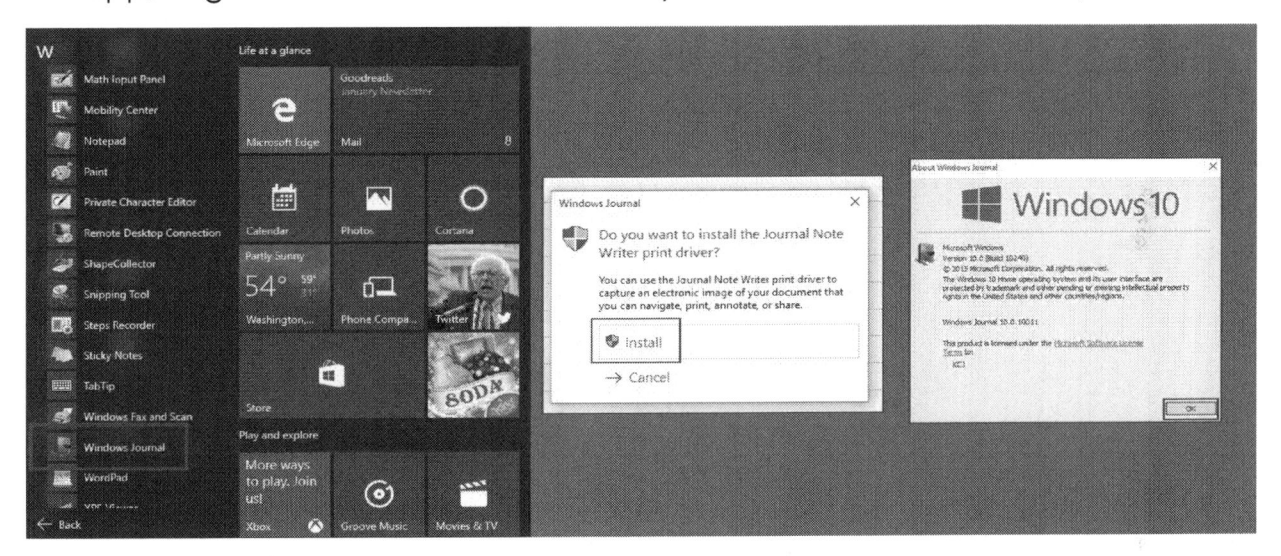

This app is very similar to the Windows Notepad Accessory app. However, in this case, you are working not with regular text but rather input from your own handwriting. From there, you can manage the notes you create as you do any other file in Windows 10 – save, create, delete, move, modify, share, etc.

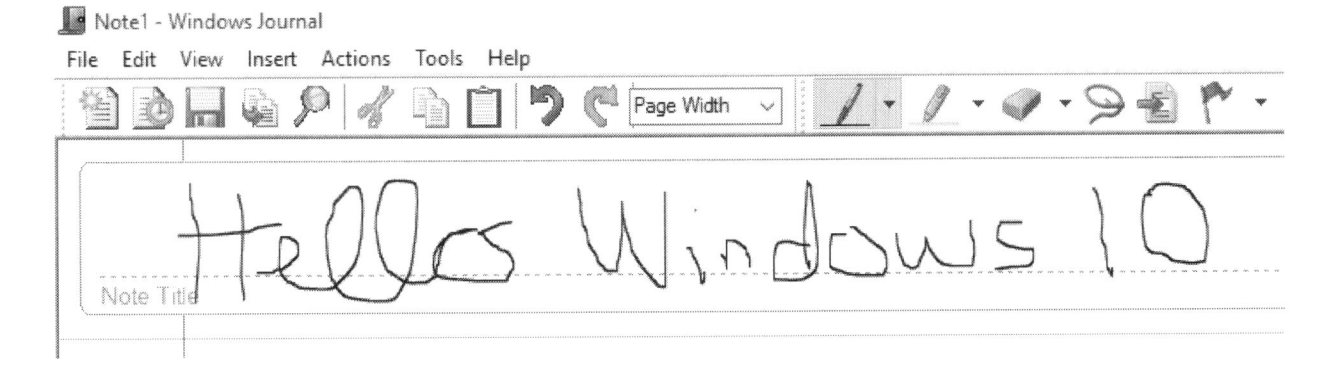

Using Windows 10 Wordpad

Wordpad is a basic word processor that comes with Windows 10. Wordpad has been a part of the Windows OS for a long time. This is because people use this app and it is a great fallback app should you have problems with another major Office Suite. The path to this app is Start Menu > All Apps > Windows Accessories > Wordpad. The three major Menu options for Wordpad are File, Home, and View. Within each of these menus are tools and resources that will help you to create, save, open, close, modify, and update your document as you need.

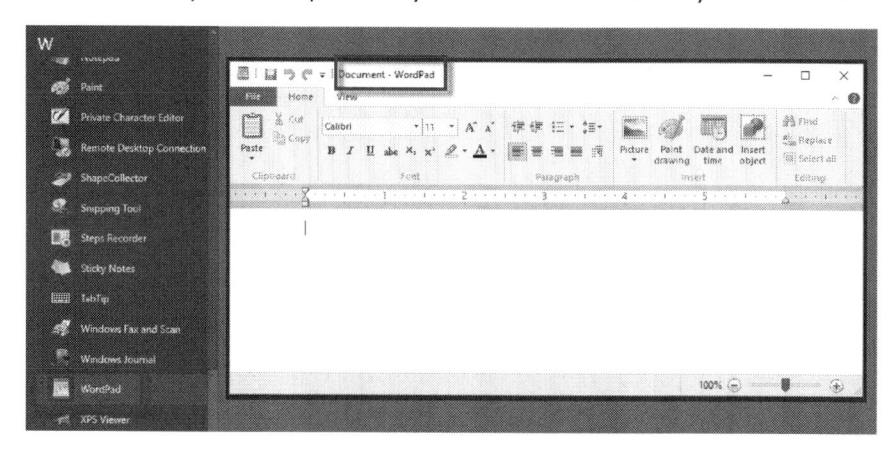

Wordpad Menu	Options Available
File	New, Open, Save, Save As, Print, Page Setup, From Scanner or Camera, Send in Email, About Wordpad, Exit
Home	Cut, Copy, Paste, Select Font – Size, Bold, Italic, Underline, Superscript, Subscript, Color, Background Color, Paragraph Left and/or Right Indent, Left Justify, Center Justify, Right Justify, General Justify, Bullets, Paragraph and Line Spacing, Picture, Paint, Date, Time, Object, Find, Replace, Select All, and more
View	Zoom In/Out, 100%, Ruler, Status Bar, Word Wrap, and Measurement Units

Using Windows 10 XPS Viewer

XPS is an acronym for "XML Paper Specification"; this is essentially a document format which can help you to view, save, digitally sign, share and also protect the inner content. To use a more humanistic description of XPS – it is a bit like having an electronic piece of paper. Please note that once an XPS document is created it cannot be undone – just like if you write out something in pen on a piece of paper – it is there. But, you can of course view it, sign it, and establish permissions as the document owner regarding its viewership. The path to this Windows 10 Accessories App is Start > All Apps > Windows Accessories > Windows 10 XPS Viewer. You will need a word processing app to create the XPS file. To create a file, go to Wordpad, for example, create then Print and Save As (.oxps) ... to the XPS document file format. Then you can see the file in the XPS Viewer app.

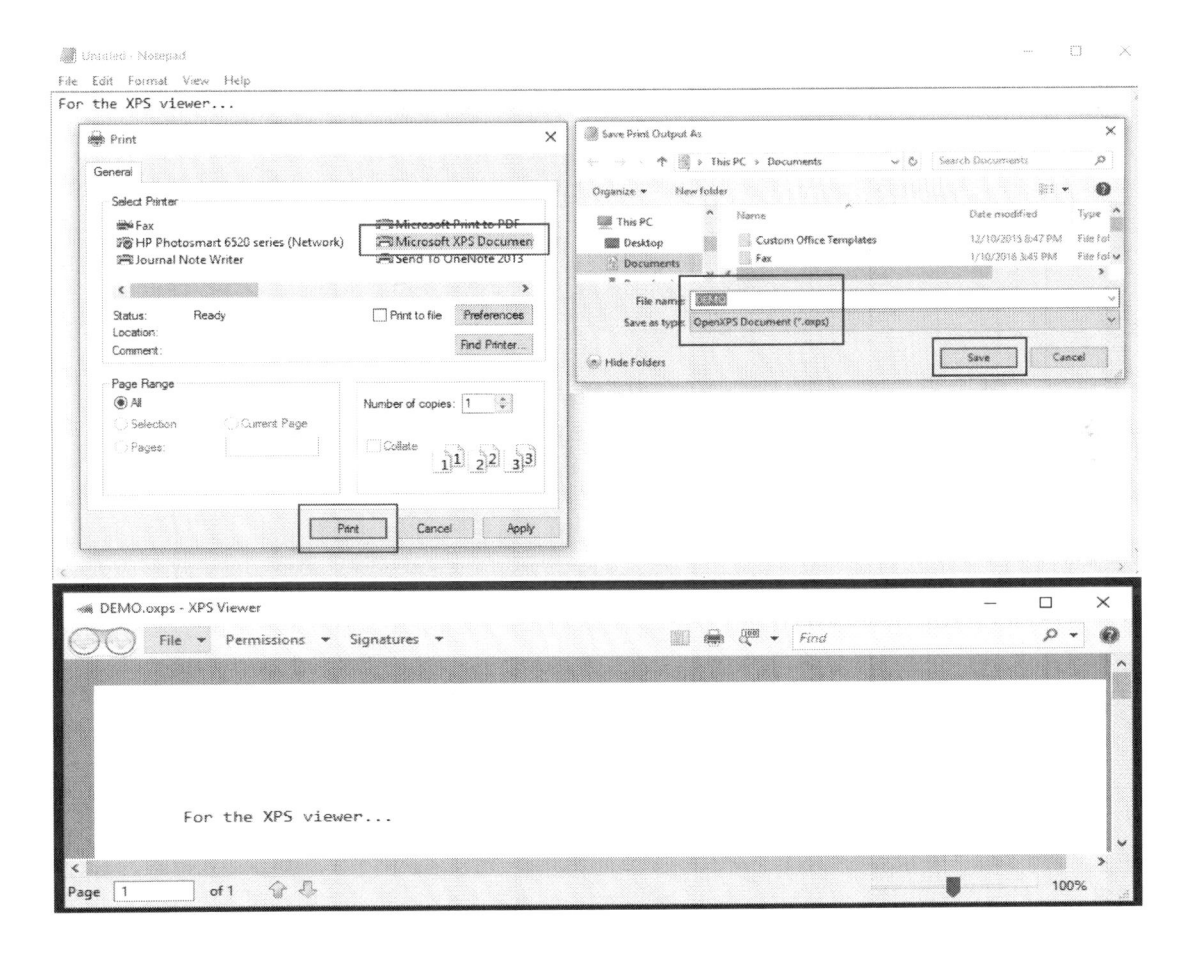

Section 15: Windows 10 Administration

Note: All of the Accessories listed in this section can be accessed *easily* by going to your Windows 10 Start Menu > All Apps > Scroll down to Windows Administrative Tools > Open the Program Listing > Make your individual selection.

Using Windows 10 Component Services

This tool should be used only by System Administrators. If you are not a System Administrator, please do not use this tool. Component Services enable you (the Windows 10 Administrator) to configure and determine which component services are to run or be disabled. Component Services are an underlying aspect of applications that run both within the Windows 10 OS and Windows applications.

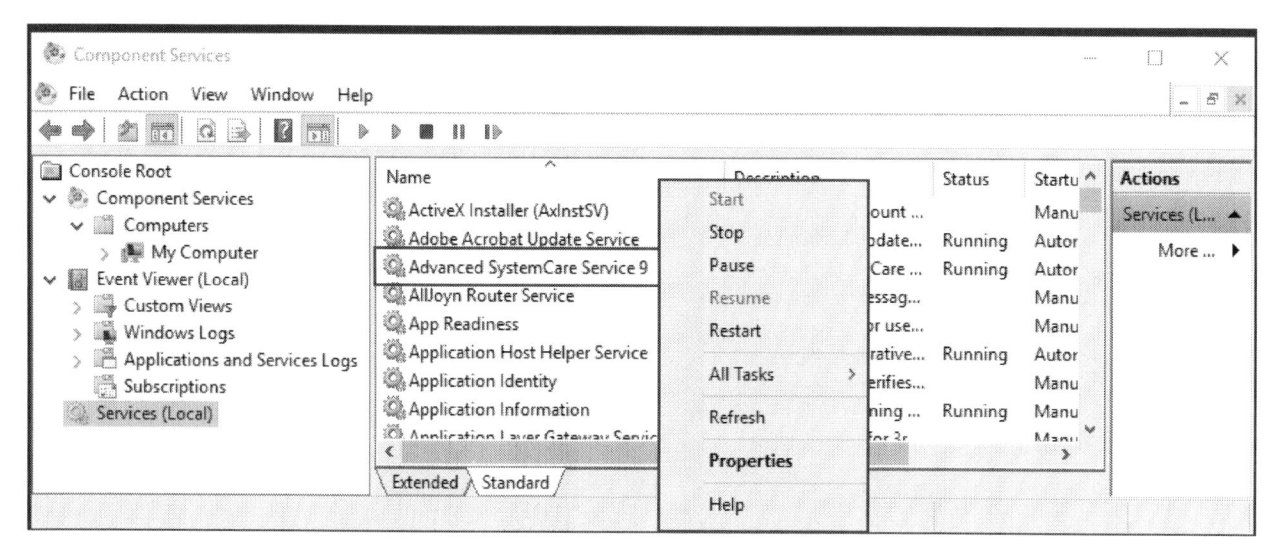

Probably the most common task in this option is to start, stop, or restart a component. Normally, this should not be necessary, but there are some resources in Windows 10 that are fragile and perhaps do not coexist well with some applications or other similar types of resources, so they might just spontaneously shut down. Here, you can restart the component service and the application should return to normal functionality. Again, this topic is mostly for System Administrators, so if you are one such individual, then you are most likely familiar with this aspect of Windows, especially from previous versions.

Using Windows 10 Computer Management

The Windows 10 Computer Management app enables you (the System Administrator) to work with important matters concerning System Tools, Storage, and Services/Applications. **This section is for System Administrators only. If you are not a System Administrator, please do not use this Windows 10 app.**

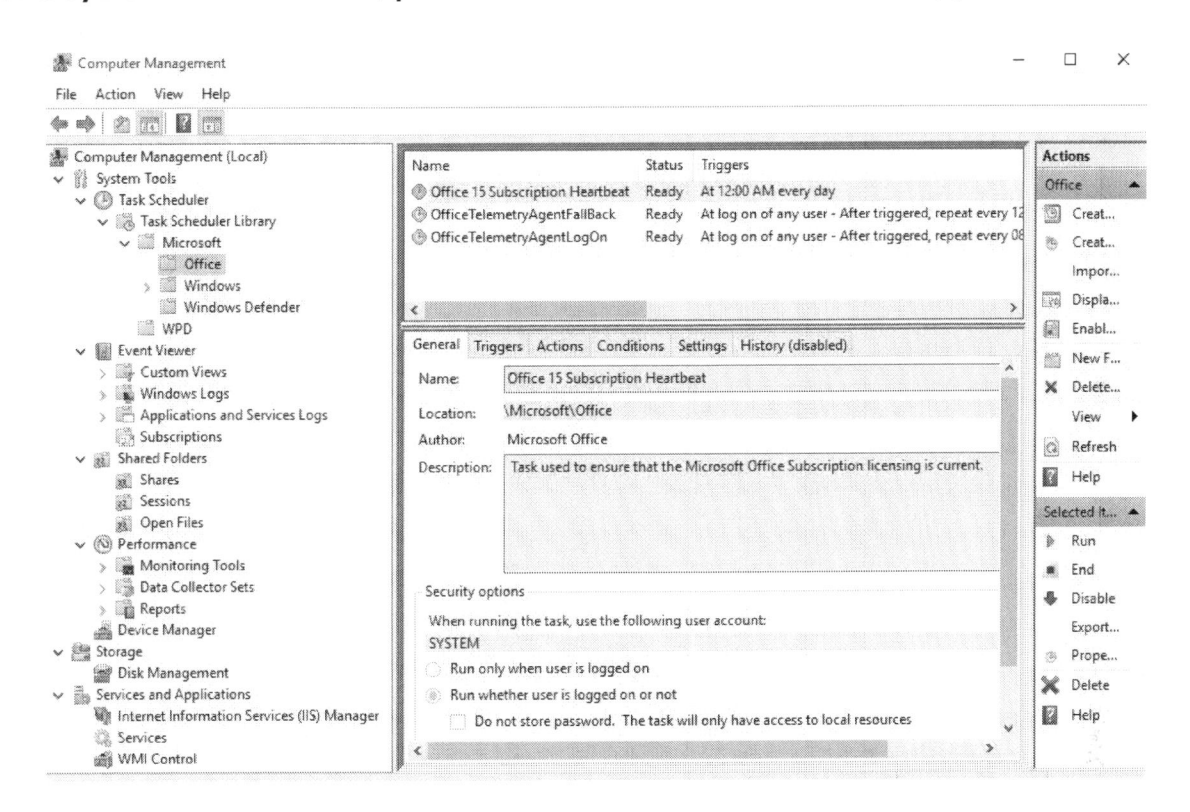

The Computer Management Tool has four main sections. They are System Tools (Task Scheduler, Event Viewer, Shared Folder, and Performance Monitoring), Storage, and Services/Applications. Task Scheduler enables you to program tasks in apps like Microsoft Office, Windows, and Windows Defender). Event Viewer enables you to see logs for both Windows as well as Applications and Services that Windows 10 can monitor. Shared Folders itemizes folder via categories such as Shares, Sessions, and Open Files. Performance let you see Windows 10 and apps on the system through the eyes of Monitoring Tools, Data Collector Sets, and Reports. This tool also lets you check on and monitor Storage via the Disk Management Tool. The final option of Services and Applications should only be handled by Senior System Administrators – as these deal with Internet Information Services (called IIS in the IT world), Services, and WMI Control.

Using Windows 10 Defrag and Optimization

Windows 10 has integrated two OS utilities which were previously known as separate applications – defrag (defragmentation) and optimization. Now, when you select this option under Windows Administrative Tools, both tools work in unison. The Analyze button works as sort of a pre-defrag/optimization resource where the disk is inspected sector-wise. Then, when you select the Optimize button, both defrag and optimize work together to get the disk to full operational wellness.

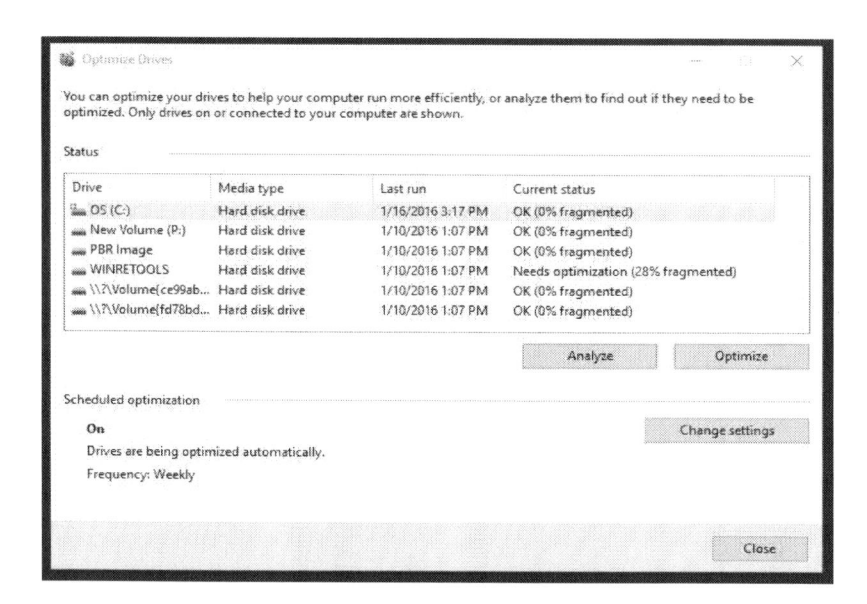

You can modify the optimization schedule by clicking on the Change Settings option that you see in the lower right-hand section of this window.

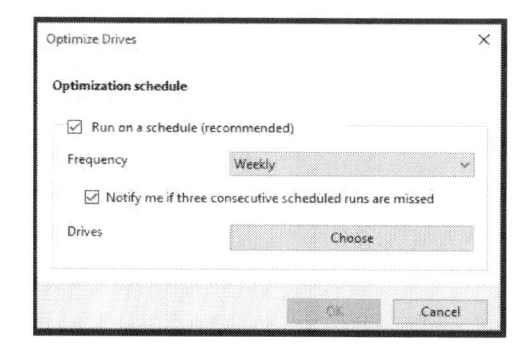

Select the optimization frequency and also specify the drives to optimize per your needs using this pop-up window. Then, after selecting OK, you return to the parent window above and can finalize all other details of your drive optimization needs.

Using Windows 10 Disk Cleanup

Go to Start Menu > All Apps > Windows Administrative Tools > Disk Cleanup. The following pop-up window is displayed. Choose the drive to clean up and press the OK button. Next, you will see a temporary pop-up window where Windows assesses the state and status of the drive before enabling this process.

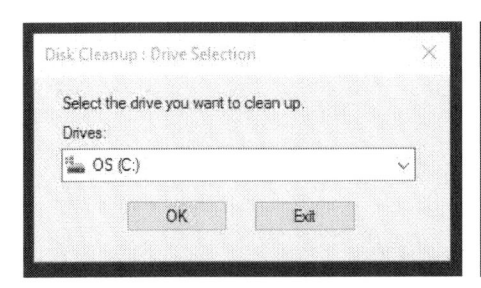

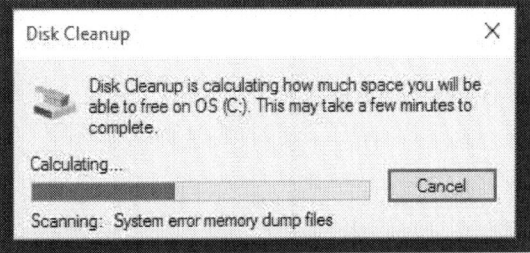

The next window that displays enables you to initiate the cleanup process. Click on the checkbox next to the file(s) you need to clean.

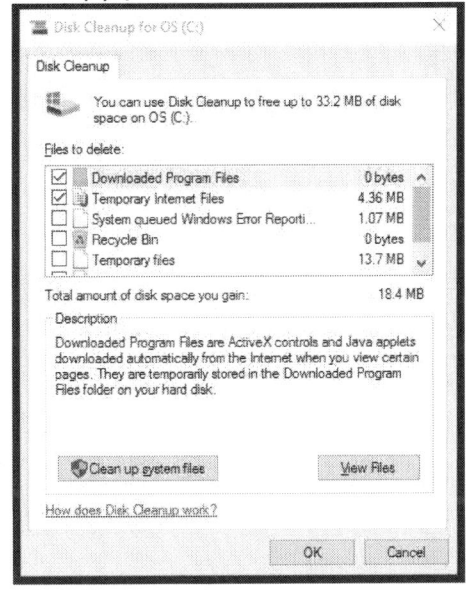

In my professional opinion, the most important files to clean up and remove from your Windows 10 system are Temporary Internet files, Temporary (local) files, and files in the Recycle Bin. Everything else is your call. Note that if you click on the cleanup system files button, this will repeat the process of Disk selection. If you click on the View Files button then the Windows Explorer will display showing the selected files. When you click OK on the Disk Cleanup window, those files that are checked are removed and with the certainty of having been done through Microsoft Windows 10 itself.

Using Windows 10 Event Viewer

This tool should only be used by System Administrators, so if you are not a System Administrator, please do not use this app. The Windows 10 Event Viewer app is a subsection of the Computer Management Tool discussed a few tips back in this book. Let us now look a bit closer at this resource.

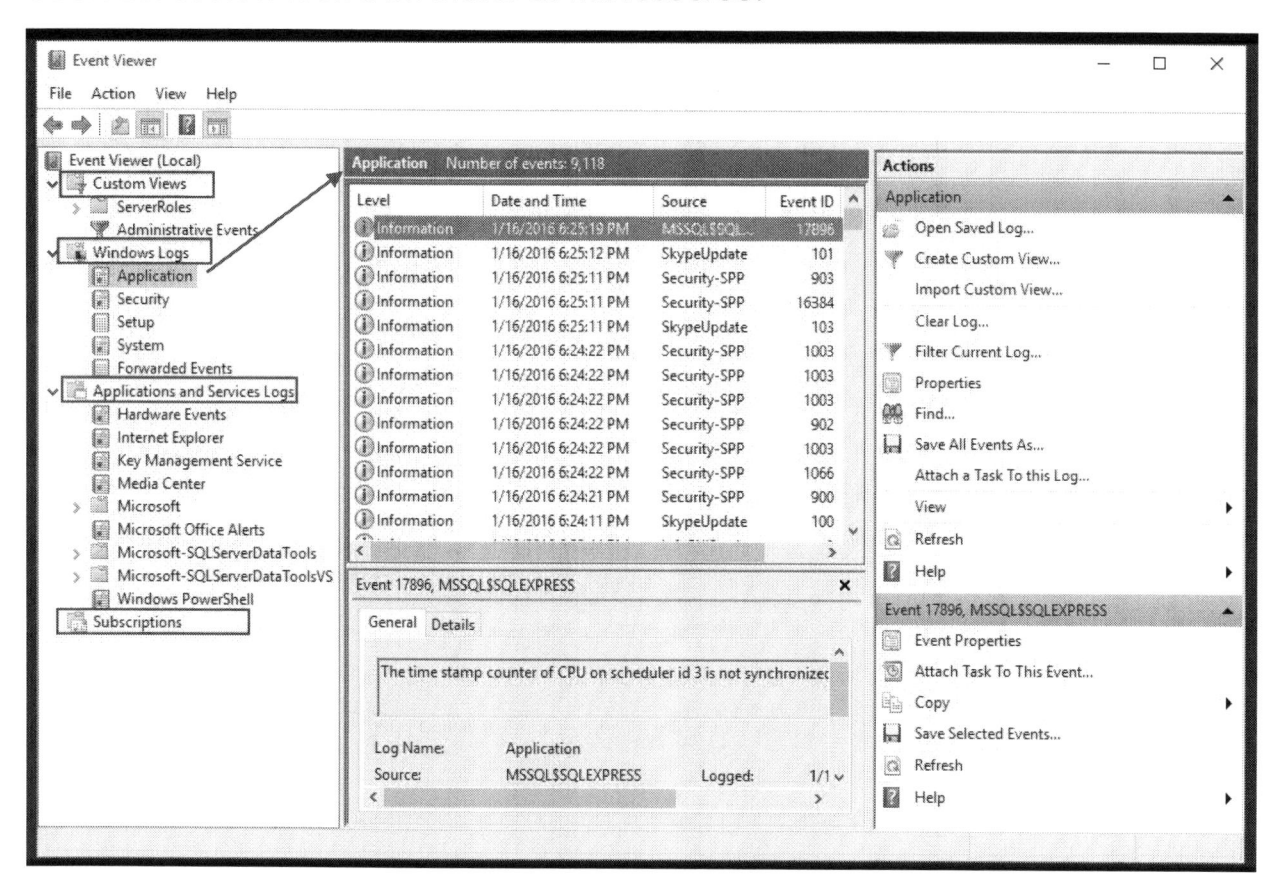

The four primary tools and system-level capabilities of the Event Viewer are Custom Views, Windows Logs, Applications/Services Logs, and Subscriptions. Custom views will depend upon Server Roles and Administrative Events. Windows Logs are a history of activities within Windows 10 per Application, Security, Setup, System, and Forwarded Events criteria. Applications and Services Logs are also a historical listing of Windows 10 events in terms of the following categories: Hardware, Internet, Key Management, Media Center, Microsoft, Microsoft Office Alerts, Microsoft – SQL Server Data Tools, Microsoft – SQL Server Data Tools (Visual Studio – this one is because I have Visual Studio on my machine), and Windows Powershell. Subscriptions are specific logs that you set up and "watch" via this option. I set up one Subscription to watch Windows Defender which is useful in checking the wellness of my machine against malware, for example.

Using Windows 10 Internet Information Services (IIS) Manager

This tool should only be used by System Administrators, so if you are not a System Administrator, please do not use this app.

Several years ago, while working at a previous job, I needed to create a Wiki for our technical publications, internally. So, using the WAMP (Windows Apache MySQL PHP) open source tools, I transformed my laptop into a server that was able to run a Wiki site. I downloaded the necessary (free) Wiki installation files from Wikimedia Foundation and soon I had a functional wiki running on my Lenovo Thinkpad laptop. Microsoft IIS is the very same, but from within the Microsoft platform.

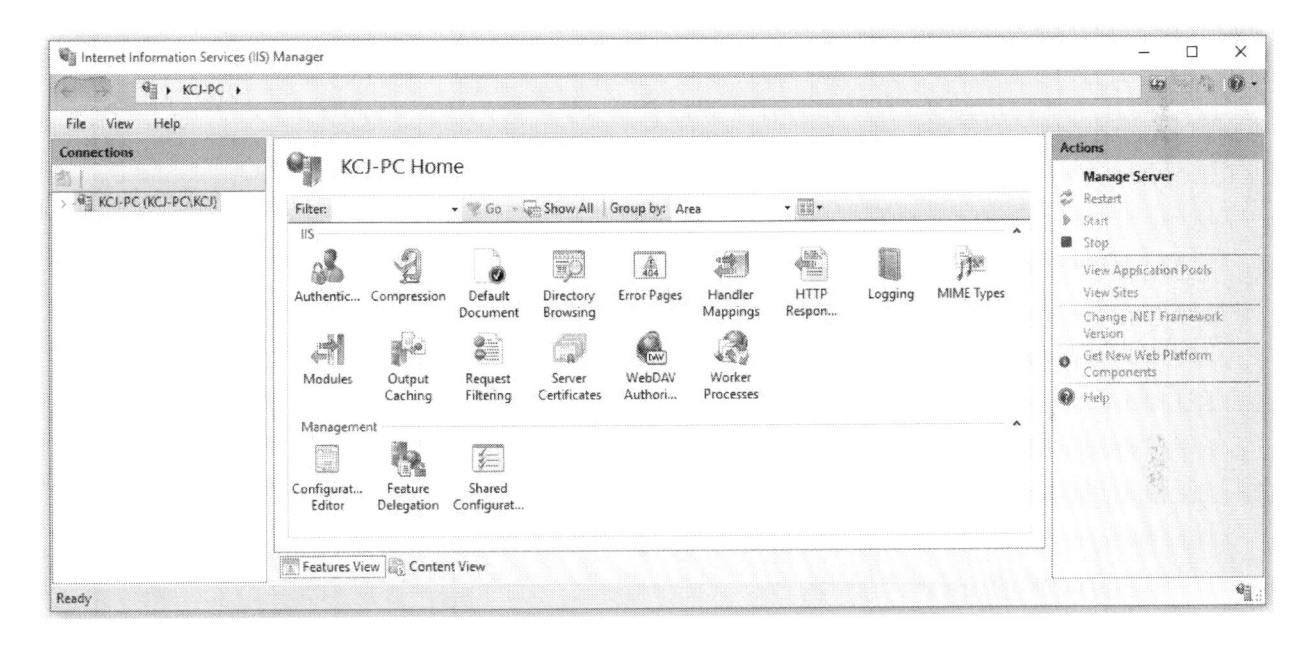

This is an *extremely* advanced topic and one that would require an entire book unto itself. So, with that said, I am going to stop here and just say that should you decide to transform your computer into a server, IIS can get you there.

Using Windows 10 Open Database Connectivity (ODBC)

This tool should only be used by System Administrators, so if you are not a System Administrator, please do not use this app. Open Database Connectivity (ODBC) finds its origins in Microsoft, back in the 1990s. Over the past twenty years, ODBC has been very useful because it enables applications and data to be ported between platforms and serves as a means of accessing and managing data – especially entire systems of data. Windows 10 features an ODBC app for 32 bit Data Administration as well as an app for 64 bit Data Administration. In the sample screen shot below, you can see how the ODBC app has picked up on the fact that I have Microsoft Office 2013 on my machine which has both MS Excel and MS Access – both are programs that can be used like a database because you can create information tables, sort, etc.

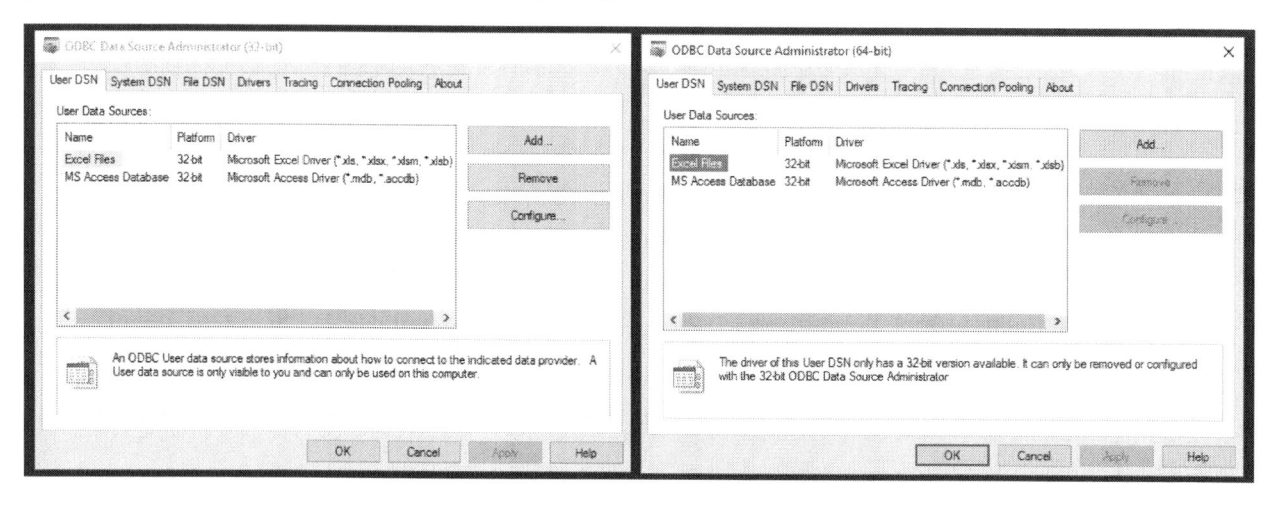

As you connect ODBC with the specific data management app – in this case MS Excel – you will need to click on the Configure button. The following window is displayed. Here, we see the Data Source, its Description, Rows to scan, and more.

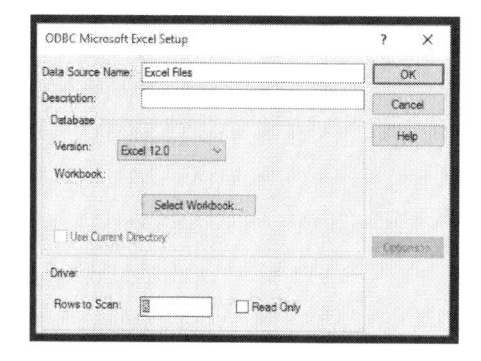

Using the Performance Monitor

This tool should only be used by System Administrators, so if you are not a System Administrator, please do not use this app.

Go to Start Menu > All Apps > Windows Admin Tools > Performance Monitor. With this resource, you can view Windows 10 performance data that is in real time or that is provided via a log. What you can do is create "data collector sets" which enable you to both configure and schedule Windows 10 performance data analysis events.

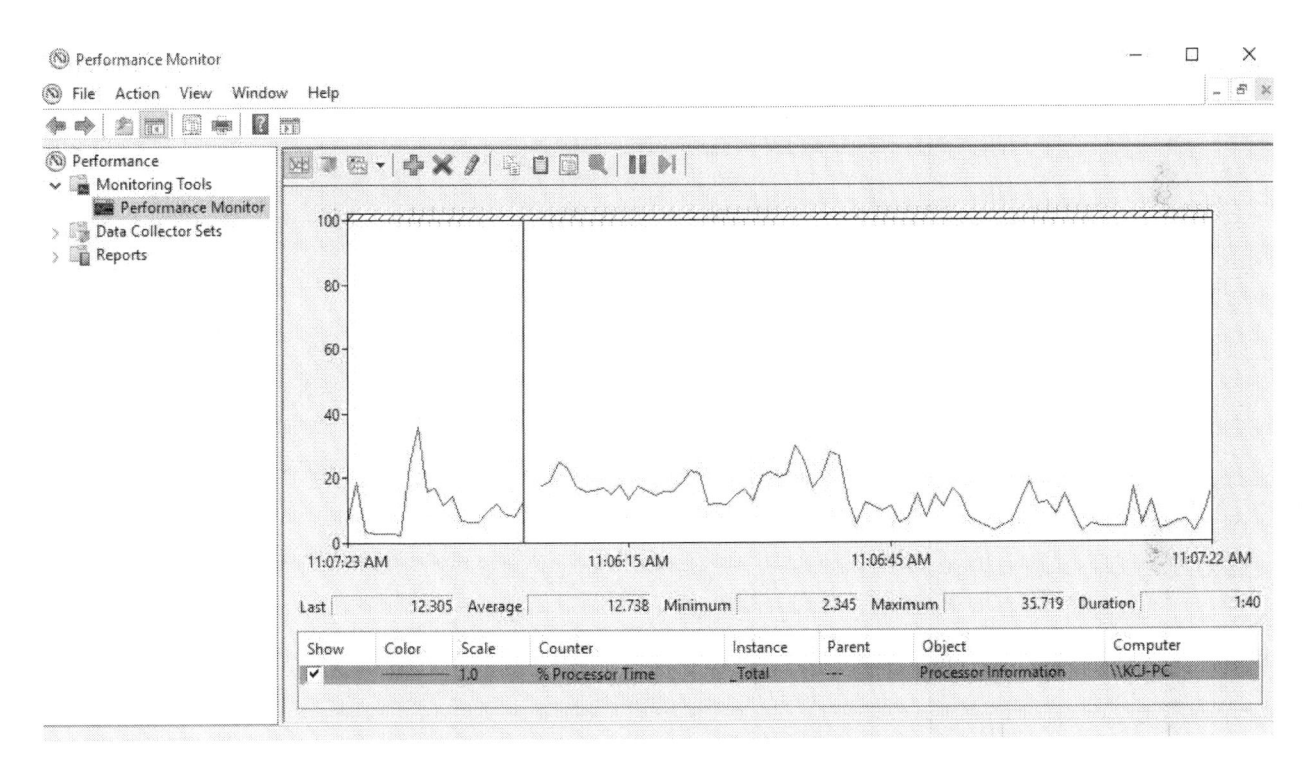

Note: The Resource Monitor (discussed on the following page) can be accessed via the Performance Monitor as well as directly via the Start Menu.

Using the Resource Monitor

This tool should only be used by System Administrators, so if you are not a System Administrator, please do not use this app.

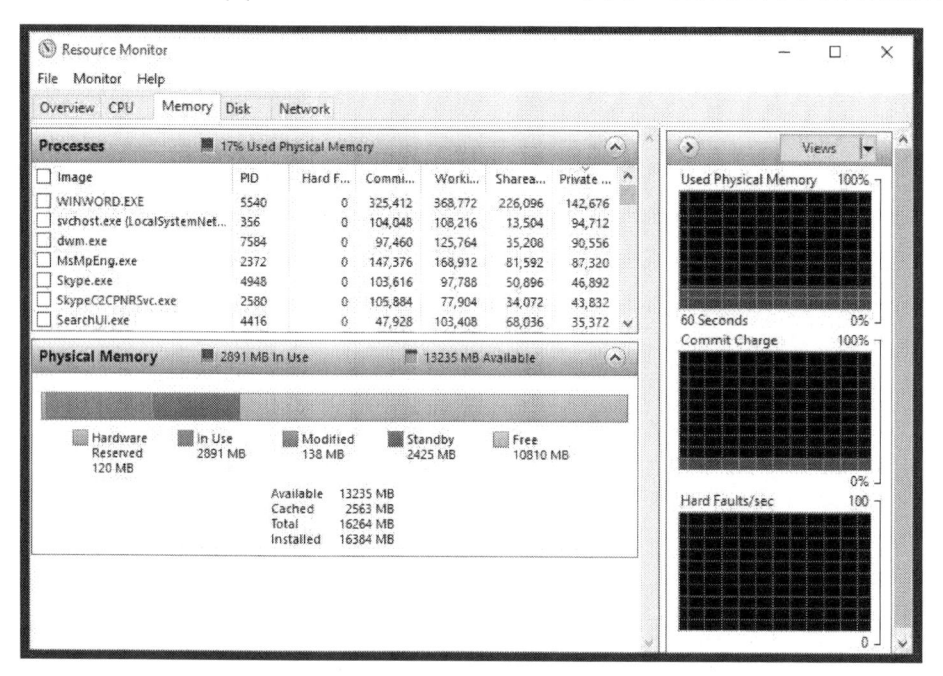

Go to Start Menu > All Apps > Windows Admin Tools > Resource Monitor.

This app enables you to see what is going on in Windows 10 – app by app and memory byte by memory byte. The Overview tab is where you can get an overview of system activity. The CPU tab enables you to see what is happening at the level of your Central Processing Unit (CPU). The Disk tab enables you to see activity per the disk you are using, in my immediate example here it is the C drive. Finally, if your computer is on a network, then you can see activity on the network that corresponds with your machine (running Windows 10).

Using Services

This tool should only be used by System Administrators, so if you are not a System Administrator, please do not use this app.

Go to Start Menu > All Apps > Windows Admin Tools > Services. This app is here to help you start, stop, configure and restart Windows Services. This is a tool which cannot be used lightly. Windows Services underlie the functionality of apps and so if a service is stopped, this could stop and app from working properly.

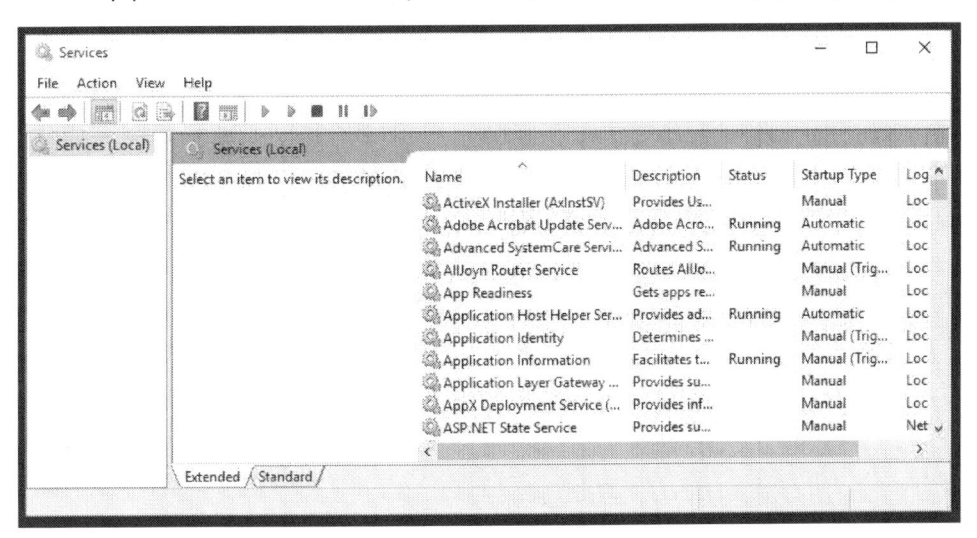

If you are absolutely sure about a service that is having problems, what you need to do is this – right click over it. A pop-up menu will be displayed and here you can use the options of the shown menu – like starting the service, pausing the service, restarting and more. There are two tabs in this app – extended services and standard services. Between these two tabs – you should be able to locate the specific service that needs your attention and manual command.

Using System Configuration

This tool should only be used by System Administrators, so if you are not a System Administrator, please do not use this app.

Go to Start Menu > All Apps > Windows Admin Tools > System Configuration.

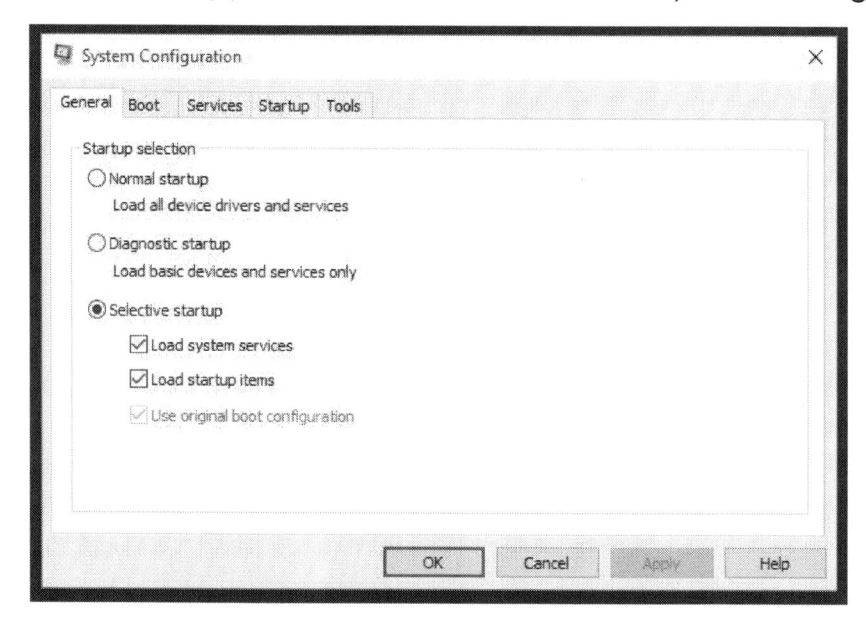

This app is a general administrative tool for the Windows 10 system. Here, you can monitor and yet update details regarding General Startup, Boot, Services, Task Manager Startup, and Tools.

I would be very careful about making changes here. Windows 10 – especially via the installation process - is able to determine, system-wise, the best path and actions for your machine (in terms of booting up, services, and more), in my humble professional opinion.

Windows has been around for twenty one years now and so sometimes technology can configure itself better than our individual selves, even as admins. So, feel free to surf the tabs you see, but only make a change when you truly understand the ramifications of what you are doing and/or changing.

Using System Information

This tool should only be used by System Administrators, so if you are not a System Administrator, please do not use this app.

Go to Start Menu > All Apps > Windows Admin Tools > System Information.

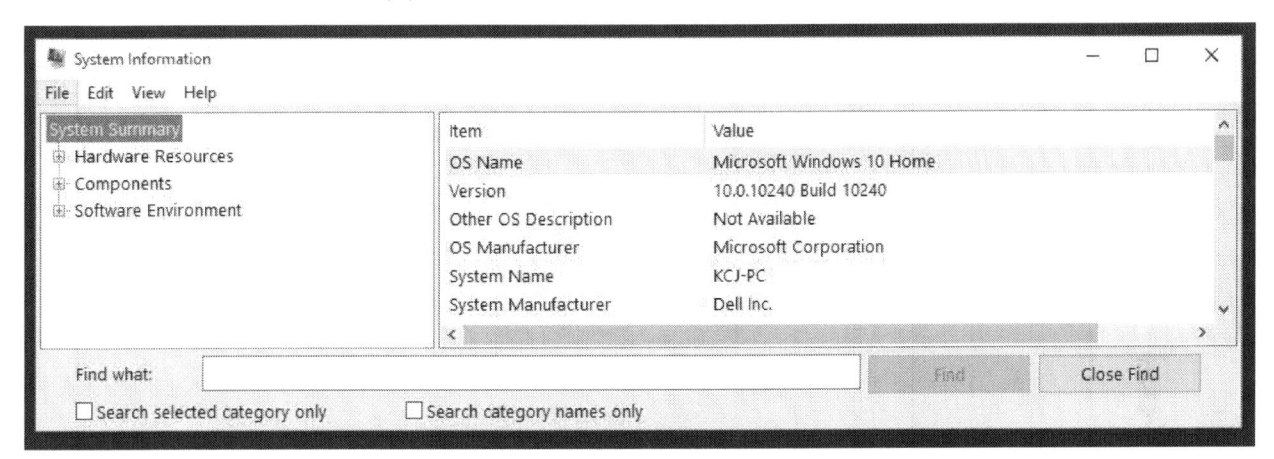

This is a great resource to use if you are troubleshooting a problem. Here, you will find absolutely every aspect of the system you have. By clicking on the right option in the left pane, you can see all details regarding Hardware Resources, Components, and the Software Environment.

Hardware Resources include Conflicts and Sharing, DMA, Forced Hardware, Input Output, IRQs, and Memory.

Component Resources include Multimedia, CD-ROM (if you have one on your computer), Sound Device, Display, Infrared, Input, Modem, Network, Ports, Storage, Printing, Problem Devices, and USB.

Software Environment Resources include System Drivers, Environmental Variables, Print Jobs, Network Connections, Running Tasks, Loaded Modules, Services, Program Groups, Startup Programs, OLE Registration, and Windows Error Reporting.

Using Task Scheduler

This tool should only be used by System Administrators, so if you are not a System Administrator, please do not use this app.

Go to Start Menu > All Apps > Windows Admin Tools > Task Scheduler.

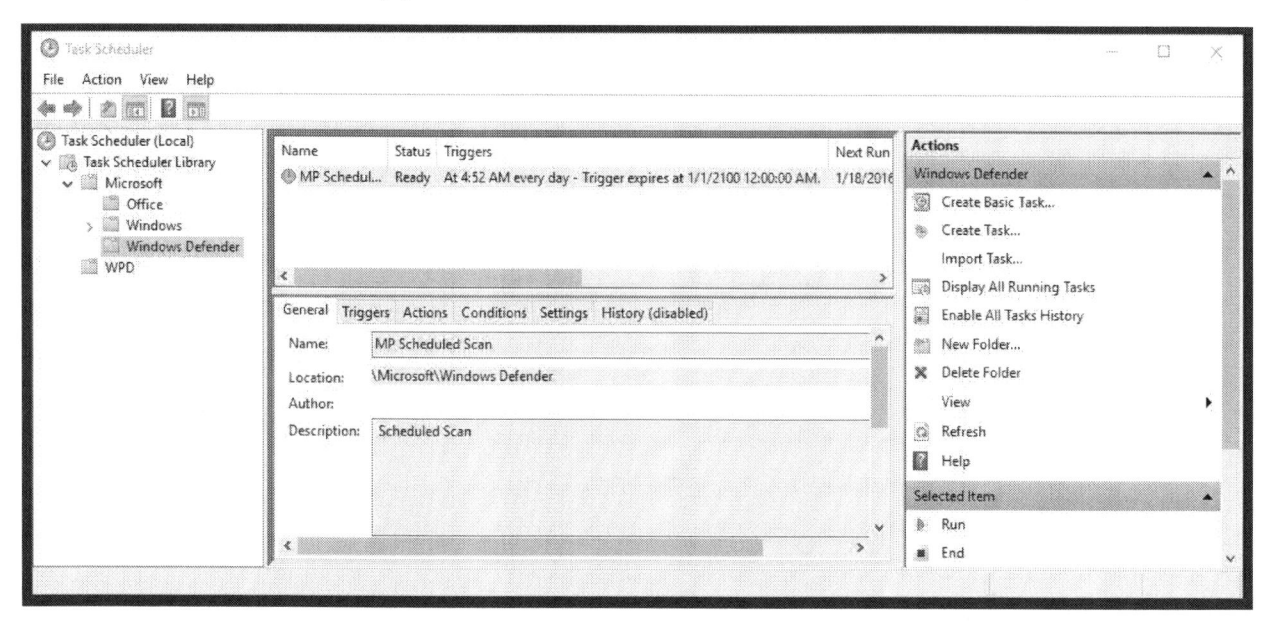

This Windows 10 Admin resource is here to help you setup and execute tasks at the OS level. Here is an example – it is good to run Windows Defender on a regular basis to ensure that your system is free of malware. Windows Defender is a great security program for your OS. So, you can set that scheduled run here in this app. Also, in the right pane as you can see, you can display all tasks that are currently running and you can also manually override a task in the bottom right pane with commands like Run and End.

Right now, I only have Office 2013 on my computer so the only tasks I can set up here are for my Windows 10 OS and Office 2013. As mentioned above, I recommend that only System Administrators use this resource – so that you do not create any unnecessary system level activities that might hamper the daily use of other Windows 10 apps.

Using Windows Firewall

This tool should only be used by System Administrators, so if you are not a System Administrator, please do not use this app.

Go to Start Menu > All Apps > Windows Admin Tools > Windows Firewall with Advanced Security.

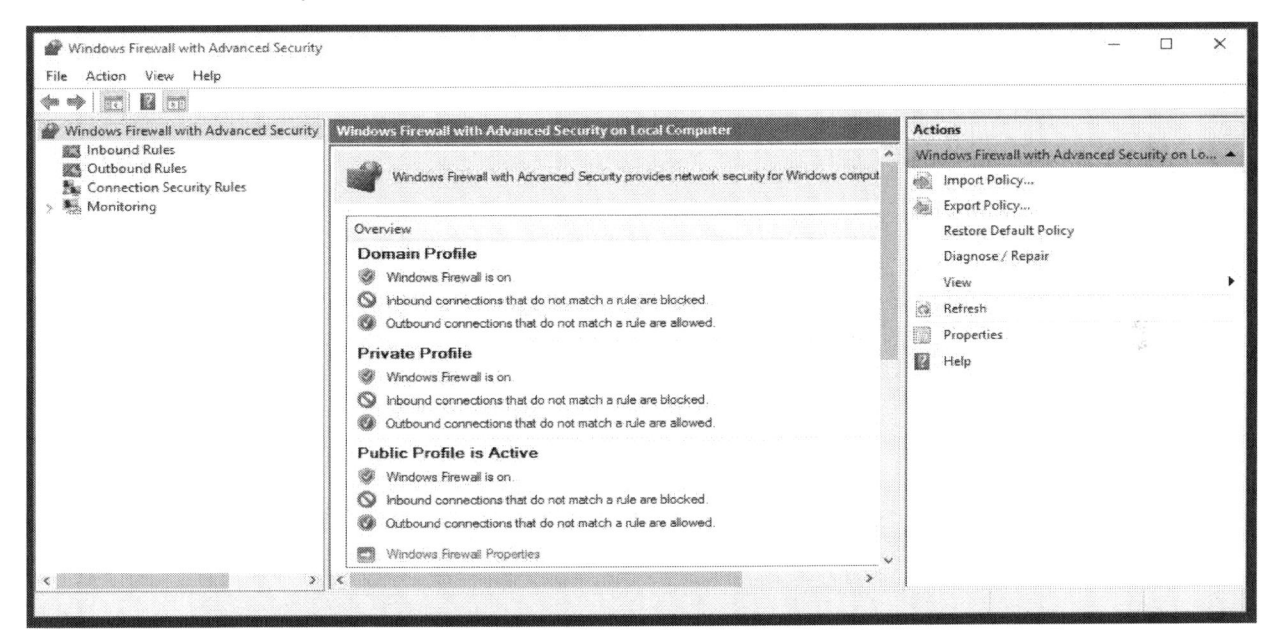

This is a brand new feature for Microsoft Windows – and it allows you to configure policies which will help you to establish strong network security for your Windows 10 computer.

With this resource, you can establish inbound firewall rules, outbound firewall rules, and connection rules. You can monitor your firewall, monitor established firewall rules, and setup security associations.

Using Windows Memory Diagnostics

Go to Start Menu > All Apps > Windows Admin Tools > Windows Memory Diagnostics. The following pop-up window is shown.

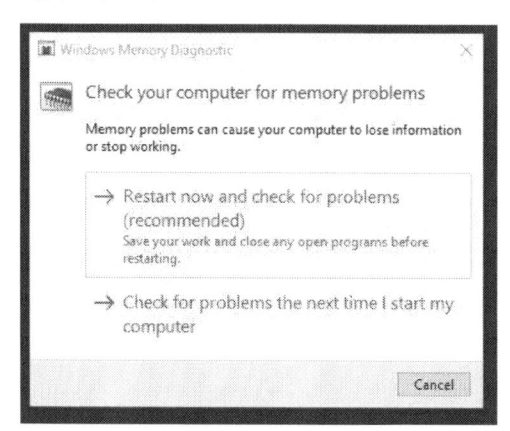

Windows 10 recommends that you select the first of the two options given in the pop-up window that is displayed. So, save your work first, then click on this link and you will see the following system level screen.

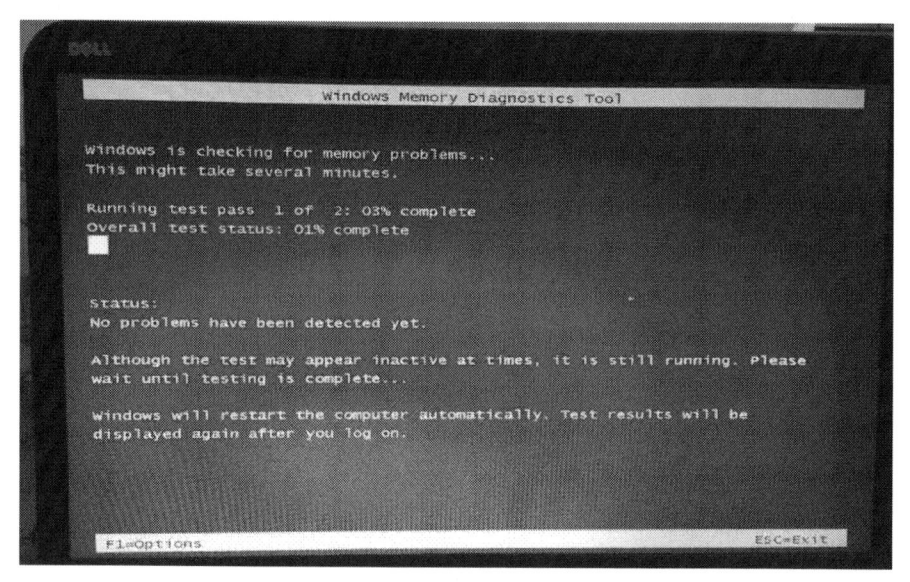

If there is one truly safe Admin Tool in Windows 10 – it is this one because all you are doing is checking on your Windows Memory. You are not changing configurations. After this tool is finished, Windows will restart. Then, you will be shown the diagnostic results after logging back in to your computer.

Using iSCSI Initiator

This tool should only be used by System Administrators, so if you are not a System Administrator, please do not use this app.

The acronym "iSCSI" stands for *Internet Small Computer Systems Interface*. iSCSI is a standard for IP (Internet Protocol) based storage networking that can connect you to external and usually distant data storage devices. As a Windows 10 user with this app, you become the "initiator" and through specific SCSI commands you send over an IP network, the data center or data-storage location on the other end can readily receive and store transmitted data as well as communicate with you, the initiator.

Go to Start Menu > All Apps > Windows Admin Tools > Using iSCSI Initiator.

If the app is not shown, you will be prompted with several pop-up windows to setup iSCSI use on your computer. If the app is shown, then your machine has been setup to work with the iSCSI protocol and subsequent data transmission.

Due to the sensitive nature of this app, I am going to stop here. This app really requires a DBA (Database Administrator) or SysAdmin (System Administrator) because you will be dealing with sensitive commands that relate to the iSCSI standard and unfortunately I do not have the space in this book to cover that topic. The specific interface could be a book unto itself. If you absolutely need to use this app, then please contact Microsoft Tech Support for Windows 10. Thanks.

Section 16: Windows 10 Ease of Access

All of the Accessories listed in this section can be accessed *easily* by going to your Windows 10 Start Menu > All Apps > Scroll down to Windows Ease of Access > Open the Program Listing > Make your individual selection.

Using Windows 10 Magnifier

The Windows 10 Magnifier app enables you to view your desktop as if you were looking through a magnifying glass. As soon as you select this app, the desktop is immediately magnified and you can use your mouse or touchpad to navigate around in this fashion. There are three degrees of magnification that you can use via your mouse – full-screen, docked, or lens. Full screen is where your whole screen is magnified. Docked simply means the magnification process is "docked" or limited to a specific portion of the desktop. While all three are like using a magnifying glass, the option of lens is that much more intense. After having fun with this app, you can press Windows logo key ⊞ + Esc. Now you should be back to a regular viewing of your desktop.

Note: I will be discussing customized use of Magnifier in the Settings section.

Using Windows 10 Narrator

Narrator is a Windows 10 app that reads selected text or text about objects on your desktop. You can use narrator to read a webpage. You can also use narrator to read information about a file.

To start Narrator, click the Windows logo key and Enter key simultaneously on your keyboard. You will see a blue box. Move that blue box to where you want narrator to read. If you are on a web page, for example, then drag and drop the bottom right-hand corner so that all text you need read is within the blue box. Narrator will first identify the webpage or document itself and then begin reading the text. After you have finished using Narrator, again click the Windows logo key and Enter key simultaneously on your keyboard. Narrator will close and also verbally tell you it is doing so.

Note: I will be discussing Narrator customization in the Settings section (a bit later in this book).

Using Windows 10 On-Screen Keyboard (OSK)

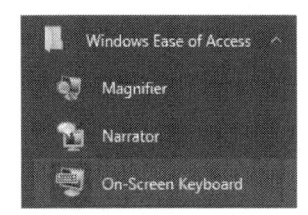

Go to your Windows 10 Start Menu > All Apps > Scroll down to Windows Ease of Access > On Screen Keyboard (OSK). This app enables you to bypass use of an external keyboard whether it be on your laptop of desktop PC. Maybe your keyboard has an issue and you have to type a paper for tomorrow at school or maybe you have something you must turn into your boss tomorrow – so besides sheer convenience and ease of use, this resource also has practical aspect.

I will address customized use of this app in Settings later on in this book. If you want to use some of the bells and whistles, if you will, that make this app fun – like sounds like the actual "typing" sound and more, then click on the Options button. You can decide on the nuances of how this app will perform for you. There is no need to have a touchscreen for this app. You can use a mouse or other pointing device to select typing inputs from the on-screen keyboard. But if you have a Surface Pro or a tablet or another device that does not necessarily have a keyboard ready to use, this is a great feature of Windows 10 to call into service. Just make sure that you have both opened this app as well as placed your cursor into the location on the screen where you are going to type....and type away. To close, just click on the X icon you see in the OSK's display window.

Using Windows 10 Speech Recognition

Microsoft Windows 10 has a fantastic resource for voice input and voice control of your Windows experience – the Speech Recognition app. As you select this tool for the first time, a wizard will walk you through each step so that it will work properly with the machine's microphone and/or headset microphone (if that is how you are interfacing). Here are the wizard's setup steps...

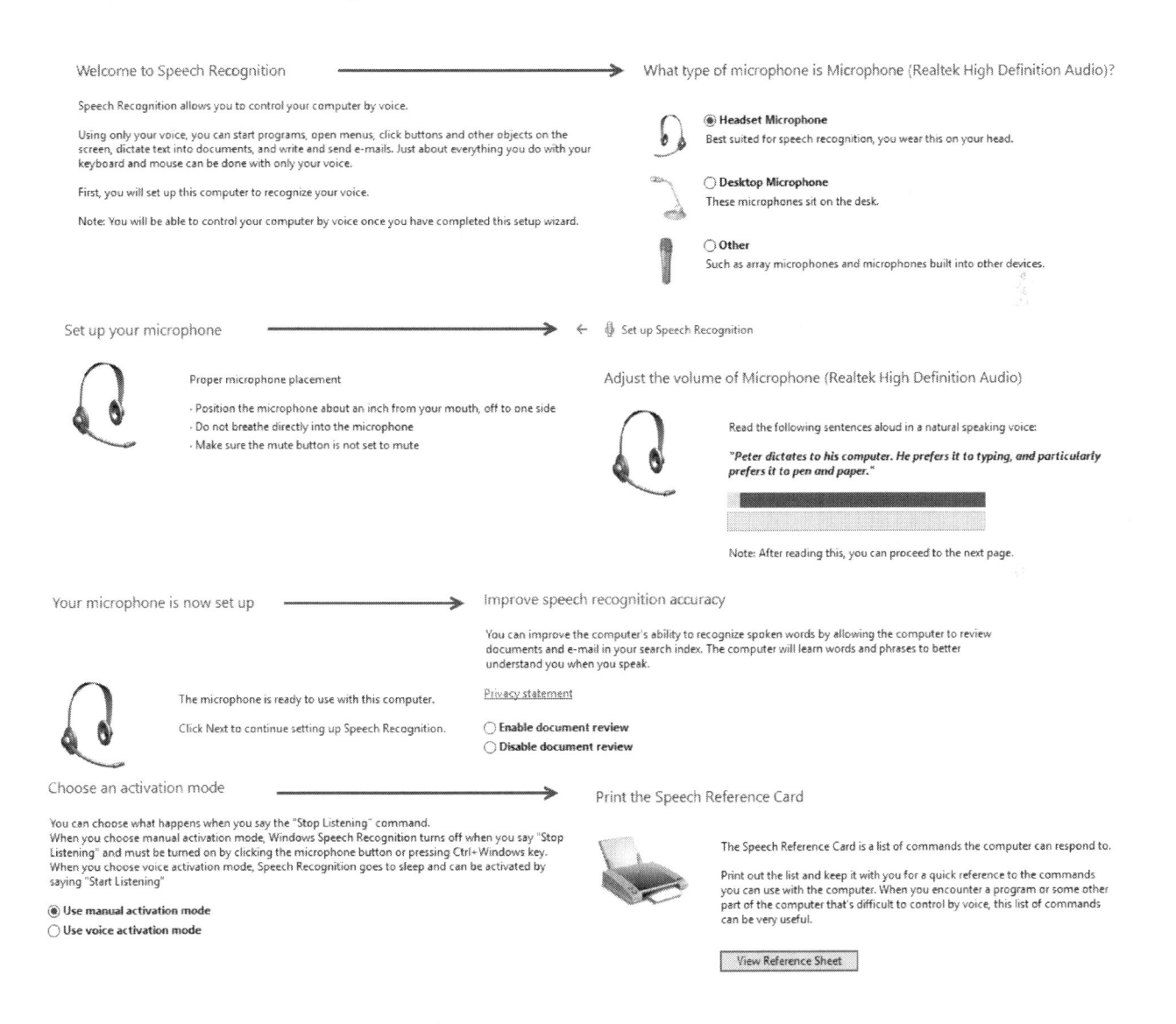

Welcome to Speech Recognition

Speech Recognition allows you to control your computer by voice.

Using only your voice, you can start programs, open menus, click buttons and other objects on the screen, dictate text into documents, and write and send e-mails. Just about everything you do with your keyboard and mouse can be done with only your voice.

First, you will set up this computer to recognize your voice.

Note: You will be able to control your computer by voice once you have completed this setup wizard.

What type of microphone is Microphone (Realtek High Definition Audio)?

- ● Headset Microphone
  Best suited for speech recognition, you wear this on your head.
- ○ Desktop Microphone
  These microphones sit on the desk.
- ○ Other
  Such as array microphones and microphones built into other devices.

Set up your microphone

Proper microphone placement
- Position the microphone about an inch from your mouth, off to one side
- Do not breathe directly into the microphone
- Make sure the mute button is not set to mute

Set up Speech Recognition

Adjust the volume of Microphone (Realtek High Definition Audio)

Read the following sentences aloud in a natural speaking voice:

"Peter dictates to his computer. He prefers it to typing, and particularly prefers it to pen and paper."

Note: After reading this, you can proceed to the next page.

Your microphone is now set up

The microphone is ready to use with this computer.

Click Next to continue setting up Speech Recognition.

Improve speech recognition accuracy

You can improve the computer's ability to recognize spoken words by allowing the computer to review documents and e-mail in your search index. The computer will learn words and phrases to better understand you when you speak.

Privacy statement

- ○ Enable document review
- ○ Disable document review

Choose an activation mode

You can choose what happens when you say the "Stop Listening" command. When you choose manual activation mode, Windows Speech Recognition turns off when you say "Stop Listening" and must be turned on by clicking the microphone button or pressing Ctrl+Windows key. When you choose voice activation mode, Speech Recognition goes to sleep and can be activated by saying "Start Listening"

- ● Use manual activation mode
- ○ Use voice activation mode

Print the Speech Reference Card

The Speech Reference Card is a list of commands the computer can respond to.

Print out the list and keep it with you for a quick reference to the commands you can use with the computer. When you encounter a program or some other part of the computer that's difficult to control by voice, this list of commands can be very useful.

[View Reference Sheet]

Once you get this app all set up, then you can start using it right away.

Because I really like this app, I am going to pin it to my taskbar for fast access. This enables me to bypass the four step route of Start > All Apps > Ease of Access > Windows Voice Recognition. If you are using a headset like I am, make sure it is plugged into your USB port, then you get started. Once the app is activated, say "start listening", as the program indicates below.

Now say "Open Windows Defender". This is what you should see.

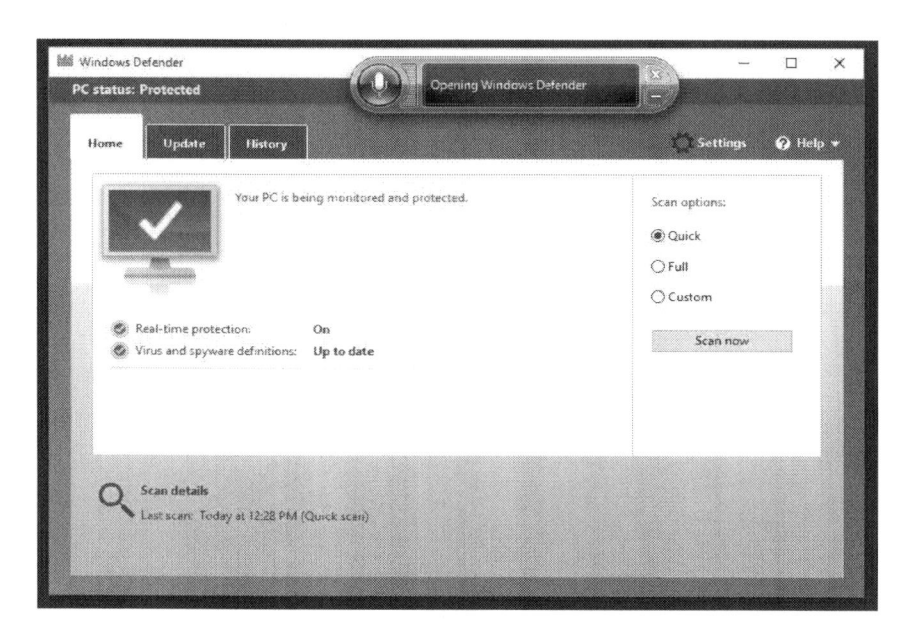

Now, let us do the opposite. Say "Close Windows Defender". Windows 10, through the Speech Recognition app, will now close Windows Defender. Cool, eh? You bet. There is one web page I want to recommend that has a complete listing of all commands for this app. Microsoft has linked this page to its Windows 10 Help website, so even though the marker is for Windows 7, the commands still stand here for the Windows 10 OS. In my humble opinion, the two most useful links on this page are common speech recognition commands and dictation.

http://windows.microsoft.com/en-us/windows/common-speech-recognition-commands#1TC=windows-7

Section 17: Windows 10 Powershell

This tool should only be used by System Administrators, so if you are not a System Administrator, please do not use this app.

Note: Powershell is essentially an advanced version of command-line DOS that also works with a Microsoft Scripting Language. Powershell is able to work with not just basic DOS commands but also advanced processes that can be given via specific scripting instructions. The following Microsoft web page covers Powershell in great detail, above and beyond the regular Microsoft Windows 10 Help page.

https://technet.microsoft.com/library/bb978526

Using Windows 10 Powershell (regular, x86, ISE, ISE x86

Go to Start Menu > All Apps > Windows Powershell. *Depending upon your machine*, select one of the following: Powershell, Powershell x86, Powershell ISE, or Powershell x86 ISE.

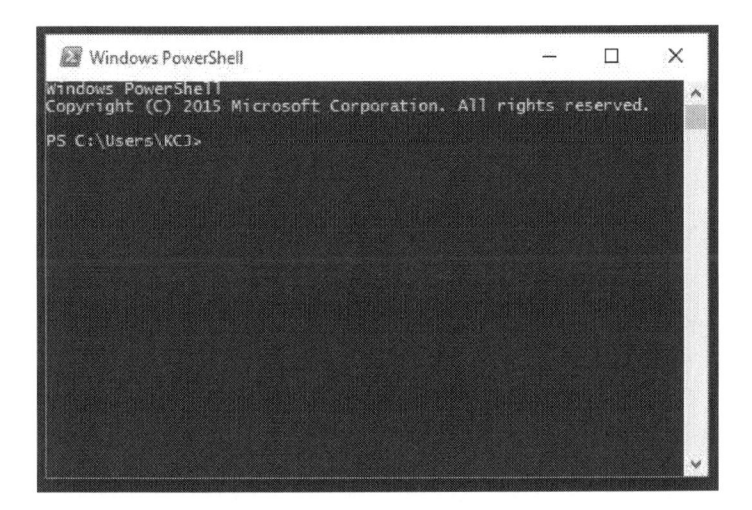

One of the easiest commands to enter is **dir** which is a simple request to Windows 10 (through a traditional DOS command) to show all directories within the currently displayed directory. So, click on the given command line to place your cursor there, type in **dir** and then press your Enter key.

Windows Powershell will show you a directory listing as requested.

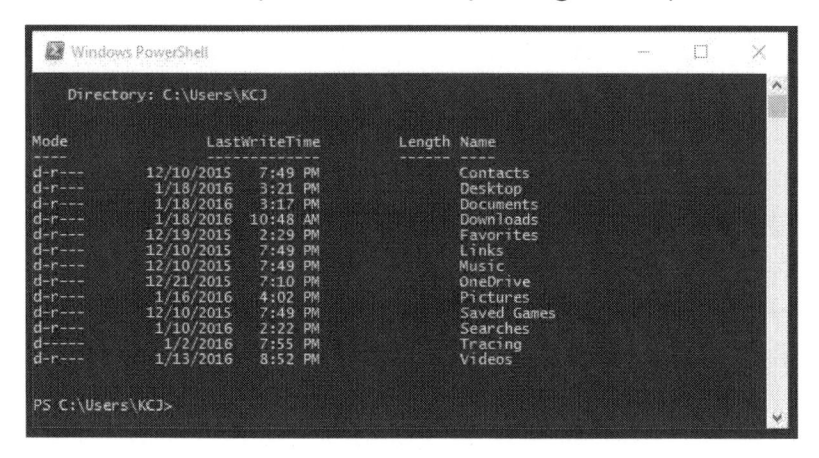

If you need to accomplish a basic system-level task (like seeing a directory listing or perhaps copying a file but not through the regular Windows GUI) and if you do not need the power of Windows Powershell (no pun intended), then I recommend you use the basic DOS prompt. All you have to do is activate your Search box at the bottom of your Home Screen with a single click, type in CMD, and press Enter. Or if you have Cortana on and are using Cortana, then say CMD. Either way, the pop-up window with your DOS prompt will be displayed. Here you can do what you must but through the DOS prompt itself without using Powershell.

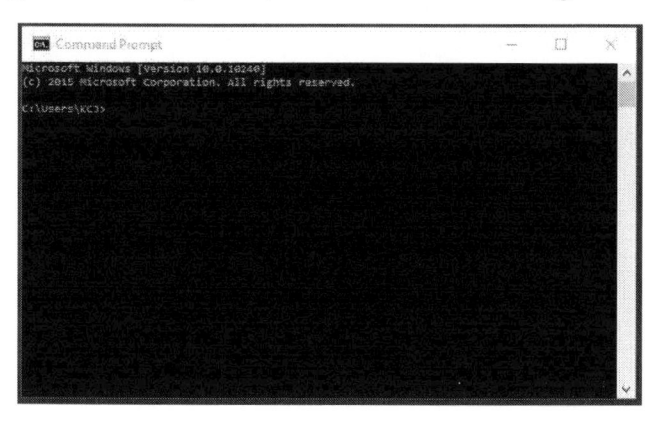

Note: To exit from both Powershell and the DOS prompt windows, type in **exit**. Press your Enter key and the command-line window should close.

Section 18: Windows 10 System Apps

All of the Accessories listed in this section can be accessed *easily* by going to your Windows 10 Start Menu > All Apps > Scroll down to Windows System > Open the Program Listing > Make your individual selection.

Windows 10 Command Prompt

The MS-DOS prompt/Command Line (CMD) option enables you to perform direct system-level operations like copying a file, creating a directory, checking on your memory, and much more.

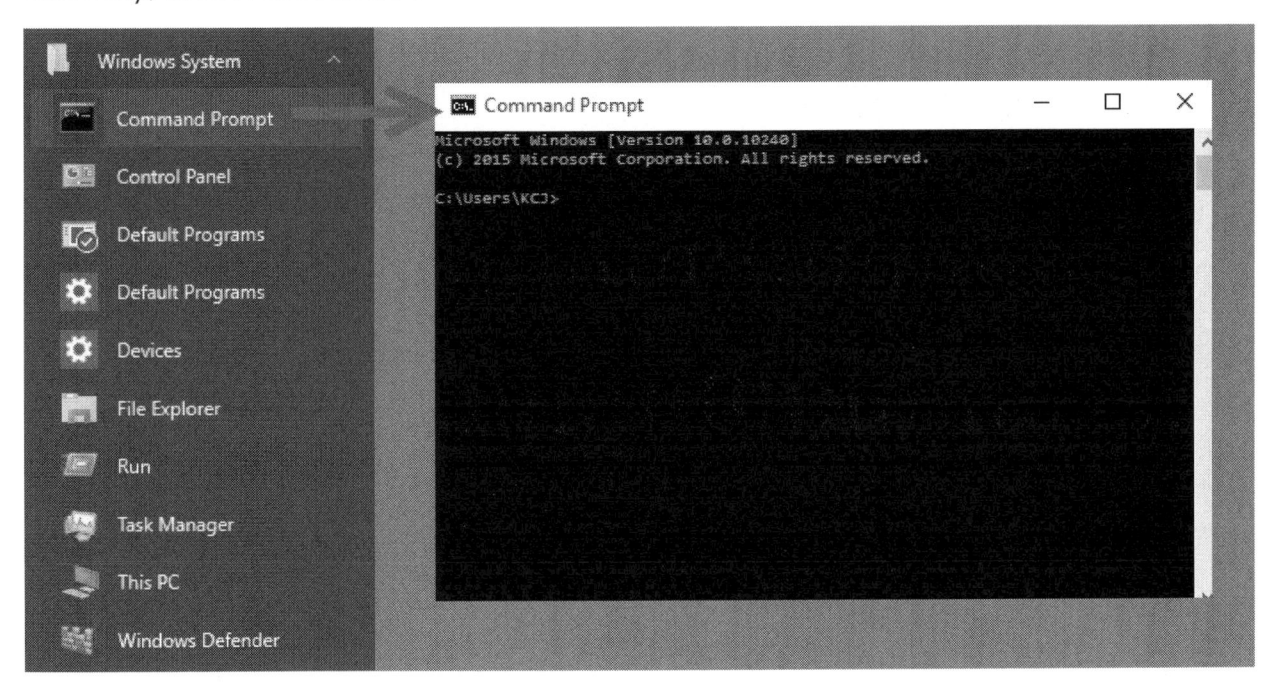

If you type in **help** at the command line (just to the right of the C: prompt), and press Enter, then MS-DOS (Microsoft DOS) will show you a list of command you can use to complete such system-level tasks. Here is a chart I put together for your convenience, with commands listed in alpha-numerical order.

MS-DOS Command	Description
ASSOC	Displays or modifies file extension associations.
ATTRIB	Displays or changes file attributes.

MS-DOS Command	Description
BREAK	Sets or clears extended CTRL+C checking.
BCDEDIT	Sets properties in boot database to control boot loading.
CACLS	Displays or modifies access control lists (ACLs) of files.
CALL	Calls one batch program from another.
CD	Displays the name of or changes the current directory.
CHCP	Displays or sets the active code page number.
CHDIR	Displays the name of or changes the current directory.
CHKDSK	Checks a disk and displays a summarized status report.
CHKNTFS	Displays or modifies the checking of a disk at boot time.
CLS	Clears the screen.
CMD	Starts a new instance of the Windows command interpreter.
COLOR	Sets the default console foreground and background colors.
COMP	Compares the contents of two files or two groups of files.
COMPACT	Displays or alters the compression of files on NTFS partitions.

MS-DOS Command	Description
CONVERT	Converts File Allocation Table (FAT) volumes to NTFS. You cannot convert the current drive.
COPY	Copies one or more files to another location.
DATE	Displays or sets the computer's system date.
DEL	Deletes one or more files.
DIR	Displays a list of files and subdirectories (within the directory that this command is given).
DISKCOMP	Compares the contents of two floppy disks.
DISKCOPY	Copies the contents of one floppy disk to another.
DISKPART	Displays or configures Disk Partition properties.
DOSKEY	Edits command lines, recalls Windows commands, and creates macros.
DRIVERQUERY	Displays current device driver status and properties.
ECHO	Displays messages or turns command echoing on or off.
ENDLOCAL	Ends localization of environment changes in a batch file.
ERASE	Deletes one or more files.
EXIT	Quits the CMD.EXE program (command interpreter) and also closes the displayed window.
FC	Compares two files or sets of files and displays the differences between them.

MS-DOS Command	Description
FINDSTR	Searches for strings in files.
FOR	Runs a specified command for each file in a set of files.
FORMAT	Formats a disk for use with Windows.
FSUTIL	Displays or configures the file system properties.
FTYPE	Displays or modifies file types used in file extension associations.
GOTO	Directs the Windows command interpreter to a labeled line in a batch program.
GPRESULT	Displays Group Policy info for machine.
GRAFTABL	Enables Windows to display an extended character set in graphics mode.
HELP	Provides (and displays) Help information for MS-DOS commands, many of which now have a correlating Windows application.
ICACLS	Displays, modifies, backs-up, or restores Access Control Lists (ACLs) for files and directories.
IF	Performs conditional processing in batch files.
LABEL	Creates, changes, or deletes the volume label of a disk.
MD	MD stands for "Make Directory" – this command creates a directory from within the directory you are in now.

MS-DOS Command	Description
MKDIR	MKDIR stands for "Make Directory" – this command creates a directory from within the directory you are in now.
MKLINK	Creates Symbolic Links and Hard Links.
MODE	Configures a system device.
MOVE	Moves one or more files from one directory to another directory.
OPENFILES	Displays files opened by remote users for a file share.
PATH	Displays or sets a search path for executable files.
PAUSE	Suspends processing of a batch file and displays a message.
POPD	Restores the previous value of the current directory saved by PUSHD (this MS-DOS command stores a directory or network path in memory so it can be returned to at any time).
PRINT	Prints a text file.
PROMPT	Changes the Windows command prompt.
PUSHD	Saves the current directory and then changes it.
RD	Removes a directory.
RECOVER	Recovers readable information from a bad or defective disk.
REM	Records comments (remarks) in batch files or CONFIG.SYS.

MS-DOS Command	Description
REN	Renames a file or files.
RENAME	Renames a file or files.
REPLACE	Replaces files.
RMDIR	Removes a directory.
ROBOCOPY	Advanced MS-DOS utility to copy files and directory trees.
SET	Displays, sets, or removes Windows environment variables.
SETLOCAL	Begins localization of environment changes in a batch file.
SC	Displays or configures services (background processes).
SCHTASKS	Schedules commands and programs (e.g. tasks) to run on a computer.
SHIFT	Shifts the position of replaceable parameters in batch files.
SHUTDOWN	Allows for the proper local or remote shutdown of a computer (machine).
SORT	Sorts input.
START	Starts a separate window to run a specified program or command.
SUBST	Associates a path with a drive letter.

MS-DOS Command	Description
SYSTEMINFO	Displays machine-specific properties and configuration information.
TASKLIST	Displays all currently running tasks.
TASKKILL	Kill or stop a running process or application.
TIME	Displays or sets the system time.
TITLE	Sets the window title for a CMD.EXE session.
TREE	Graphically displays the directory structure of a drive or path.
TYPE	Displays the contents of a text file.
VER	Displays the Windows version.
VERIFY	Tells Windows whether to verify that your files are written correctly to a disk.
VOL	Displays a disk volume label and serial number.
XCOPY	Copies files and directory trees.
WMIC	Displays WMI information inside interactive command shell.

Note: To see more information on how to use each command listed here, see the command-line reference section of the Microsoft Windows 10 Online Help.

Windows 10 Control Panel

Windows 10 has done something remarkable – it has created a really nice Settings interface which incorporates all options *and more* in what we used to know (in Windows 7 and 8 for example) as Control Panel. We are creatures of habit, are we not? Microsoft knows this. So, in the same way Microsoft brought back the Start Menu as the true starting place on your Home Screen, it has also *retained* the Control Panel option for diehard fans of Windows going back several versions who know this path as "the way" to update programs on the computer and perform other administrative tasks that are common to the Windows experience. And so it is. Control Panel (CP). If you love Control Panel as much as I do, go ahead and pin it to your Start Menu or Task Menu. There you go. Now, you can go directly there in one simple click or navigation. I will, however, be covering all Categories you see in the following sample screen shot in my Settings write-up, which begins in Section 19. But, of course, you can navigate directly to what you need via the CP interface – System and Security, Network and Internet, Hardware and Sound, Programs, User Accounts, Appearance and Personalization, Clock (and Language and Region), and Ease of Access.

Windows 10 Default Programs (CP)

Go to Start Menu > All Apps > Windows System > Default Programs (CP).

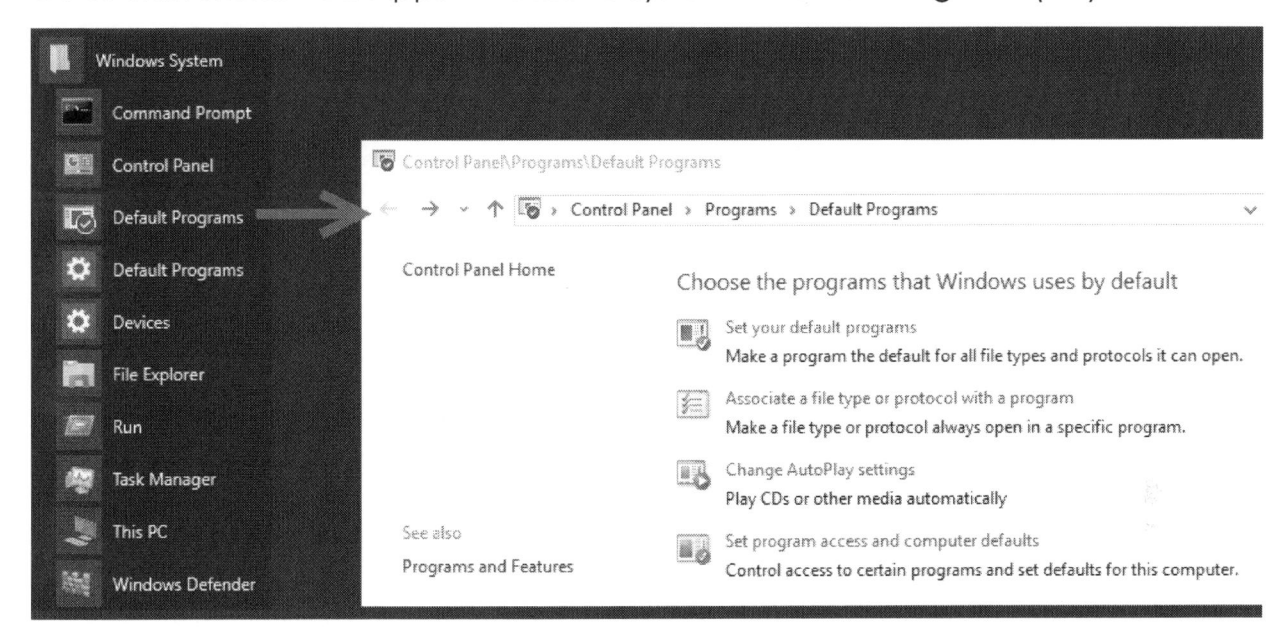

This particular Start Menu option is for Default Programs via the Control Panel interface. As you can see in the sample screen shot above, Default Programs is an option within the CP directory called Programs. Here, you have four major tasks that can be accomplished. *First*, you can establish default programs that will run when your computer is started. Example: Click on this link and you will see a listing of programs on your computer. Let us select the Calculator app – it will now be moved to the right pane. Save this change and the next time you boot your computer – the Calculator app will be running so you can use it immediately. *Second*, you can associate file types or protocols with a program. Here is an example – usually Microsoft Word works with file extensions of .doc or .docx. You can also see HTML files in Microsoft Word, so if you use this option to associate HTML files with Microsoft Word, then Word can immediately work with this new association. *Third*, you can change (e.g. update) Autoplay settings. Regardless of the media player you have on your computer, you can use this option to fine tune file formats and media details to expedite your media experience. Fourth, you can use this option to set program access and computer defaults. The default options here are Microsoft (Windows), Non-Microsoft, and Custom – for web browsing, e-mail and more. Just follow the prompts that Microsoft Windows 10 provides.

Windows 10 Default Programs (Settings)

Go to Start Menu > All Apps > Windows System > Default Programs (Settings).

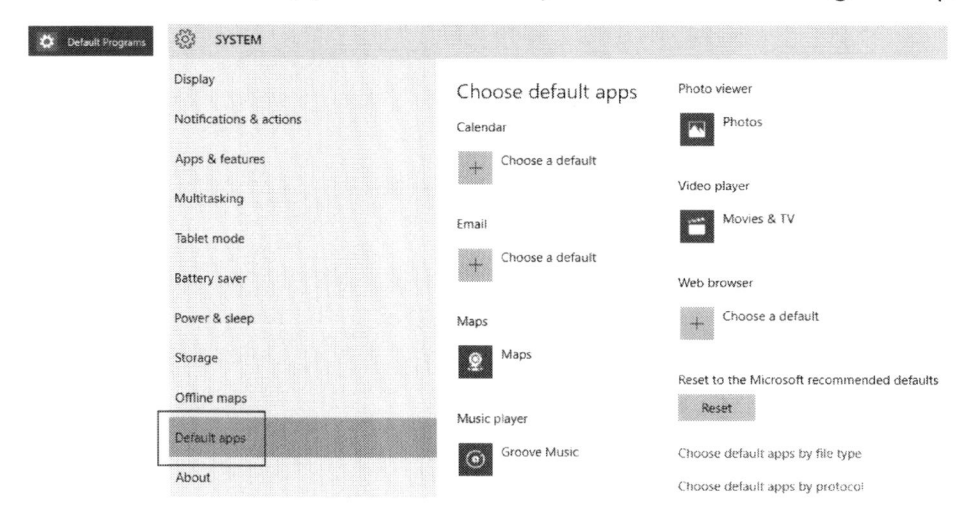

Select, here, Default apps and you will be able to accomplish all that you could accomplish in the previous tip. The only difference between the previous tip and this one is the route and interface to Default Programs (the former tips via the older Control Panel interface and this one via the Settings interface). In this particular interface – as you can see – it is very easy to add or change the defaults. Click on a Plus (+) icon to add – in the example above we have yet to add a default Calendar and Email app as well as Web browser. For the ones that are already there, you can single click on the existing default and a pop-up window is shown where you can make a change.

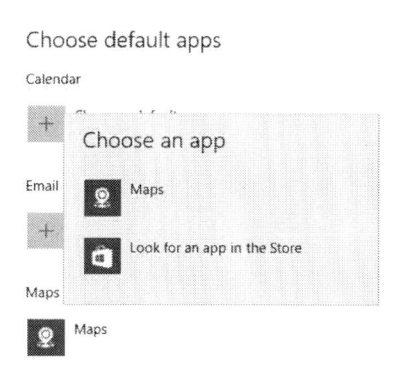

If you cannot decide what to do, you can always choose defaults that Microsoft can set for you (e.g. Reset to the Microsoft recommended defaults). Sometimes when you are new to an app or platform the vendor (e.g. Microsoft) has a pretty good idea of your needs as a new user. You can always change this later.

Windows 10 Devices

Go to Start Menu > All Apps > Windows System > Devices.

This path is an alternative path to a key part of the Settings app which I will be covering in the final part of this book. This is what Windows 10 displays for you.

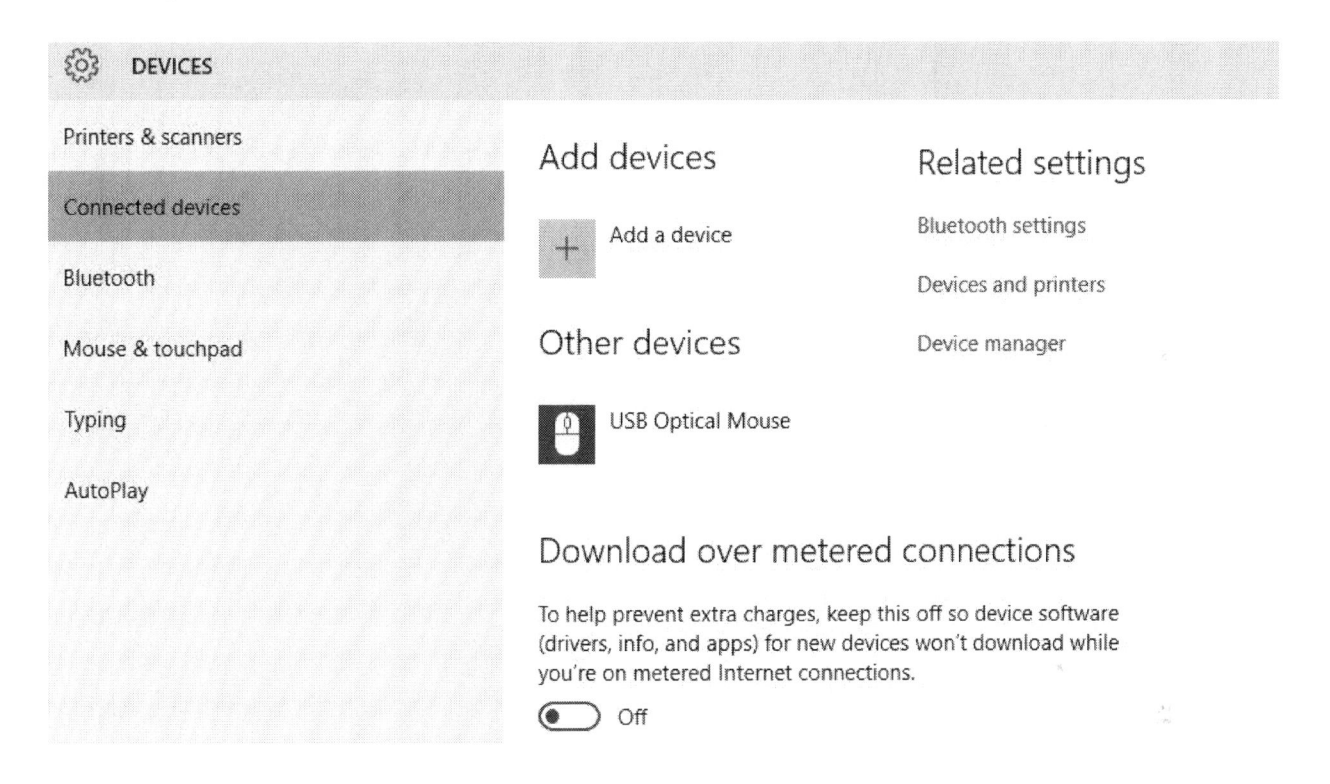

There are six major sections to the Devices component of Settings. They are: Printers and Scanners, Connected Devices (which is shown above), Bluetooth, Mouse and Touchpad, Typing, and Autoplay.

Even though you see the *Add a Device* button in the same screen shot above, for the post part, Windows will manage this process without any human involvement. So, if you get a PC with Windows 10 or upgrade your machine to Windows 10, this OS should fare well in terms of recognizing devices with which it must interface.

File Explorer (formerly Windows Explorer)

Go to Start Menu > All Apps > Windows System > File Explorer.

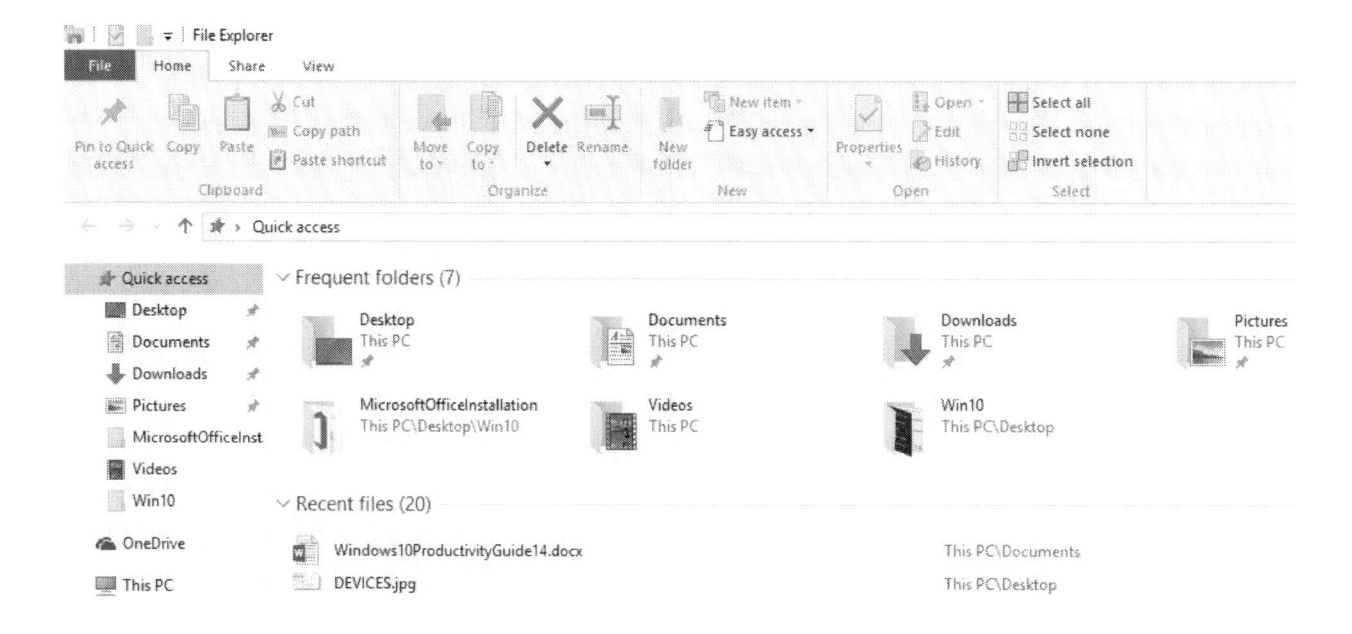

If I had to give just one "composite" tip for you to access the improved features of the longstanding Windows Explorer (now "File Explorer") – it is this – the *right click* of your mouse over the folder, icon, file, space, for "that" which you seek to do. This of course requires you to be a semi-proficient user of the Windows (File) Explorer to understand this – but you do, right? I am assuming that most of you will understand this. *Here is an example ...*

I want to see my options for an image file called "Coffee_ProgrammersCup.jpg". So ... I RIGHT click on my mouse over the file (with the file first selected of course). A pop-up window/menu is shown and this window shows me everything I can do with respect to the file.

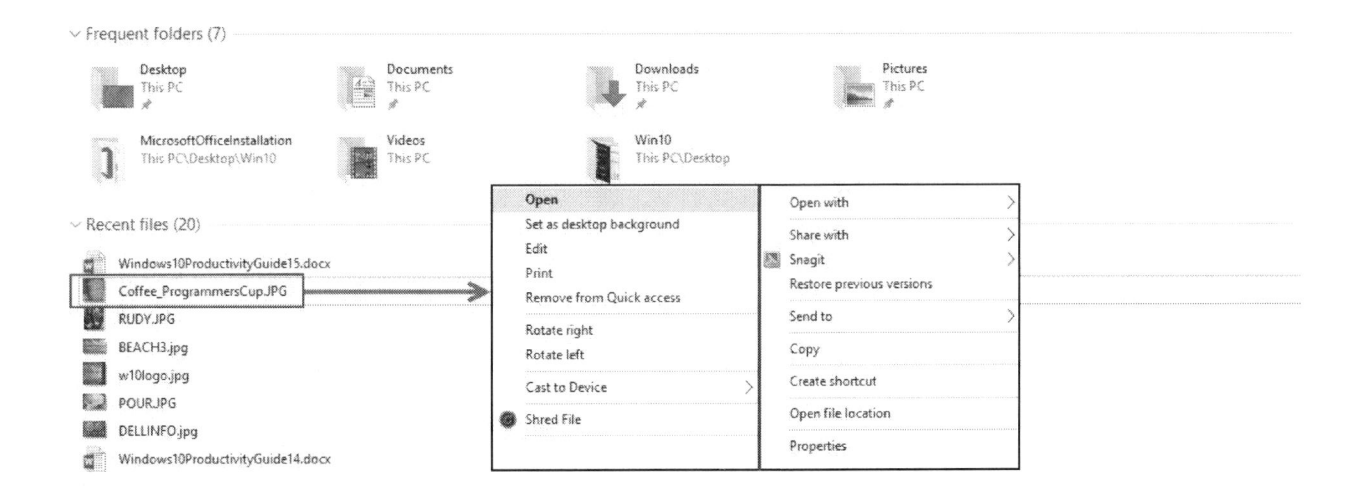

Let us now select a folder instead of a file. What I do is first single left-click on the folder and then right click on my mouse. This is the pop-up window you should see that has options related to the folder from within the File Explorer's capabilities. Notice the difference of options between a file and folder.

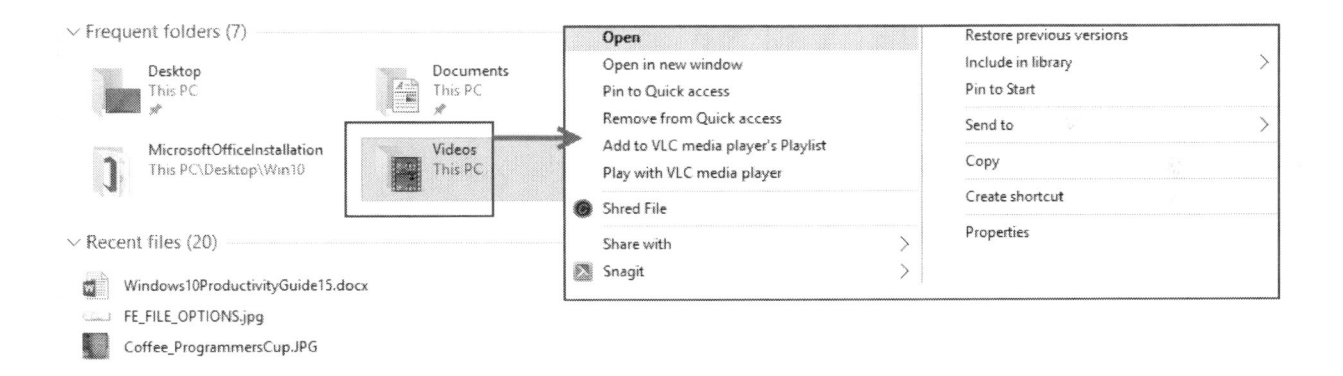

Finally, let us click on a blank space within the File Explorer. Just give a single left click with your mouse. Then, single click with the right button of your mouse. You are presented with a pop-up window/menu as follows. This is what you can do regarding this space – view icons in different sizes as well as refresh the explorer window.

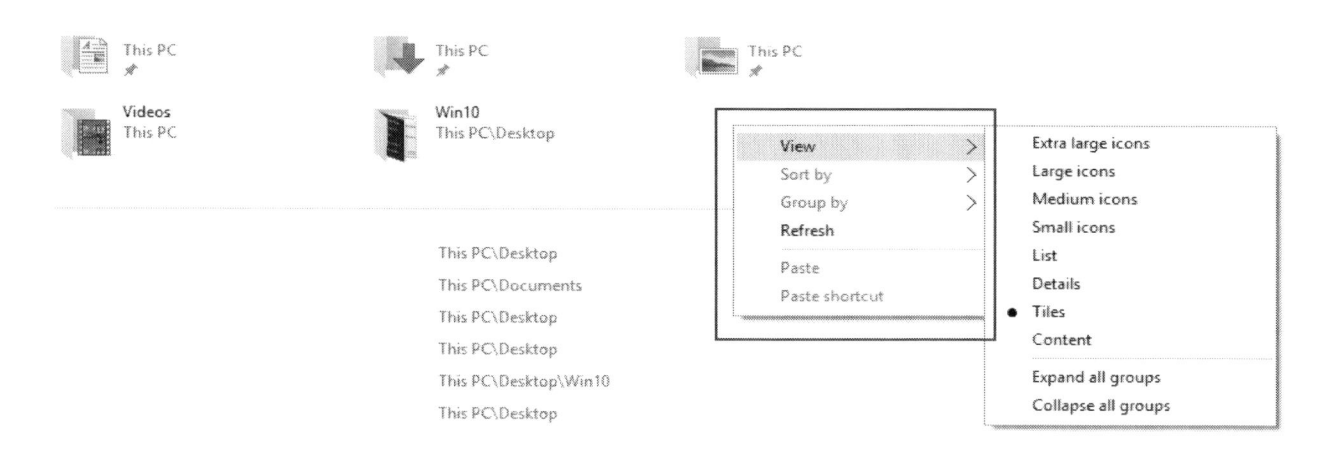

Please note that the pop-up windows do not show absolutely all options available for the selected object. There are additional options shown in menus in the top part of the window. The key here is to make sure you first single-click to select the object for which you see to employ a Windows maintenance operation. Then you can use menus above as well as use the right-button click on your mouse to find the specific command you need.

Windows 10 for Seniors and Beginners, ® All Rights Reserved, Keith Johnson   Page 116

Windows 10 Run

Run is essentially a command-line app that runs right up front within Windows 10 itself. You can just click on the Windows Logo Key ⊞+ R to access Run. This is what you should get ...

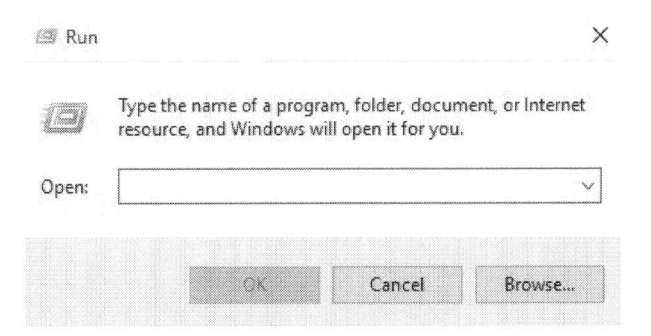

This option is best used by System Administrators. If you are not a Sys Admin, there really is no need for you to use this option. You should be able to do 99% of your daily tasks via regular Windows apps and resources. In any case, here is the list of commands you can give from within the Run app and here are the tasks they accomplish:

Task	What you must type in Run
Open Documents Folder	documents
Open Videos folder	videos
Open Downloads Folder	downloads
Open Favorites Folder	favorites
Open Recent Folder	recent
Open Pictures Folder	pictures

Task	What you must type in Run
About Windows dialog	winver
Add Hardware Wizard	hdwwiz
Advanced User Accounts	netplwiz
Advanced User Accounts	azman.msc
Backup and Restore	sdclt
Bluetooth File Transfer	fsquirt
Calculator	calc
Certificates	certmgr.msc
Change Computer Performance Settings	systempropertiesperformance
Change Data Execution Prevention Settings	systempropertiesdataexecutionprevention
Change Data Execution Prevention Settings	printui
Character Map	charmap
ClearType Tuner	cttune

Task	What you must type in Run
Color Management	colorcpl
Command Prompt	cmd
Component Services	comexp.msc
Component Services	dcomcnfg
Computer Management	compmgmt.msc
Computer Management	compmgmtlauncher
Connect to a Projector	displayswitch
Control Panel	control
Create A Shared Folder Wizard	shrpubw
Create a System Repair Disc	recdisc
Data Execution Prevention	systempropertiesdataexecutionprevention
Date and Time	timedate.cpl
Default Location	locationnotifications
Device Manager	devmgmt.msc

Task	What you must type in Run
Device Pairing Wizard	devicepairingwizard
Diagnostics Troubleshooting Wizard	msdt
Digitizer Calibration Tool	tabcal
DirectX Diagnostic Tool	dxdiag
Disk Cleanup	cleanmgr
Disk Defragmenter	dfrgui
Disk Management	diskmgmt.msc
Display	dpiscaling
Display Color Calibration	dccw
Display Switch	displayswitch
DPAPI Key Migration Wizard	dpapimig
Driver Verifier Manager	verifier
Ease of Access Center	utilman
EFS Wizard	rekeywiz

Task	What you must type in Run
Event Viewer	eventvwr.msc
Fax Cover Page Editor	fxscover
File Signature Verification	sigverif
Font Viewer	fontview
Game Controllers	joy.cpl
IExpress Wizard	iexpress
Internet Explorer	iexplore
Internet Options	inetcpl.cpl
iSCSI Initiator Configuration Tool	iscsicpl
Language Pack Installer	lpksetup
Local Group Policy Editor	gpedit.msc
Local Security Policy	secpol.msc
Local Users and Groups	lusrmgr.msc
Location Activity	locationnotifications

Task	What you must type in Run
Malicious Software Removal Tool	mrt
Manage Your File Encryption Certificates	rekeywiz
Microsoft Management Console	mmc
Microsoft Support Diagnostic Tool	msdt
Mouse	main.cpl
NAP Client Configuration	napclcfg.msc
Narrator	narrator
Network Connections	ncpa.cpl
New Scan Wizard	wiaacmgr
Notepad	notepad
ODBC Data Source Administrator	odbcad32
ODBC Driver Configuration	odbcconf
On-Screen Keyboard	osk
Paint	mspaint

Task	What you must type in Run
Pen and Touch	tabletpc.cpl
People Near Me	collab.cpl
Performance Monitor	perfmon.msc
Performance Options	systempropertiesperformance
Phone and Modem	telephon.cpl
Phone Dialer	dialer
Power Options	powercfg.cpl
Presentation Settings	presentationsettings
Print Management	printmanagement.msc
Printer Migration	printbrmui
Printer User Interface	printui
Private Character Editor	eudcedit
Problem Steps Recorder	psr
Programs and Features	appwiz.cpl

Task	What you must type in Run
Region and Language	intl.cpl
Registry Editor	regedit
Registry Editor 32	regedt32
Remote Access Phonebook	rasphone
Remote Desktop Connection	mstsc
Resource Monitor	resmon
Resultant Set of Policy	rsop.msc
SAM Lock Tool	syskey
Screen Resolution	desk.cpl
Securing the Windows Account Database	syskey
Services	services.msc
Set Program Access and Computer Defaults	computerdefaults
Share Creation Wizard	shrpubw
Shared Folders	fsmgmt.msc

Task	What you must type in Run
Signout	logoff
Snipping Tool	snippingtool
Sound	mmsys.cpl
Sound recorder	soundrecorder
SQL Server Client Network Utility	cliconfg
Sticky Notes	stikynot
Stored User Names and Passwords	credwiz
Sync Center	mobsync
System Configuration	msconfig
System Configuration Editor	sysedit
System Information	msinfo32
System Properties	sysdm.cpl
System Properties (Advanced Tab)	systempropertiesadvanced

Task	What you must type in Run
System Properties (Computer Name Tab)	systempropertiescomputername
System Properties (Hardware Tab)	systempropertieshardware
System Properties (Remote Tab)	systempropertiesremote
System Properties (System Protection Tab)	systempropertiesprotection
System Restore	rstrui
Task Manager	taskmgr
Task Scheduler	taskschd.msc
Trusted Platform Module (TPM) Management	tpm.msc
Turn Windows features on or off	optionalfeatures
User Account Control Settings	useraccountcontrolsettings
Utility Manager	utilman
Volume Mixer	sndvol
Windows Action Center	wscui.cpl

Task	What you must type in Run
Windows Activation Client	slui
Windows Anytime Upgrade Results	windowsanytimeupgraderesults
Windows Disc Image Burning Tool	isoburn
Windows Explorer	explorer
Windows Fax and Scan	wfs
Windows Firewall	firewall.cpl
Windows Firewall with Advanced Security	wf.msc
Windows Journal	journal
Windows Media Player	wmplayer
Windows Memory Diagnostic Scheduler	mdsched
Windows Mobility Center	mblctr
Windows Picture Acquisition Wizard	wiaacmgr
Windows PowerShell	powershell

Task	What you must type in Run
Windows PowerShell ISE	powershell_ise
Windows Remote Assistance	msra
Windows (Create) Repair Disc	recdisc
Windows Script Host	wscript
Windows Update	wuapp
Windows Update Standalone Installer	wusa
Windows version	winver
WMI Management	wmimgmt.msc
WordPad	write
XPS Viewer	xpsrchvw

As an example …

Here is what typing "winver" into **Run** (and then clicking OK) gives us …

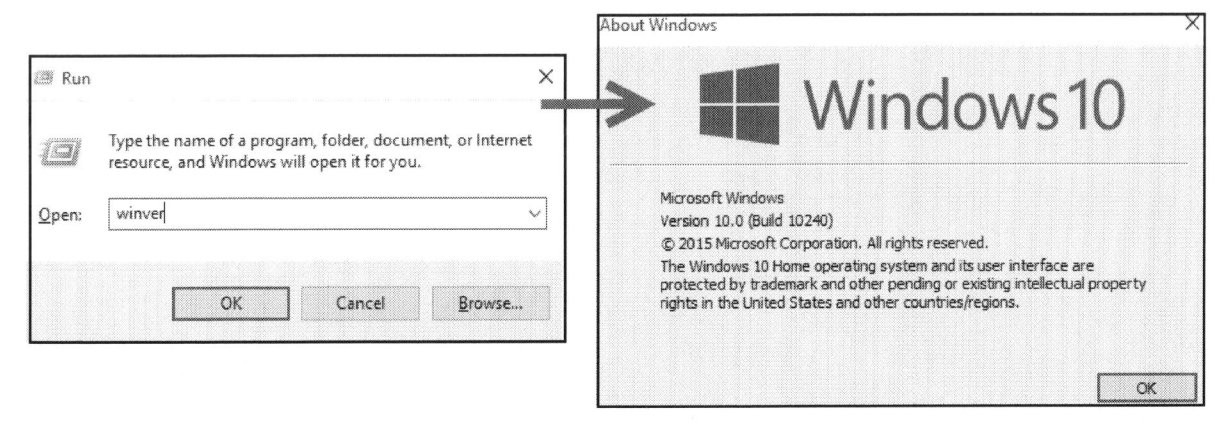

As a second example …

Here is what typing "utilman" into **Run** (and then clicking OK) gives us …

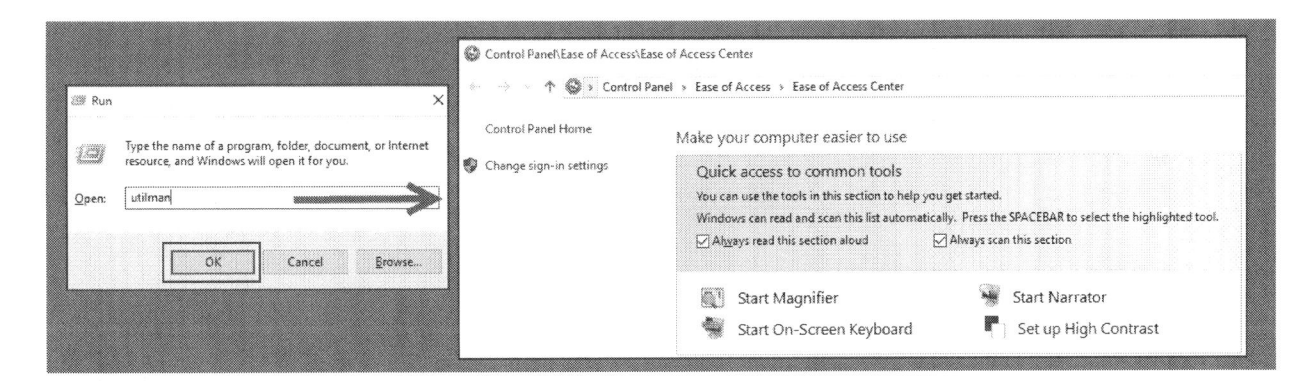

Note: The Run window also has a Browse button option. Here you can surf the Windows (File) Explorer to find the file, app, or folder you want to access and open. As long as the item you select has a supporting app or means to access or show, you are all set. If that is not the case, you will have to find such a resource on the web. Fear not because there are many great free open-source tools on the web should you find yourself in this situation.

Windows 10 Task Manager

There are two ways to access your Windows 10 Task Manager. The first - as most of you know – is Control + Alt + Delete keys (press these keys at the same time). The second is for you to use this path: Start > All Apps > Windows System > Task Manager. Here is what you should see, either way …

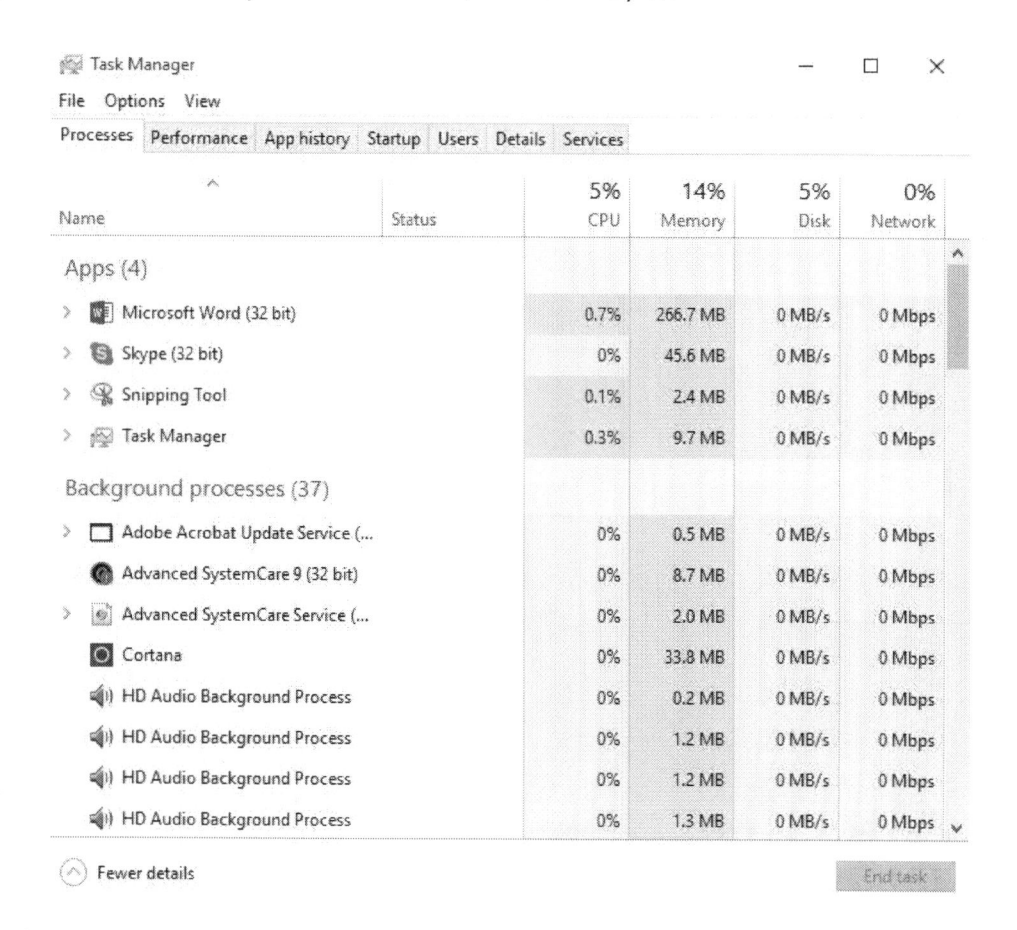

Task Manager					
File Options View					
Processes Performance App history Startup Users Details Services					
Name	Status	5% CPU	14% Memory	5% Disk	0% Network
Apps (4)					
> Microsoft Word (32 bit)		0.7%	266.7 MB	0 MB/s	0 Mbps
> Skype (32 bit)		0%	45.6 MB	0 MB/s	0 Mbps
> Snipping Tool		0.1%	2.4 MB	0 MB/s	0 Mbps
> Task Manager		0.3%	9.7 MB	0 MB/s	0 Mbps
Background processes (37)					
> Adobe Acrobat Update Service (...		0%	0.5 MB	0 MB/s	0 Mbps
Advanced SystemCare 9 (32 bit)		0%	8.7 MB	0 MB/s	0 Mbps
> Advanced SystemCare Service (...		0%	2.0 MB	0 MB/s	0 Mbps
Cortana		0%	33.8 MB	0 MB/s	0 Mbps
HD Audio Background Process		0%	0.2 MB	0 MB/s	0 Mbps
HD Audio Background Process		0%	1.2 MB	0 MB/s	0 Mbps
HD Audio Background Process		0%	1.2 MB	0 MB/s	0 Mbps
HD Audio Background Process		0%	1.3 MB	0 MB/s	0 Mbps
Fewer details					End task

A "task" is an "active operation" of some kind running within the Microsoft Windows 10 platform. It could be a full app – it could also be a component or service of an app. The Task Manager prominently features seven tabs that reveal everything that is going on within Windows 10 on your machine – Processes, Performance, Application History, Startup, Users, Details, and Services. This option is best used by System Administrators, however, if you really have a pressing need to use this resource, you can. Most of the time, people go to the Task Manager when an application gets locked up for some reason. Here, you can close or shut down the program, leave the Task Manager, and then relaunch the program from your Windows Home Screen.

Windows 10 This PC

Go to Start Menu > All Apps > Windows System > This PC. Microsoft Windows 10 will access the File Explorer and show information according to this vantage point of "this PC". Your computer should show - for devices and drives - at least the OS (C:) drive – I have a DVD RW Drive and a second partition on my computer, that is why these other two are shown for This PC.

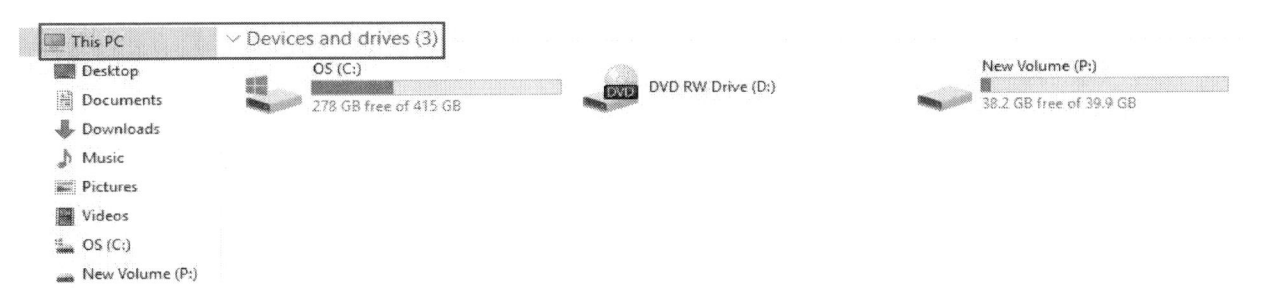

Your computer should also show, via This PC, major navigational highpoints like Desktop, Documents (folder), Downloads (folder), Music (folder), Pictures (folder), Videos (folder), and icons for your present drives (at least the C: drive). As I mentioned in the section covering the Windows (File) Explorer, to know what you can or cannot do here – single click on the icon in question first. Then, single right click on your mouse or mousepad to open the pop-up window showing your available navigational options. From there, you can choose as you need. When I am here at this window, I like to check the status of my C: drive. So, single click (left mouse button) on OS C: and then single right click to access the pop-up window/menu. Select Properties. You should see something like this ....

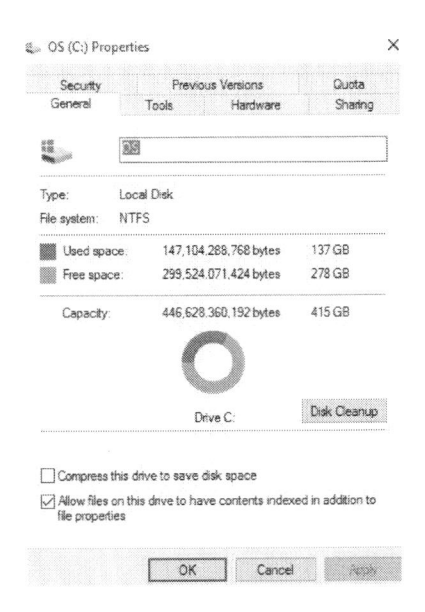

There are a total of seven tabs for the Properties window. They are as follows: General, Tools, Hardware, Sharing, Security, Previous Versions, and Quota.

The General Tab reveals information about hard disc space and provides a link to the Windows 10 Disk Cleanup utility program.

The Tools Tab provides links to two utility programs - Error Checking and Optimization and Defragmentation - where you can provide additional care for your drive:

The Hardware Tab shows all information related to the physical drives on your machine – hard disk, media, and otherwise.

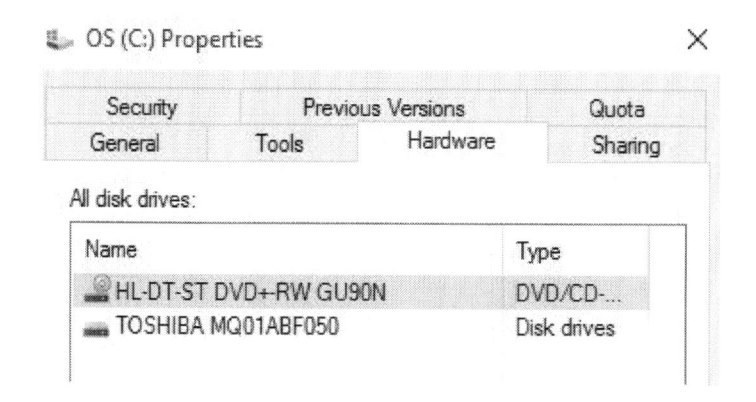

The Sharing Tab shows files and folders that are shared via the established Network, if there is one.

The Security Tab shows all users and user groups to which security can be applied. Simply single click on the user or user group and click on the Edit button to create or update applied security – like Read, Write, Modify, Full Control, etc.

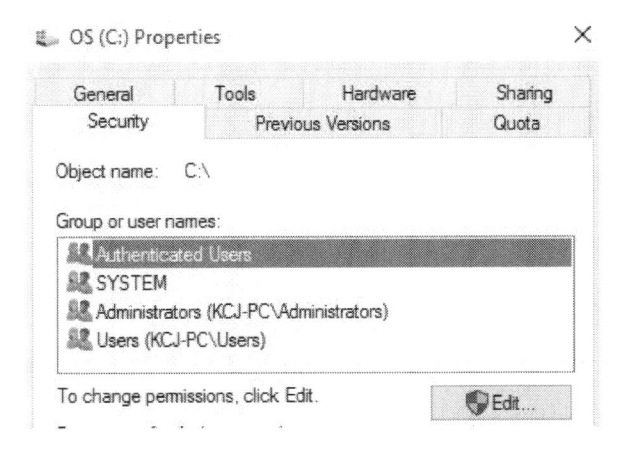

The Previous Versions Tab shows folders and more according to restore points that you have established in the past – a way of time-stamping so that you can return to earlier versions according to those time-stamps (e.g. previous versions).

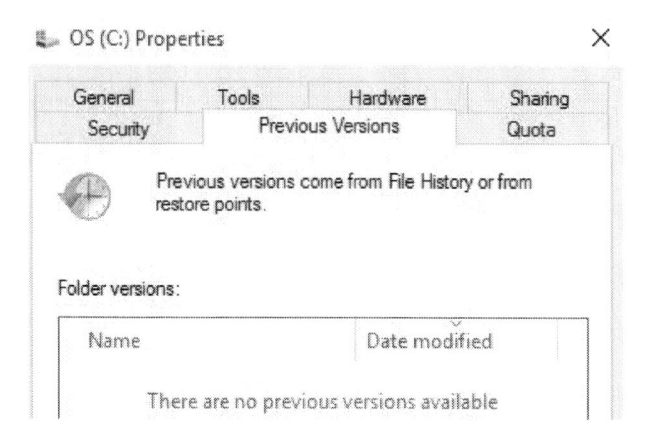

The Quota Tab shows disk space management tools. Click on the Show Quota Settings button and Windows 10 opens the Quota Settings window. Here you can setup and establish what you need per user and hard disk space he or she is allowed to have. You can also set up a log notification if a limit is exceeded.

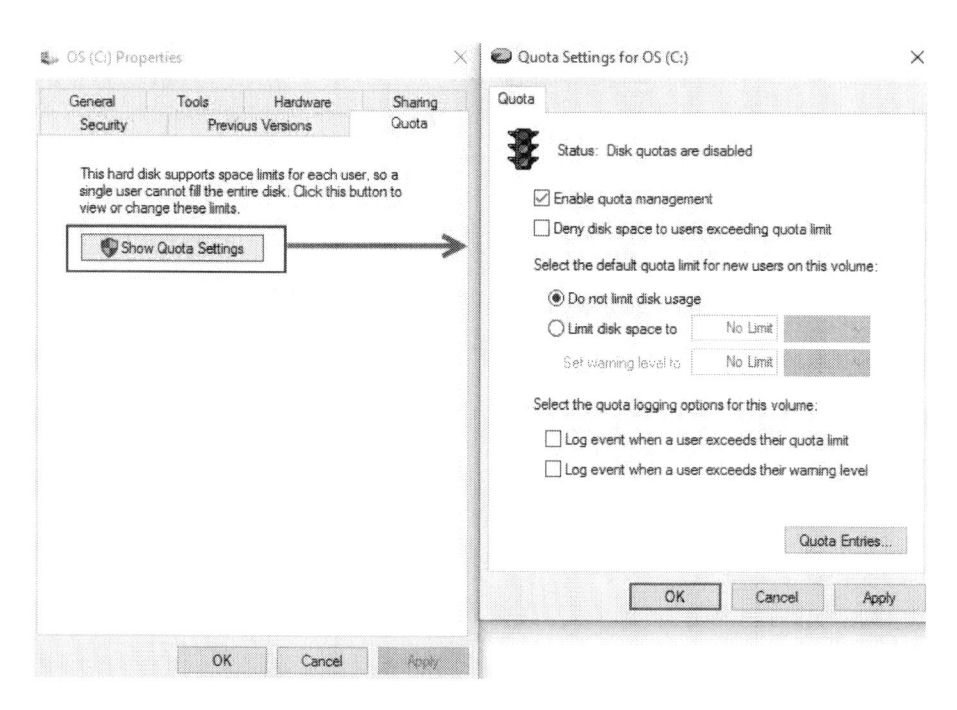

Windows 10 Defender

Go to Start Menu > All Apps > Windows System > Windows Defender.

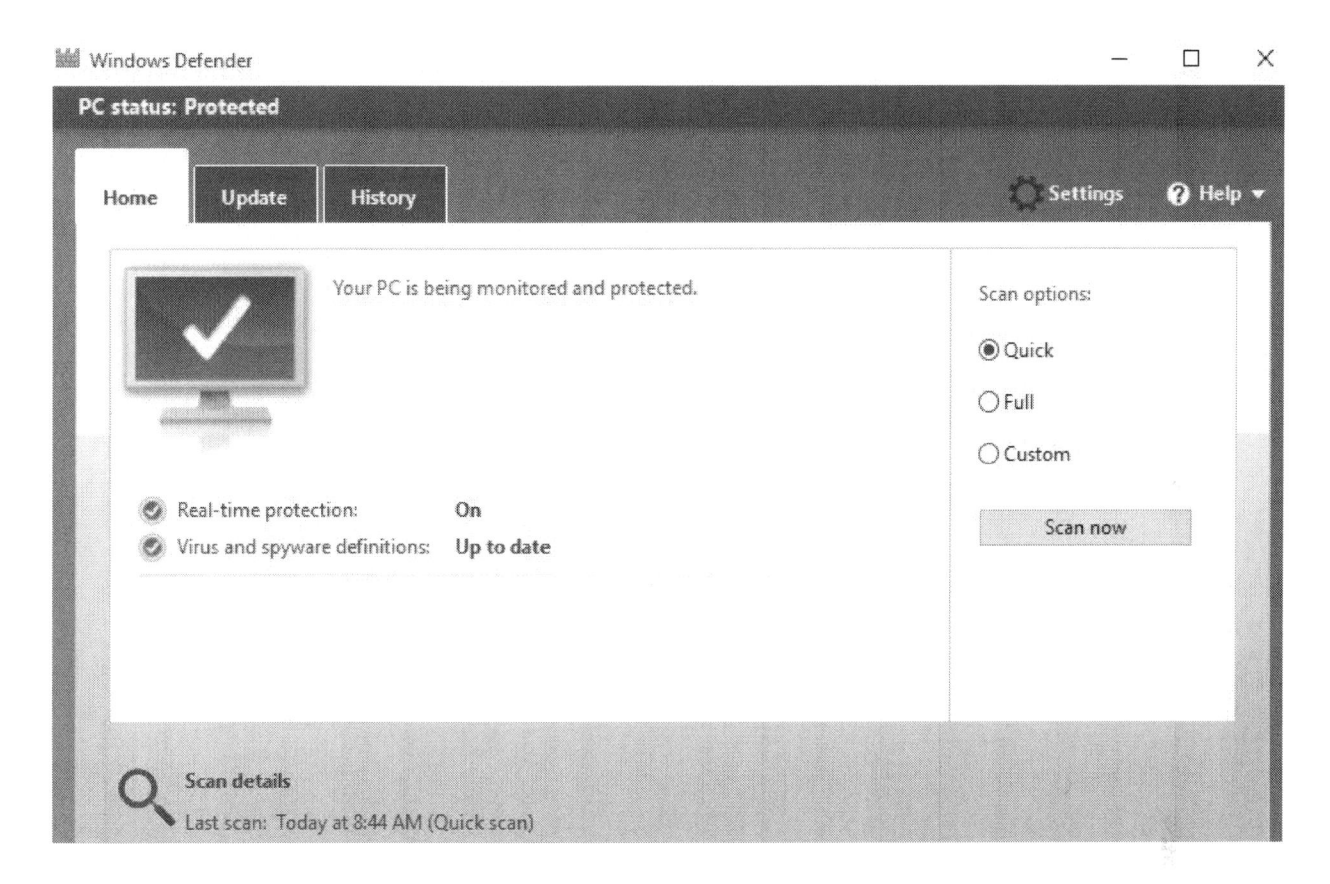

[Screenshot of Windows Defender window showing PC status: Protected, with Home/Update/History tabs, "Your PC is being monitored and protected." message, Real-time protection: On, Virus and spyware definitions: Up to date, Scan options (Quick, Full, Custom) with Scan now button, and Scan details showing Last scan: Today at 8:44 AM (Quick scan)]

Windows Defender has been a key "security" player for the Windows OS for quite some time now (but was called Security Essentials). While it is difficult to see any changes to the user interface, rest assured Microsoft has done its homework regarding viruses and malware that is out there. So, via your Microsoft updates, Defender – every time it is run – endeavors to keep your machine bug-free and malware-free. You can do quick scans, full scans, and custom scans of your drives. There are also tabs where you can check into see available updates as well as the history of scans you have run. Just select the type of scan you want to run and click on the Scan now button. If there are issues, then Defender gives you a chance to quarantine or delete files that are deemed unstable. Quick updates usually can be done within several minutes depending on the size of your drive. Full scans however can last several hours.

Section 19: Windows 10 Total Apps – Listing

We have already covered many Windows 10 apps thus far in this book. However, let us now go through a table which has both the app as well as a description so we know - from head to toe – exactly what Windows 10 Home provides.

Windows 10 App	**Description**
3D Builder	This app lets you create and print out your own 3D models.
Alarms and Clock	This app lets you utilize a Windows-based alarm, world clock, timer, and stopwatch.
Calculator	This app features a standard calculator, a scientific calculator, a programmer calculator, and a converter that can work with the following: volume, length, weight and mass, temperature, energy, area, speed, time, power, data, pressure, and angles.
Calendar	This app works with your Microsoft profile that is connected to your copy of Windows 10. You can view time per day week, month and more. You can schedule events and setup alerts and more.

Windows 10 App	Description
Camera	This app works with the Camera on your computer. If your Camera conforms to the hardware requirements of Windows 10 Hello, then the Camera app can be used to setup a retina scan where Windows recognizes you and therefore you can bypass normal login protocol such as a username and password. This is a work in progress right now from the Microsoft end so you need to check with Microsoft Help Online to see the latest list of Cameras that are able to perform a retina scan and see if the Camera on your machine is on this list. The Camera of course, aside from this task, can be used to record not just pictures but also video. Just open the app and follow the instructions per the interface you see (e.g. click on the photo or view button as needed).
Get Office	As of the writing of this book, Microsoft is pushing Office 365. As a Tech Writer, I work with MS Office every day. Office is a great business and productivity suite. However, Office is not cheap. A free alternative can be found with LibreOffice. You can download this program at this URL: https://www.libreoffice.org/

Windows 10 App	Description
Get Skype	Skype has become the de-facto standard for Over-The-Web communications (especially VoIP – Voice Over Internet Protocol). Skype today features tremendous quality in text, phone calls, video and more. You are given a basic free account and from there you can select paid services if you need. But for most the free account has just about everything you will need. You can share files and stay in touch with people from around the world in a timely way. The Get Skype app installs Skype on your local drive but you can also access Skype from its main portal www.skype.com.
Groove Music	This is a new app for Microsoft Windows. Groove can be used to play your current music collections as well as create and listen to new and customized playlists. Groove Music lets you save music to OneDrive and get music from the Microsoft Store as well as from on your computer itself.
Mail	Mail is an app similar to Inbox by Google where you can work with your Outlook.com e-mails.

Windows 10 App	**Description**
Maps	This app is very similar to Google Maps where you can see a location, get directions, search for a location, create a list of favorites and see cities in 3D.
Microsoft Edge	Edge is the new Microsoft browser that is replacing Internet Explorer. At the present time, Microsoft has discontinued support for IE versions through v10. There is still support for the latest version which is v11 but Microsoft is indirectly encouraging users to switch over to Edge as a definitive web browser. I cover Edge in the earlier part of this guide.
Microsoft Solitaire Collection	Today, Solitaire on Windows 10 is better than ever. You can play as a guest or via your Microsoft account and there are many games above and beyond the traditional solitaire game.
Movies and TV	This app is a portal for your computer through which you can both order and watch movies, TV programs and more.

Windows 10 App	Description
News	This app is a portal for your computer through which you can get the latest world news and information. This app works through the same sources as MSN.
OneDrive	In the same way that you can have Google Drive fast access through a drive icon on your Local Explorer, the OneDrive drive icon provides the same access to your Microsoft OneDrive cloud account. If you are not logged in, then this app directs you to the login window for OneDrive. If you are already logged into your Microsoft account, then you are automatically redirected to your OneDrive account (Explorer view).
People	This app directs you to the Contacts aspect of your Microsoft Hotmail/Outlook account. You can add or delete contacts as well as initiate communications here, as long as you are logged into your Microsoft account.

Windows 10 App	Description
Phone Companion	Use this app to SYNC your Microsoft Account and Windows 10 experience (especially Cortana) with your smartphone – which could be a Windows phone, Android phone, or Apple (iOS) phone.
Photos	Use this app to organize your photos into collections, albums and folders.
Settings	You can access Settings via Start > All Apps > Settings, Start > Settings, and Settings *directly* if you have pinned this icon to your Taskbar or created a shortcut on your desktop. All paths lead you to the Settings section of Windows 10 – a full discussion of this section is *next* in this guide – we are almost there!
Sports	This app is a portal for your computer through which you can get the latest sports news and information. This app works through the same sources as MSN.
Store	The app directs you to the Microsoft Store and this is where you can find all kinds of cool apps, music, TV, movies, games and more.

Windows 10 App	**Description**
Twitter	The Twitter app connects you directly with the Twitter platform (for tweeting) without having to go through your web browser. If you do not have an account, then there is an option for you to sign-up. For those of you with an account, you can log in or if you are already logged in, then this app connects you directly with your Twitter account.
Voice Recorder	Use this app to record your voice or something you want to say. You need to click on the Record icon to initiate this process. The next time you access this app, you will see a listing of all recordings which you can both playback as well as share.
Weather	This app is a portal for your computer through which you can get the latest weather-related news and information. This app works through the same sources as MSN.

Windows 10 App	Description
Windows Accessories	This is a major folder in your Windows 10 Start Menu that features all sorts of dynamic and useful accessory applications that can help you in many ways. All accessory apps are covered in earlier parts of this guide.
Windows Administrative Tools	This is a major folder in your Windows 10 Start Menu. All tools within this folder are here to help expedite your Admin duties or accomplish Admin tasks. These tools are recommended for use by System Administrators but they can be used by regular users as long as such users are aware of the consequences of working with these advanced tools and system-related commands and directives therein.
Windows DVD Player	This app enables you to enjoy DVDs of all kinds as well as data, music and game CDs.
Windows Ease of Access	This is a major folder in your Windows 10 Start Menu. All tools in the Ease of Access folder are designed to help you create a more personalized experience in Windows above and beyond just clicking and typing.

Windows 10 App	Description
Windows Feedback	This is an app designed to help you communicate your Windows 10 user experience with Microsoft. As you open this app/window, select the app or resource about which you want to share your experience(s).
Windows Media Player	As I mentioned earlier in this guide, if you have upgraded to Windows 10 from Windows 7 or 8, there is a great chance that Windows 10 has *deleted* your Windows Media Player. However, that did not happen to me. My Windows Media Player is still here – alive and ticking. Should you be as fortunate, then this is a great resource with which you can play music and more and create personalized play lists. If you do not have this app, here is a download link you can use to get it back and install it once again: http://windows.microsoft.com/en-us/windows/download-windows-media-player

Windows 10 App	Description
Windows Powershell	This is a major folder in your Windows 10 Start Menu (via All Apps). Powershell is essentially a command-line app where you can drive Windows 10 via specific DOS-level scripts. This app is best utilized by System Administrators and if it is to be used by regular users – they must know the specifics of the operations they are conducting lest they mess up or delete or misconfigure something in a way that is unfixable.
Windows System	This is a major folder in your Windows 10 Start Menu (via All Apps). Windows System includes many great programs like Control Panel, Device, Run, Task Manager, and Windows Defender. Like Powershell programs (apps), Windows System apps are designed to be used primarily by System Administrators, however, if users are aware of the details of the app and what they do and how to use it, then important system-level tasks can be accomplished directly and safely.
Xbox	Windows 10 can be used as the Operating System for the Microsoft Xbox for gaming and more. This guide is intended, however, for computers and not the Xbox.

Section 20: Windows 10 Settings – Overview

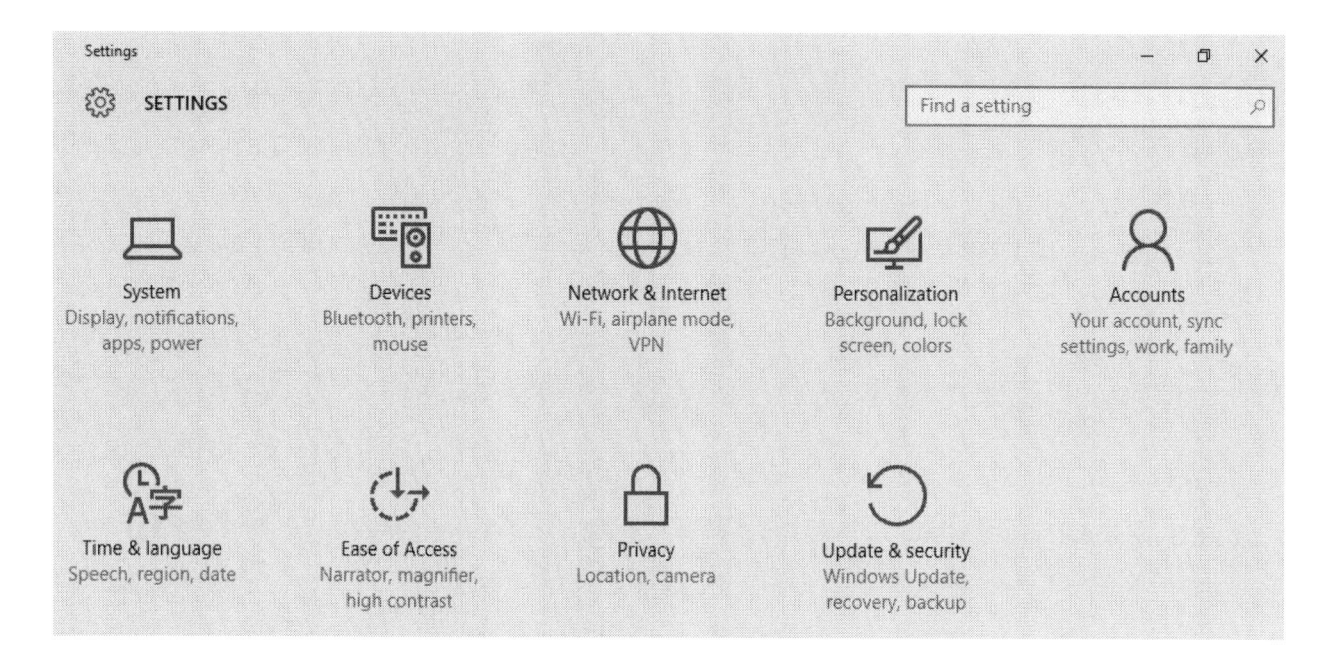

Thus far in this guide – three major aspects of Windows have been covered – installation and user login/access, navigation (especially the new and improved Start Menu), and apps (applications, programs, and more). Now, I would like to cover the fourth major aspect – Settings. Through Settings you can customize your Windows 10 experience greatly. Up until this point, what you have seen is the experience of using Windows 10 according to default settings that Microsoft sets up for you through the Windows 10 complete install or Windows 10 upgrade. For most people, default settings are fine and will take you far. But still, there are times when you will want to customize certain aspects of your Windows experience and for that reason I am covering Settings here.

The major Settings categories to be covered are as follows: System, Devices, Network and Internet, Personalization, User Accounts, Time and Language, Ease of Access, Privacy, and finally Updates and Security. In addition to navigating through these icons in the General Settings Window, you can use the Search box located at the upper right hand corner. Simply type in the Settings aspect you want to address and Windows 10 will show you what is available per this request. You can access Settings directly from the Start Menu as well as Pin it to your Taskbar or create a shortcut on your Desktop if you think you will be using it frequently.

Section 21: Windows 10 Settings for System – Overview

Go to Start > Settings > System and Windows 10 displays the following ...

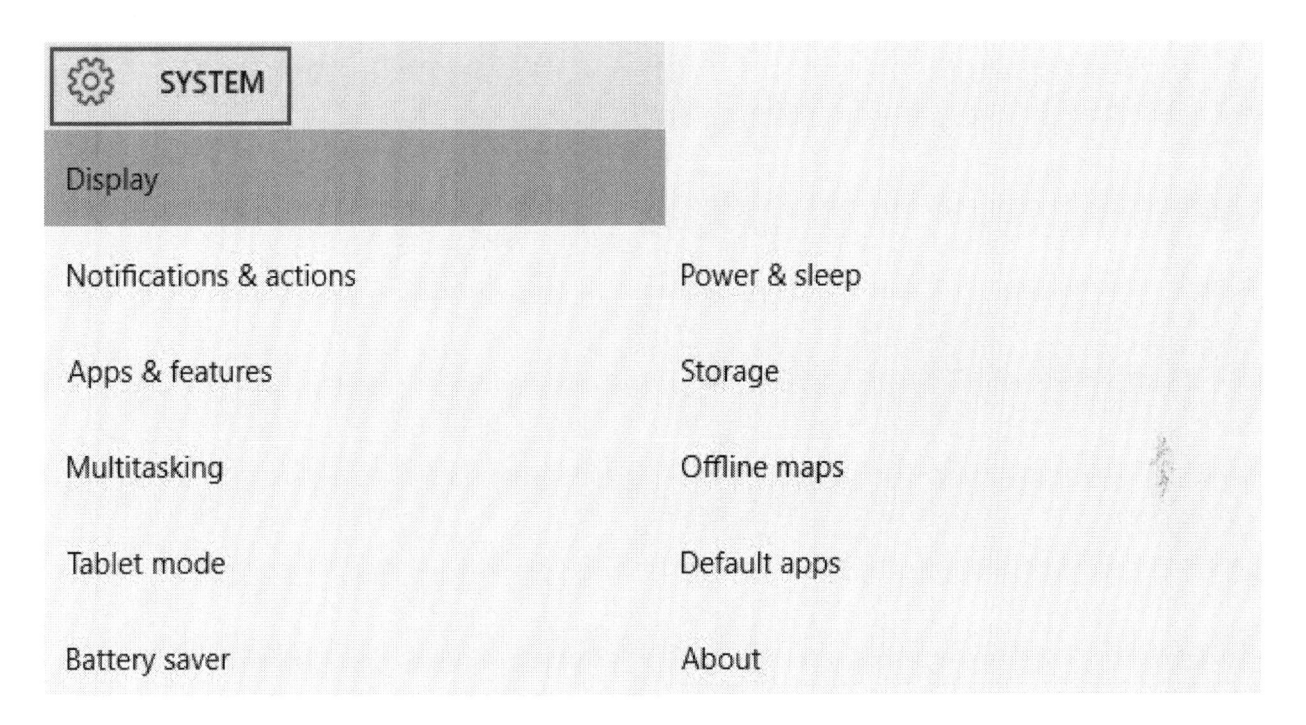

⚙ SYSTEM	
Display	
Notifications & actions	Power & sleep
Apps & features	Storage
Multitasking	Offline maps
Tablet mode	Default apps
Battery saver	About

The System Settings you can customize here include ...

1. Display
2. Notifications and Actions
3. Applications and Features
4. Multitasking
5. Tablet Mode
6. Battery Saver
7. Power and Sleep
8. Storage
9. Offline Maps
10. Default Apps
11. About

Section 22: Windows 10 System Display

Go to Start > Settings > System > Display.

The Display System Settings enable you have the display that is best for you. You can use both basic and advanced options as you need.

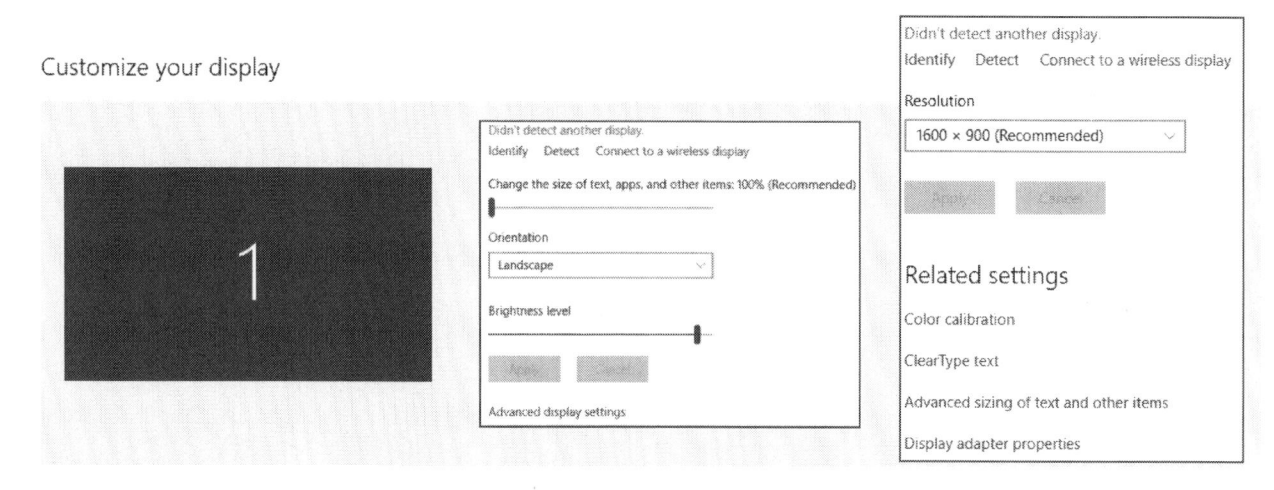

Customize your display

Depending on the number of screens/displays you have – that is what will show in blue. For me, here, I have just my laptop screen display so you just see #1. With Display settings, you can establish the size that text, apps, and more are displayed. You can also setup the Display Orientation per Landscape, Portrait and more. You can setup the Brightness of the display. If what you have chosen is good and meets your needs then click on the Apply button.

However, if you need further customization – click on the Advanced Display Settings link. The window farthest to the right is shown. Go through the options here to make sure Display Resolution, Color Calibration, ClearType and Sizing of Text and Display Adapter Properties are the best they can be for you. Then, click on the Apply button to finalize your choices.

Section 23: Windows 10 System Notification

Go to Start > Settings > System > Notifications and Actions.

The System Notification and Action Settings enable you to determine exactly what Windows is allowed to show you (or notify you about) during your Windows experience.

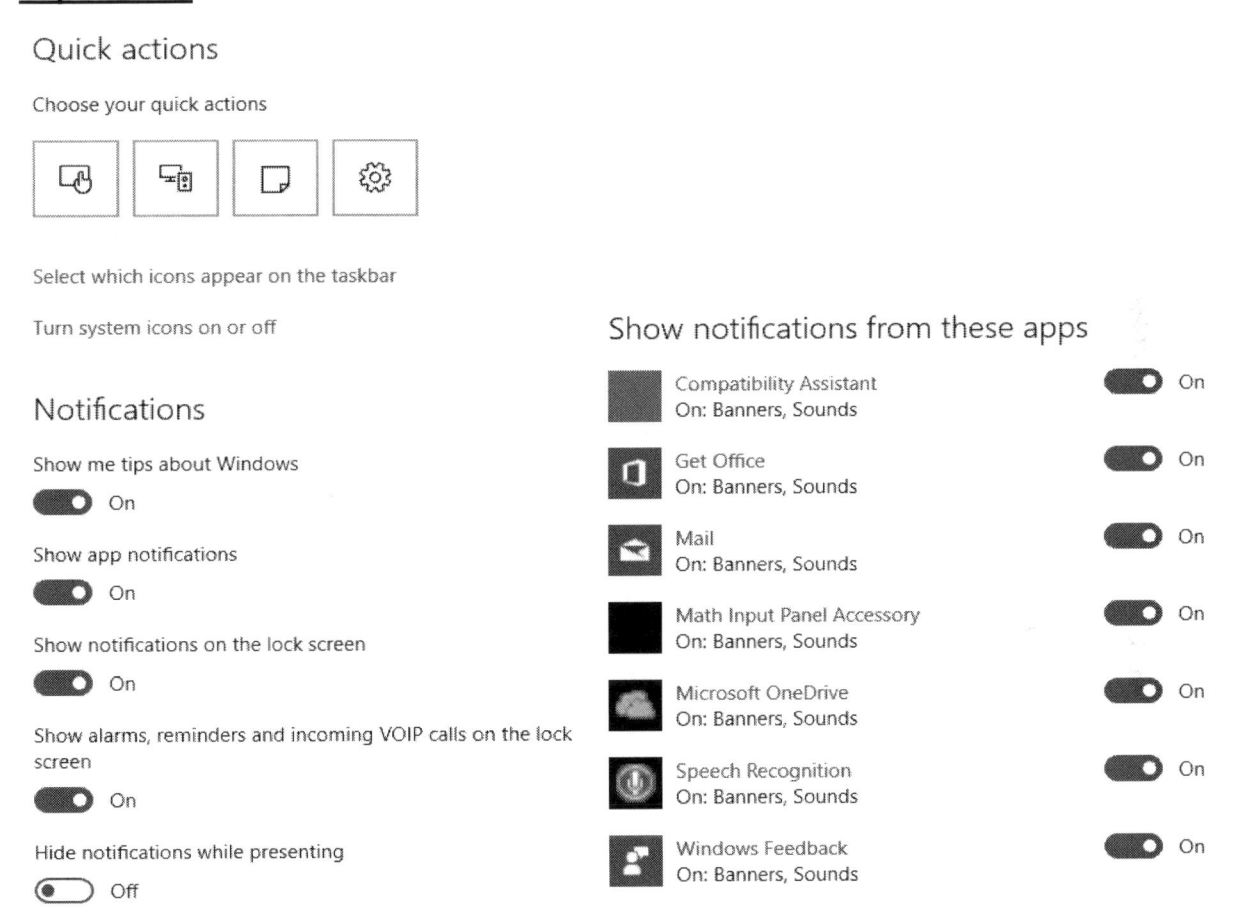

Quick actions

Choose your quick actions

Select which icons appear on the taskbar

Turn system icons on or off

Notifications

Show me tips about Windows
On

Show app notifications
On

Show notifications on the lock screen
On

Show alarms, reminders and incoming VOIP calls on the lock screen
On

Hide notifications while presenting
Off

Show notifications from these apps

Compatibility Assistant — On
On: Banners, Sounds

Get Office — On
On: Banners, Sounds

Mail — On
On: Banners, Sounds

Math Input Panel Accessory — On
On: Banners, Sounds

Microsoft OneDrive — On
On: Banners, Sounds

Speech Recognition — On
On: Banners, Sounds

Windows Feedback — On
On: Banners, Sounds

Here you can decide on major notifications, app notifications, icons that appear on your taskbar (use the link to open the selections pop-up window), and system icons to be displayed (use the link to open the selections pop-up window). The Quick Actions section of this Settings Option enables you to choose the type of display as well as Settings options for other aspects of System Settings – but I will be covering these in detail in the following pages. It is important you understand the implications of these before randomly just selecting them out of thin air.

Section 24: Windows 10 System Apps and Features

Go to Start > Settings > System > Apps and Features.

It is through Apps and Features that you can manage the presence of apps (e.g. programs) on your Windows 10 computer.

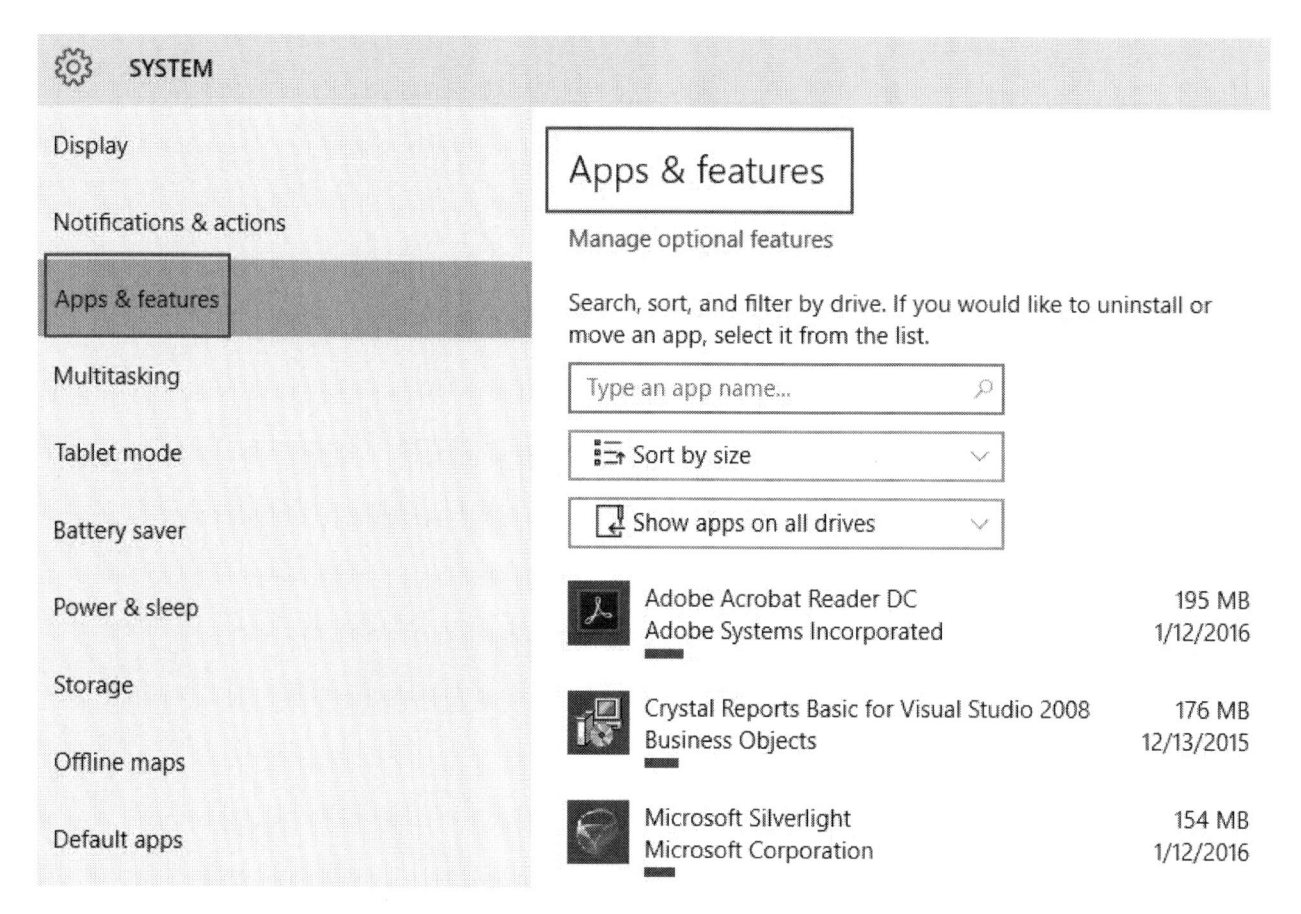

{image of System settings showing Apps & features panel with Display, Notifications & actions, Apps & features (selected), Multitasking, Tablet mode, Battery saver, Power & sleep, Storage, Offline maps, Default apps on the left. On the right: Apps & features, Manage optional features, "Search, sort, and filter by drive. If you would like to uninstall or move an app, select it from the list.", Type an app name..., Sort by size, Show apps on all drives, Adobe Acrobat Reader DC — Adobe Systems Incorporated — 195 MB — 1/12/2016, Crystal Reports Basic for Visual Studio 2008 — Business Objects — 176 MB — 12/13/2015, Microsoft Silverlight — Microsoft Corporation — 154 MB — 1/12/2016}

Apps and Features is the latest version of the longstanding "Programs and Features" section of your Control Panel – where you could see programs installed on your computer and also uninstall programs if that was necessary. You can do all this and more in Apps and Features. Unlike Programs and Features from Windows 7 and 8, Apps and Features enables you to show only a small listing of apps per your Search criteria (use the Type an app name box). You can also Search by app size and/or see apps by drive or all drives. So, in some searches, you might see one or two apps, on other searches you might see most apps on your computer. Single clicking on the app enables you to access an Uninstall button which completes that operation.

You can also click on the Manage Optional Features link.

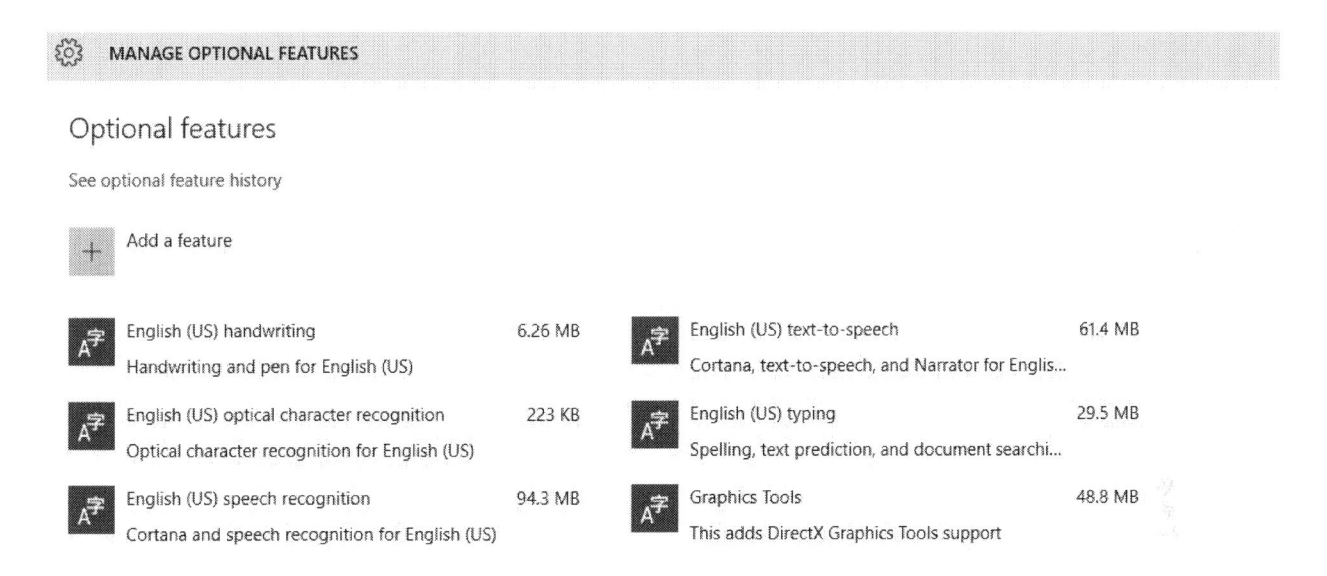

⚙️ MANAGE OPTIONAL FEATURES			

Optional features

See optional feature history

➕ Add a feature

English (US) handwriting	6.26 MB	English (US) text-to-speech	61.4 MB
Handwriting and pen for English (US)		Cortana, text-to-speech, and Narrator for Englis...	
English (US) optical character recognition	223 KB	English (US) typing	29.5 MB
Optical character recognition for English (US)		Spelling, text prediction, and document searchi...	
English (US) speech recognition	94.3 MB	Graphics Tools	48.8 MB
Cortana and speech recognition for English (US)		This adds DirectX Graphics Tools support	

This window works in the same way the parent window works – by single clicking on the Feature (which is like an app), you can see whether it can be managed or uninstalled. To add a feature, use the + Add a feature icon. To see the history of features on your computer, click on the See optional feature history button. To return to the parent window, click on the back arrow that is shown at the top of the window.

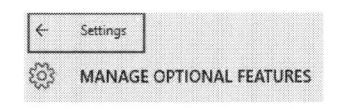

← Settings
⚙️ MANAGE OPTIONAL FEATURES

Optional features

Section 25: Windows 10 System Multitasking

Go to Start > Settings > System > Multitasking.

The Multitasking option in System Settings enables you to fine tune user interface details that can contribute to your overall productivity. These two details are Snap and Virtual Desktops.

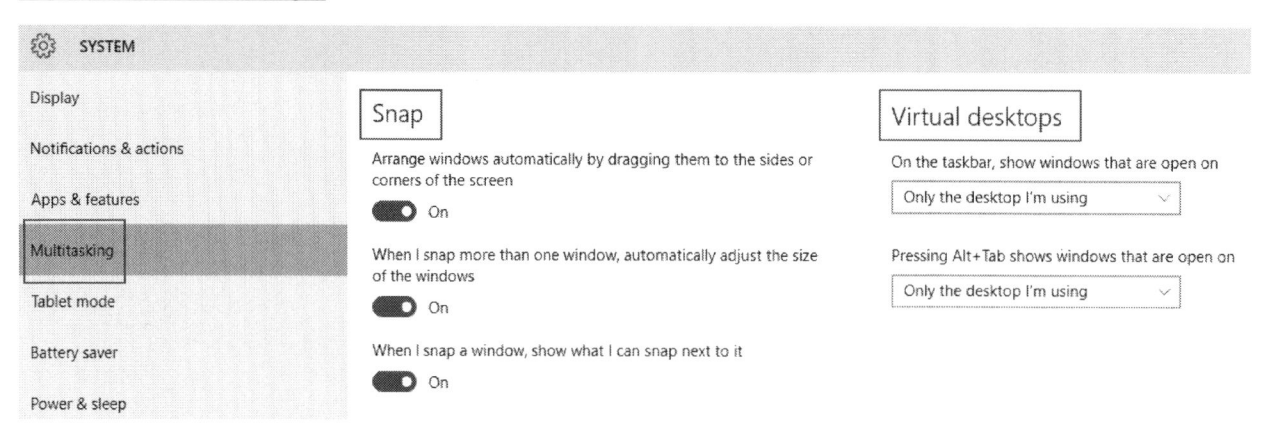

Snap refers to the behavior of displayed windows and their sizing. Snap means the window will take on a specific and determined size and shape as opposed to being one that is free-floating and possibly showing over another window. When you click "On" for all options you see above, windows are shown but they do not interfere with other windows that are also open. This makes it easier to work between different "windows" as you multitask and do several things simultaneously from within Windows 10.

Virtual Desktops are not a topic I have covered in this guide because this is an advanced topic for System Administrators and chances are you are not going to be working with Virtual Desktops. However, if that is the case, and you do have a Virtual desktop (which is a platform within a platform), there are options you have regarding how windows are shown. The drop-down menus for each option show what is available for you.

Section 26: Windows 10 System Tablet Mode

Go to Start > Settings > System > Tablet Mode.

If your computer has a touch screen, then it can operate in Tablet mode. Otherwise, this System Setting does not apply to your computer.

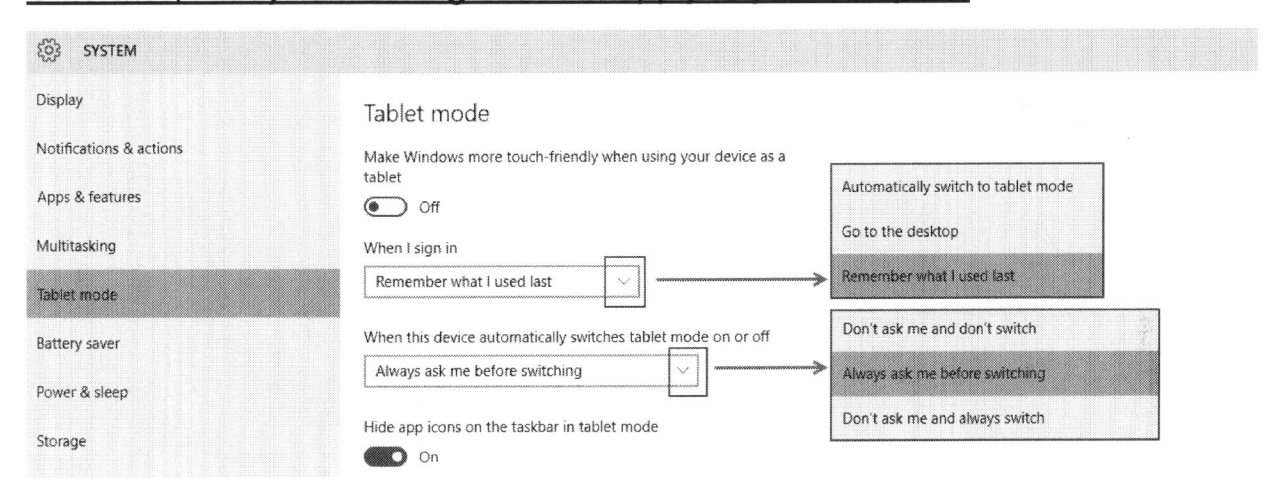

There are four ways to customize the use of your touch-screen computer in tablet mode. They are as follows ...

1. Make Windows more touch-friendly when using your device as a tablet – slide this setting to ON for best results.

2. When I sign in, choose one of the following three options: automatically switch to tablet mode, go to the desktop, or remember what I used last.

3. When this device automatically switches tablet mode on or off, choose one of the following three options: don't ask me and don't switch, always ask me before switching, or don't ask me and always switch.

4. Hide app icons on the taskbar in tablet mode? For no, leave this option off. For yet, leave this option on.

Section 27: Windows 10 System Battery Saver

Go to Start > Settings > System > Battery Saver.

If you are using battery power frequently, this Setting can help you with the computer's battery energy-level and charge-management process.

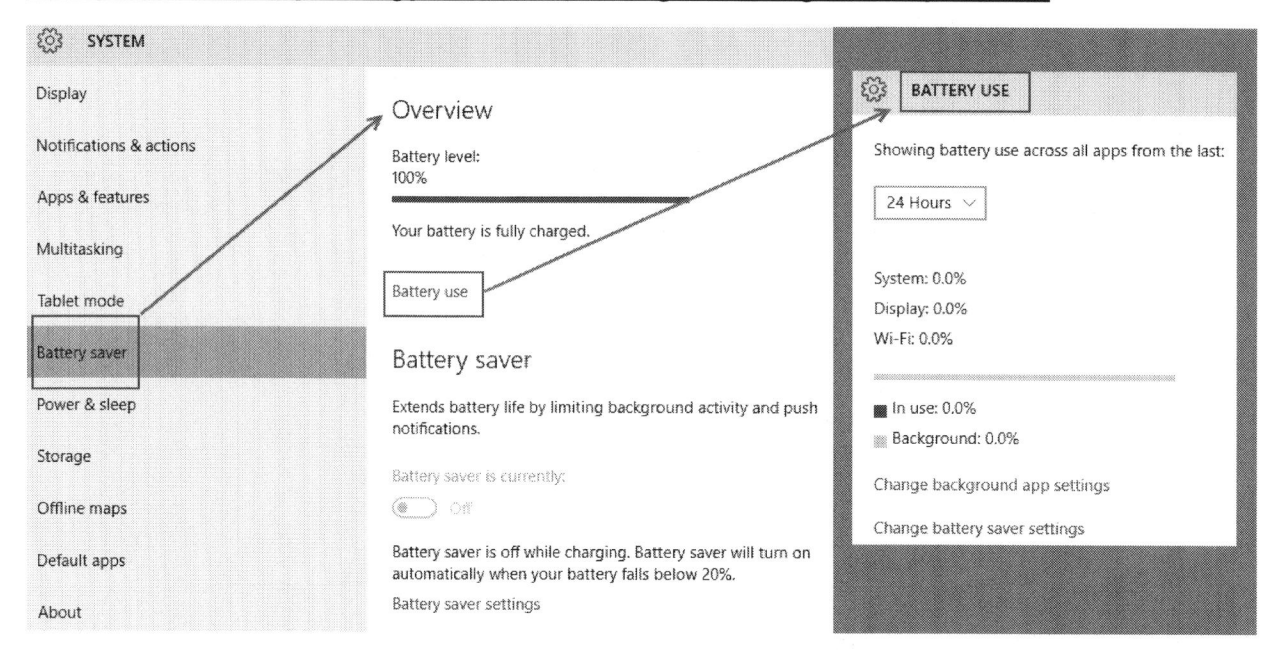

This is a very simple Settings option. Battery Saver has two main parts – Overview and Battery Saver. Overview shows you the current status of your computer's battery and its Battery use link opens a window showing these details which you can manage as necessary. The second option is Battery Saver. You need to click on the Battery saver settings link to open this window where you can make appropriate selections:

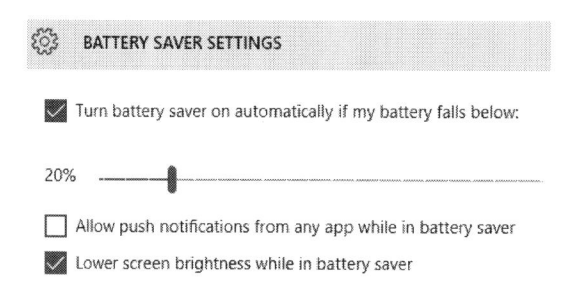

Section 28: Windows 10 Power and Sleep

Go to Start > Settings > System > Power and Sleep.

Use the Power and Sleep Settings option to manage energy flow to your computer's screen and main hardware.

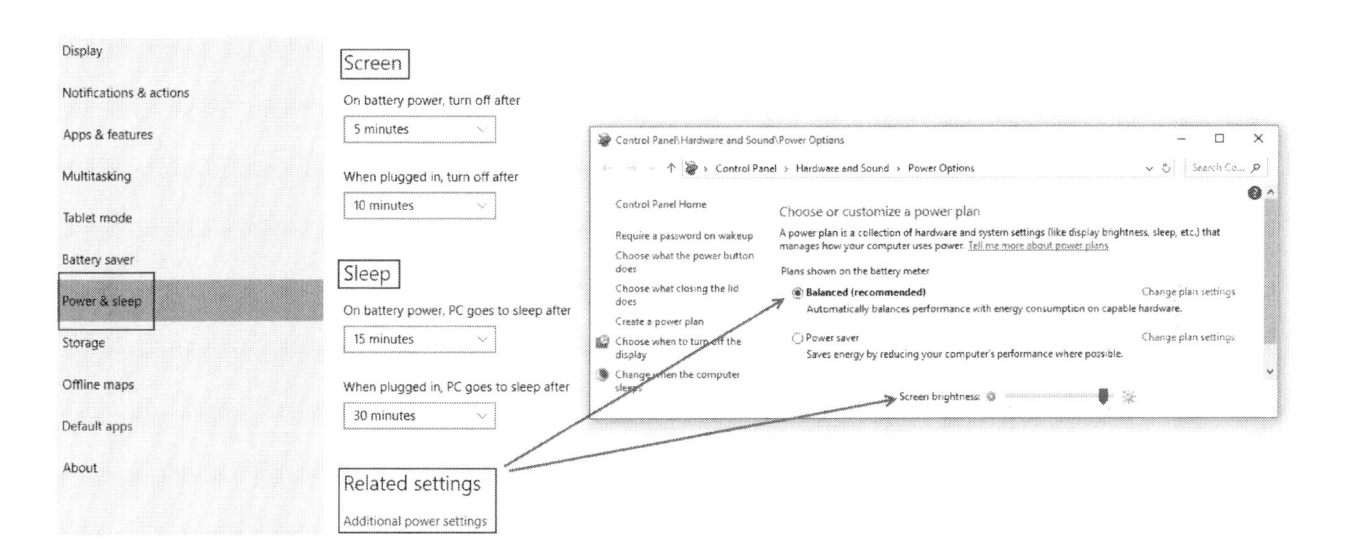

For Screen – you can specify the amount of time before the computer is turned off while on battery power and also while it is plugged into an electrical outlet.

For Sleep – you can specify the amount of time before the PC goes to sleep while on battery power and also while it is plugged into an electrical outlet.

Note: Should you decide to manage your computer's power further, then click on the Related Settings (Additional power settings) link. A window that looks like the former Control Panel interface is shown. There are several options here, but the two most important ones are Balanced Power and Power User. Make your choice wisely to optimize power and how it charges your computer overall.

Section 29: Windows 10 Storage

Go to Start > Settings > System > Storage.

Use the Storage Settings option to manage how information is saved.

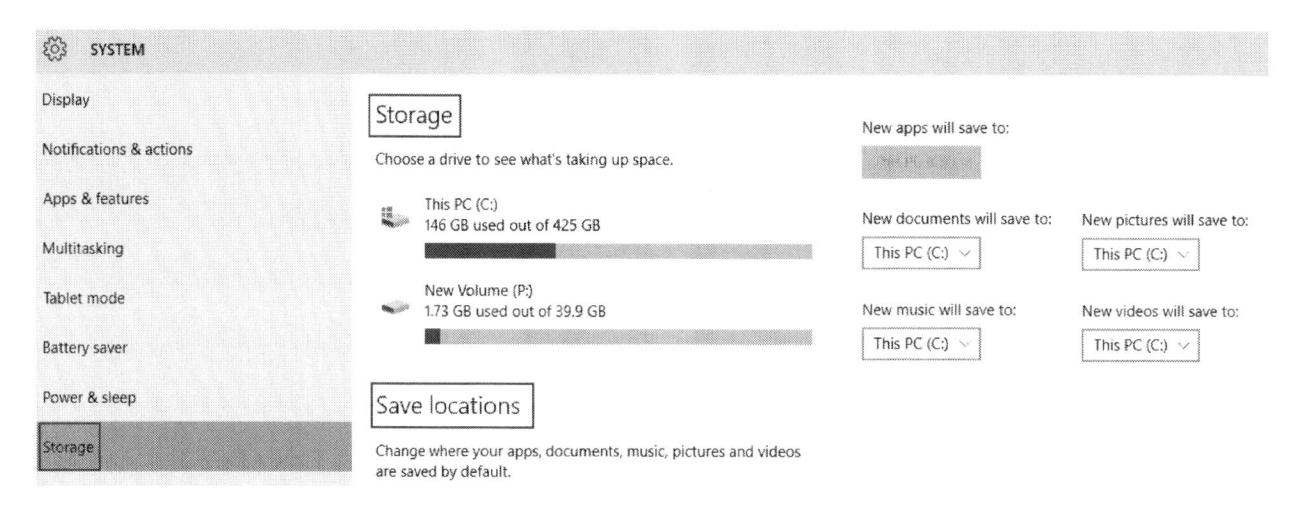

As you can see in the same screen shot above, I have two main drives – my C drive and also a second partition I have labeled P. I use the C drive to save 99% of my files but use the P drive to do some work with open source tools like WAMP.

So, with that said, the options available for apps being saved is only my C drive because Windows 10 is only installed on the C drive. However, new documents, new music, new pictures, and new videos can be saved on both the C and P drives because they do not require Windows 10 to be saved.

Section 30: Windows 10 Offline Maps

Go to Start > Settings > System > Offline Maps.

Use the Offline Maps Settings option to manage maps that you can use on your computer when you are offline.

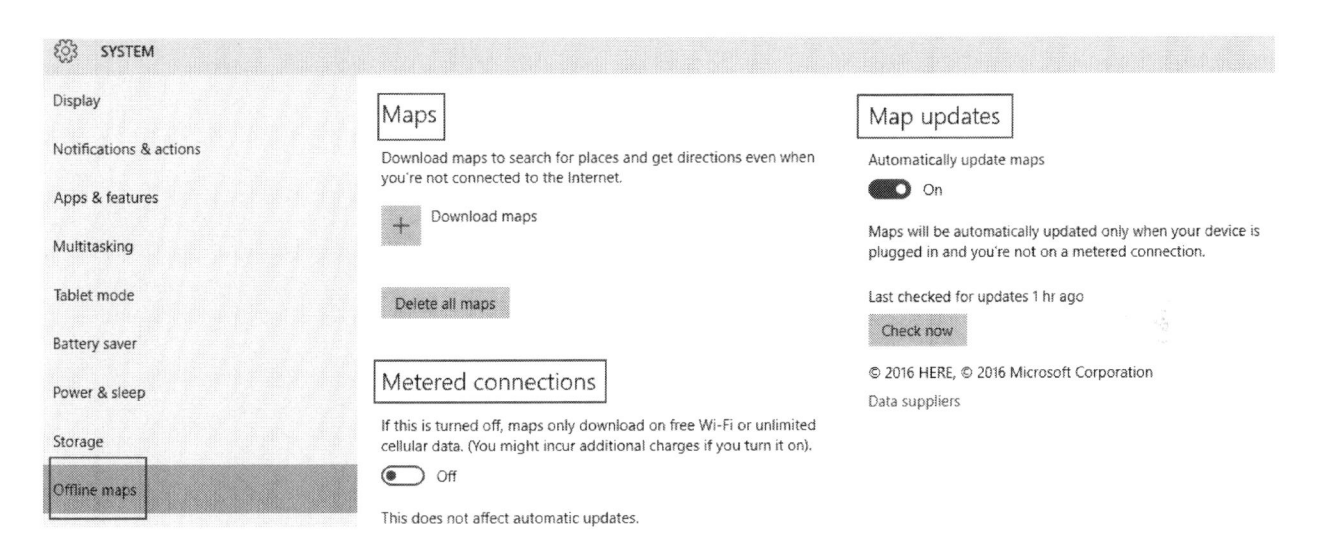

This System Settings option has three major parts – Maps, Metered Connections and Map Updates. Maps is where you can actually download maps to your computer. Metered Connections is where you can manage data consumption of your computer should you not have a Wi-Fi connection available. Finally, Map Updates (if kept "On") allows for automatic updates to downloaded maps so they stay up-to-date. This is a great resource of you depend on maps and especially if you go to areas that have no Wi-Fi readily available.

Section 31: Windows 10 Default Apps

Go to Start > Settings > System > Default apps.

Use the Default apps System Settings option to manage apps that Windows recognizes as the primary app for the category indicated here.

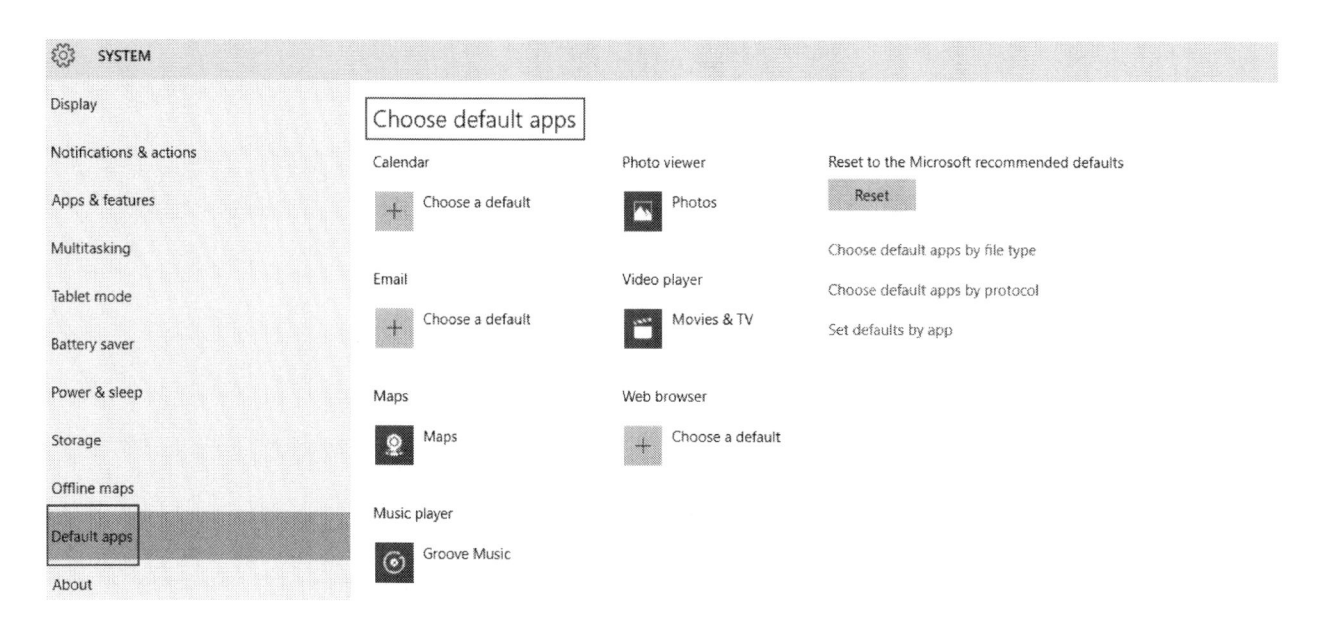

Windows 10 starts you off with common applications categories like Calendar, Email, Maps, Music Player, Photo Viewer, Video Player, and Web Browser. Click on either the + icon or the image next to the app to update it or verify it. You can further set your apps through three more options...

1. Choose default apps by file type

2. Choose default apps by protocol

3. Set defaults by app

Finally, if there are issues of any kind regarding one or more apps that have been set as defaults and that do not work properly or you don't want to personally manage apps in this way, you can select the Reset button which gives Microsoft permission to set the default apps.

Section 32: Windows 10 "About"

Go to Start > Settings > System > About.

Use the About System Settings option to manage your Windows 10 Product ID and other machine-related information to help you optimize your Windows 10 experience.

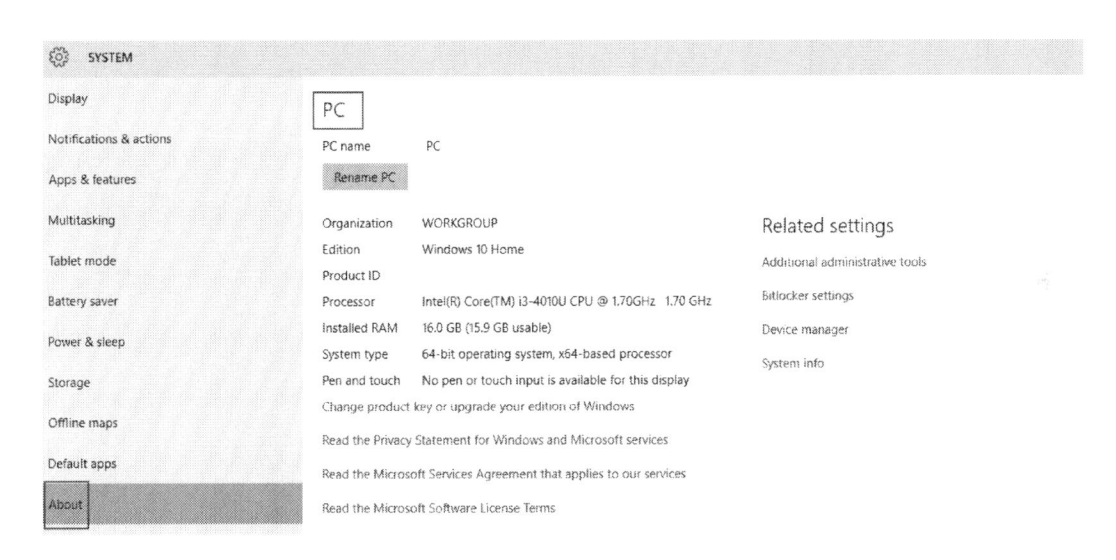

The "About" System Settings window enables you to rename your PC if you must as well as (1) change product key or upgrade Windows edition, (2) read the privacy statement for Windows 10 and Microsoft services, (3) read the Microsoft Services Agreement that applies to Windows 10 services, (4) read the Microsoft Software License Terms document for users, (5) administrate additional Windows 10 tools, (6) administrate settings for BitLocker (you need to have at least Windows Pro for this option), (7) administrate your Device Manager resource, and/or (8) check your latest system info.

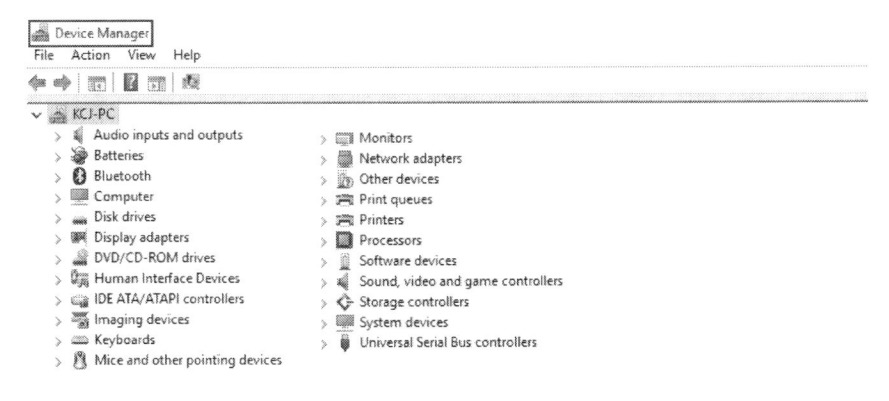

Section 33: Windows 10 Settings for Devices – Overview

Go to Start > Settings > System > Devices.

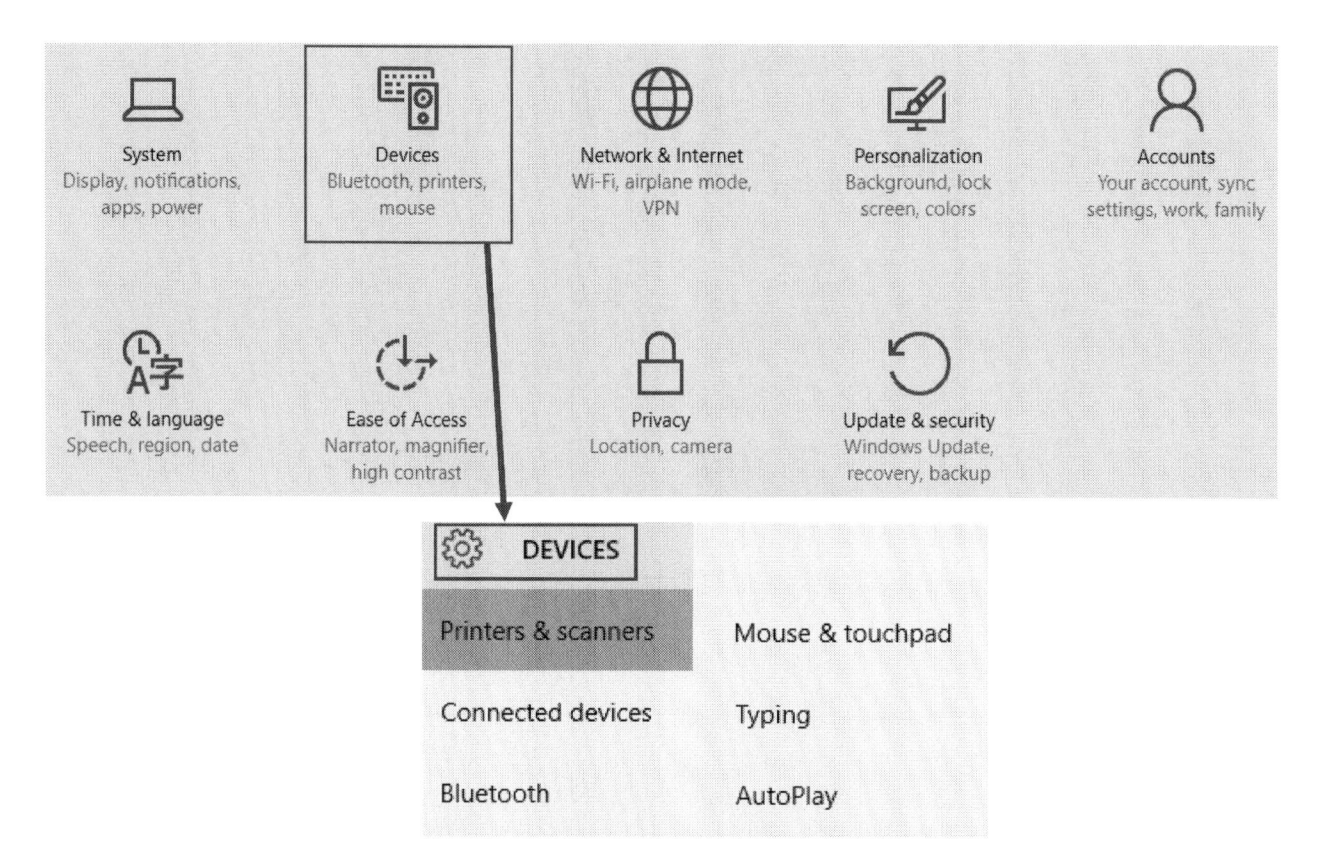

Use the Devices System Settings option to manage the following hardware that interface with your Windows 10 Operating System – Printers and Scanners, Connected Devices, Bluetooth, Mouse and Touchpad, Typing, and Autoplay.

Section 34: Windows 10 Settings for Printing/Scanning

Go to Start > Settings > System > Devices > Printers and Scanner.

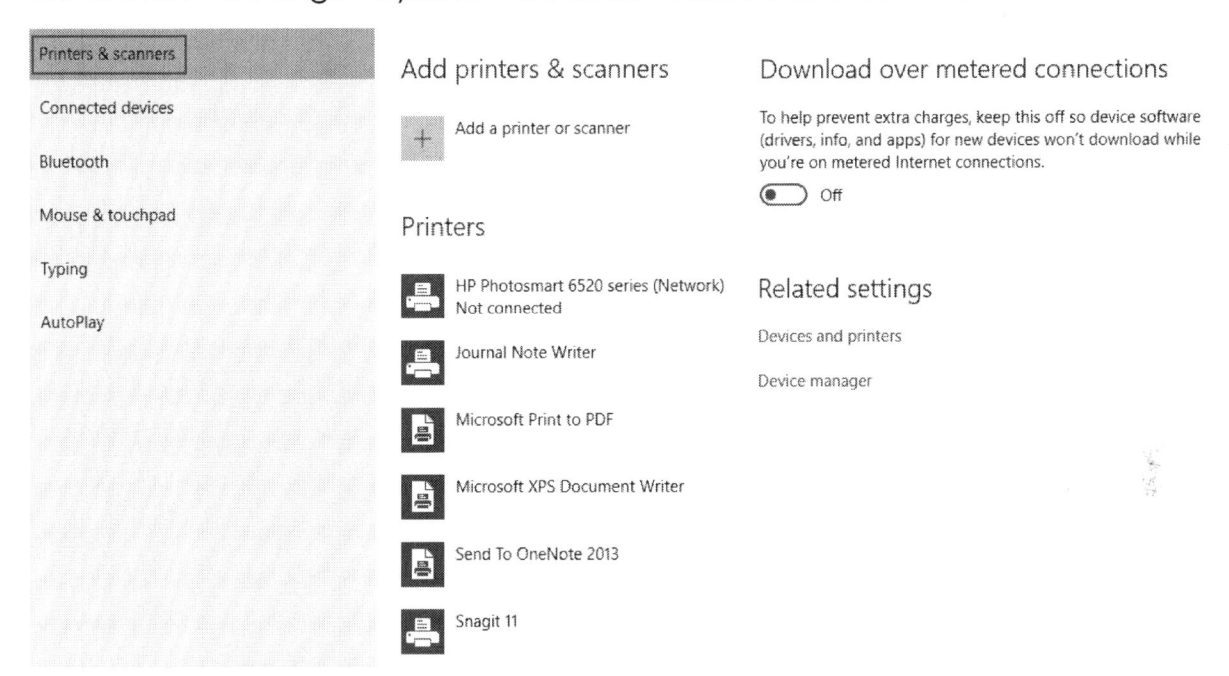

In this Settings option, you can add printing and scanning devices as well as remove them. To add a device to your system, click on the + button that you see in the sample screen shot above. Windows 10 automatically attempts to refresh your Printers/Scanners list but if you do not see your device listed, then click on the "the printer that I want isn't listed" link and you are directed to a pop-up window where you can resolve this through an Add Printer wizard.

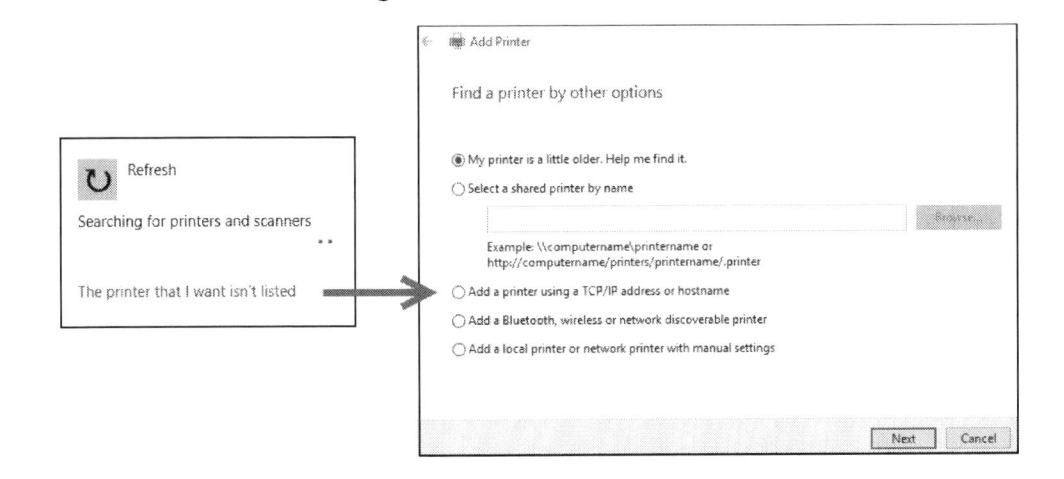

Just follow the steps of this wizard-window and you should be able to get your Printers/Scanners list updated. If you are really having problems, contact the vendor (manufacturer) of the device for troubleshooting support. Make sure the Printer/Scanner has a driver that is compatible with Windows 10.

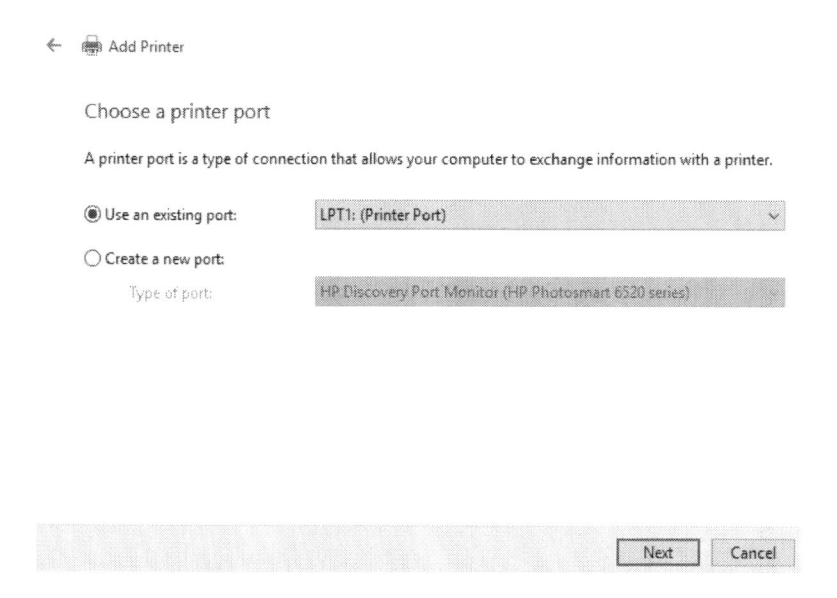

← Add Printer

Choose a printer port

A printer port is a type of connection that allows your computer to exchange information with a printer.

● Use an existing port: LPT1: (Printer Port)
○ Create a new port:
   Type of port: HP Discovery Port Monitor (HP Photosmart 6520 series)

Next   Cancel

There is also, in this Settings option, a section called "Download over Metered Connection". This setting is recommended to remain *OFF* to save you money so that you do not unnecessarily get charged for downloads outside of your WiFi or established data account.

If there are additional concerns related to your Printers/Scanners connected to your computer, Windows 10 provides two additional links for quick access so you can get more related information – Devices and Printers and Device Manager.

Section 35: Windows 10 Settings for Connected Devices

Go to Start > Settings > System > Devices > Connected Devices.

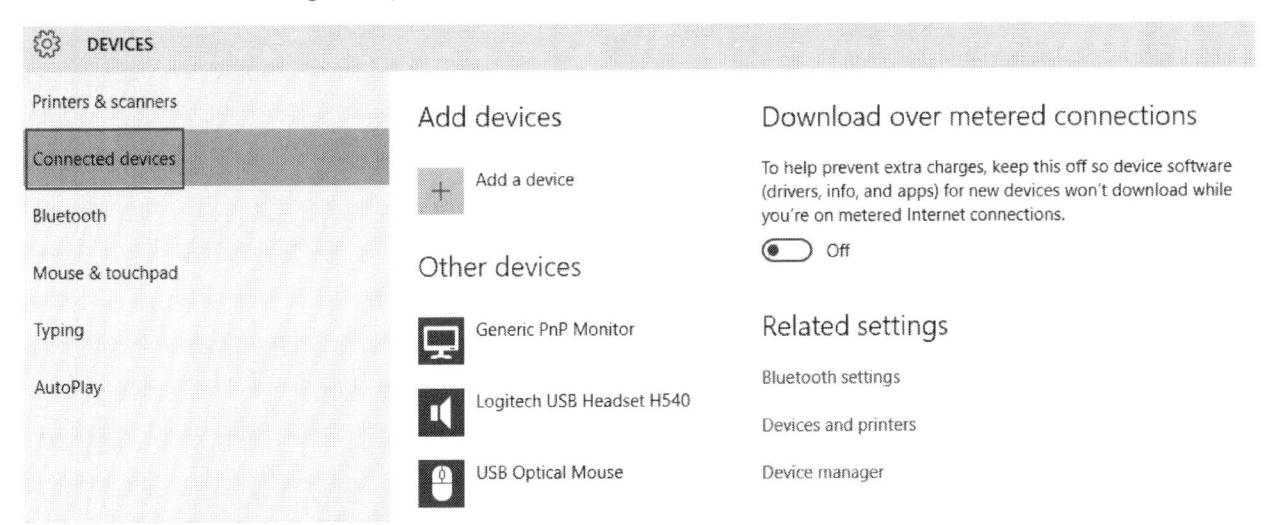

DEVICES		
Printers & scanners	**Add devices**	**Download over metered connections**
Connected devices	+ Add a device	To help prevent extra charges, keep this off so device software (drivers, info, and apps) for new devices won't download while you're on metered Internet connections.
Bluetooth		
Mouse & touchpad	**Other devices**	⬤ Off
Typing	Generic PnP Monitor	**Related settings**
AutoPlay	Logitech USB Headset H540	Bluetooth settings
		Devices and printers
	USB Optical Mouse	Device manager

In this Settings option, you can add connected devices as well as remove them. To add a device, click on the + button (as shown in the sample screen shot above). Windows 10 will automatically update your Devices list (called Other Devices). As you can see, I have a second monitor (Generic PnP Monitor), as well as a Logitech USB Headset and Logitech (Optical) Mouse listed in Windows 10 as Other Devices.

This Settings option works the same way as Printers/Scanners regarding the Download over metered connections option. Keep this OFF so that you don't get charged for an Internet connection outside your usual WiFi or data account, especially during downloads.

Should there be any additional concerns regarding Other Devices, Windows 10 provides you with three links so that you can get more information if this is necessary – Bluetooth settings, Devices and Printers, and Device Manager.

Section 36: Windows 10 Settings for Bluetooth

Go to Start > Settings > System > Devices > Bluetooth.

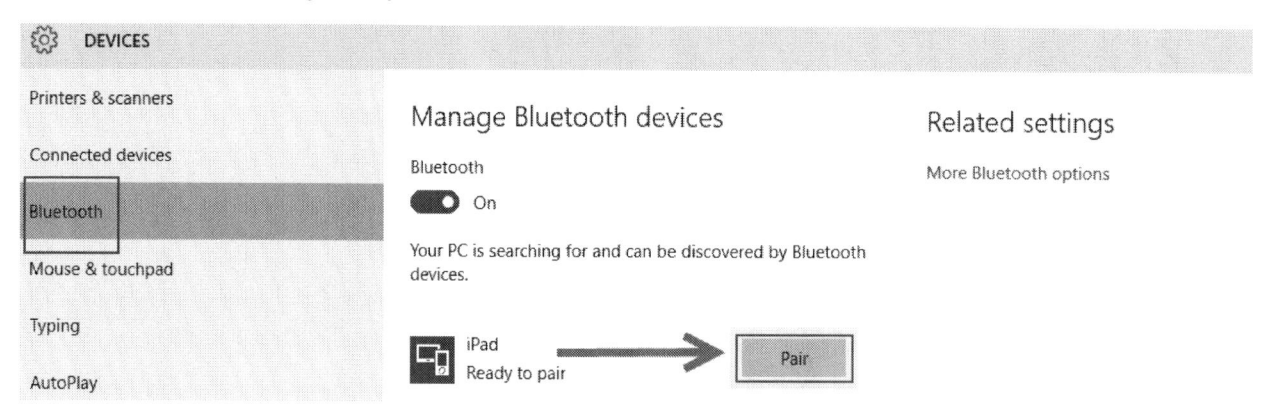

This Settings option enables you to manage Bluetooth-enabled devices and their connections to your computer running Windows 10. You must of course turn this setting ON for this option to work. From there, Windows 10 will be able to sense Bluetooth-enabled devices that can be connected or "paired" with the computer. To continue with the process, click on the device listed and then the "Pair" button that is displayed. If you have difficulty with the connection, click on the More Bluetooth options link and you can try different checkboxes to help Windows 10 and the Bluetooth-enabled device to connect (pair).

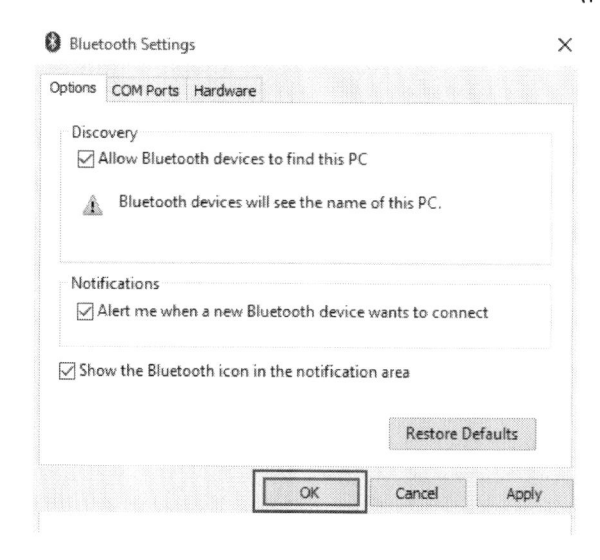

Section 37: Windows 10 Settings for Mouse/Touchpad

Go to Start > Settings > System > Devices > Mouse and Touchpad.

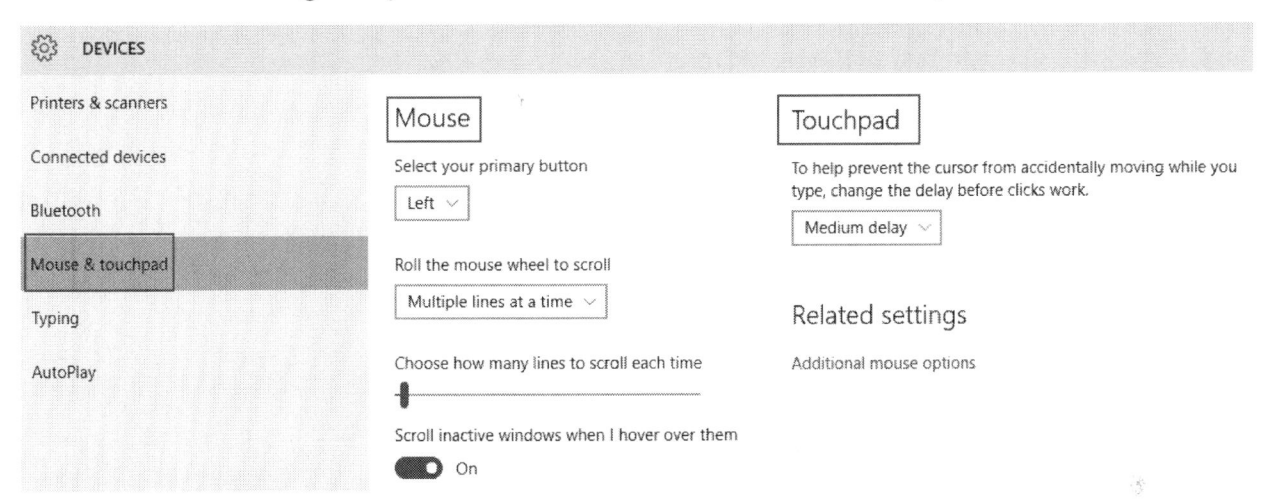

This Settings option enables you to manage your mouse and/or touchpad and how they are connected to your computer running Windows 10.

Options available for the Mouse include (1) selecting the primary button, (2) rolling the mouse wheel to scroll, (3) choosing how many lines to scroll each time (you scroll), and (4) scroll inactive windows when I hover over them (On/Off).

Options available for the Touchpad include (1) no delay (always on), (2) short delay, (3) medium delay, and (4) long delay regarding how long before a click actually works (to help prevent the cursor from accidentally moving while you type). Use the drop-down menu that this Settings option provides you. For additional mouse options, click on this Related Settings link for reference. Windows displays the old Control Panel window for Mouse Properties.

Section 38: Windows 10 Settings for Typing

Go to Start > Settings > System > Devices > Typing.

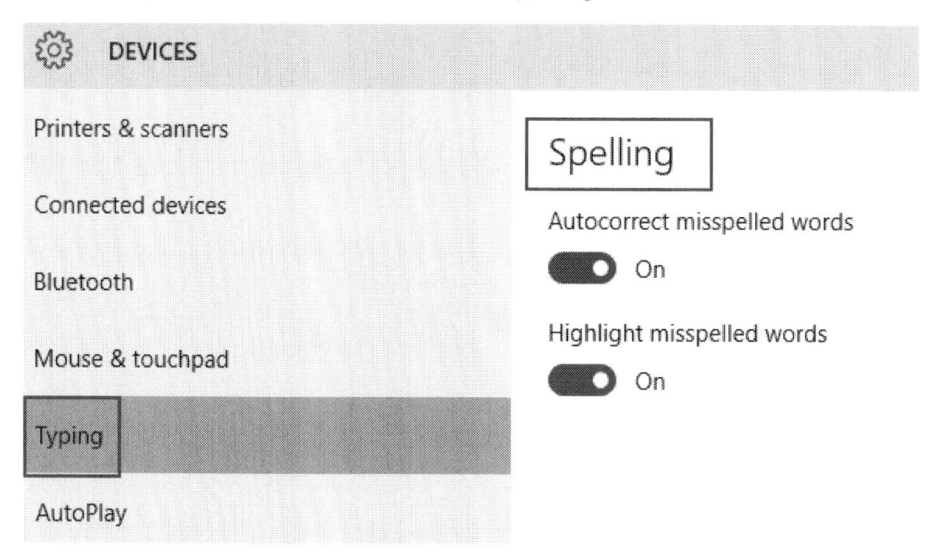

This Settings option gives you the chance to manage your typing on your computer's keyboard.

What you need to do is turn two Spelling settings to ON. They are (1) autocorrect misspelled words and (2) highlight misspelled words. If you turn either or both of these off, then the Spelling settings that are off will not help you to manage your typing in those specific respects. My recommendation is to leave both ON at all times.

Section 39: Windows 10 Settings for Autoplay

Go to Start > Settings > System > Devices > Autoplay.

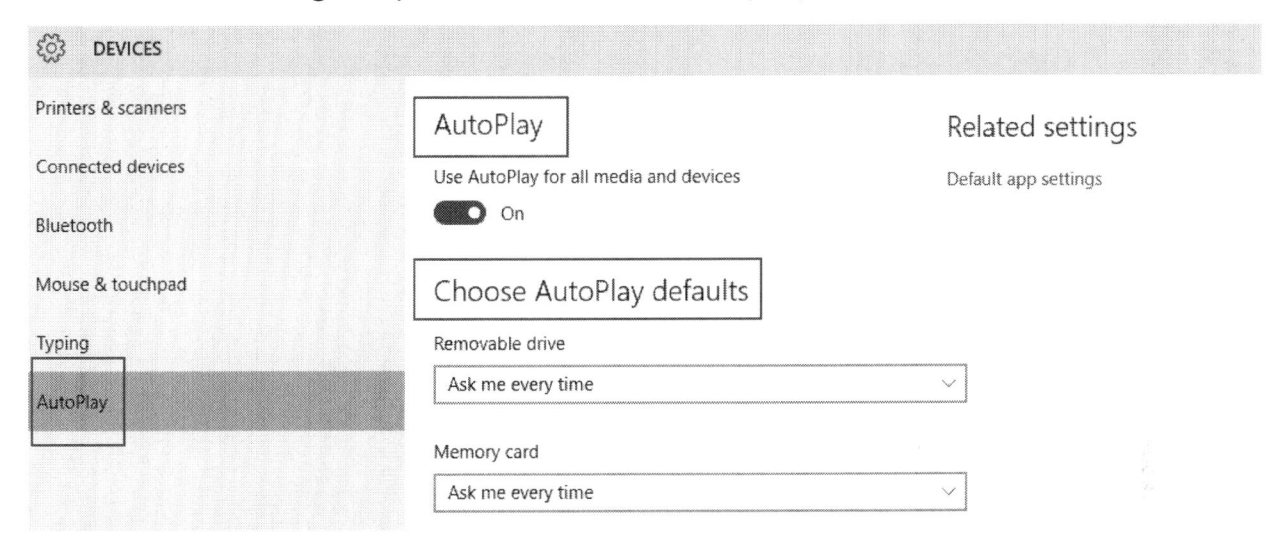

The Autoplay Settings option in Windows 10 enables you to configure your computer such that it can play a CD or DVD automatically when it is loaded into your local CD/DVD player.

Make sure (as you see in the sample screen shot above) Autoplay is ON.

For my laptop here – Autoplay has detected two defaults that I can configure. Each machine will be different so most likely what you see will be a bit different. Still, the same logic applies. There are drop-down menus for each default and you can choose how that default is to be configured. I like to be asked if I really want to play the CD or DVD in case I am busy with something else and it also helps me to verify that the drive is working nicely. So, I have chosen "ask me every time". You can select according to your needs and best interests here. Notice that there is not a "Save" button like in older versions of Windows because Windows 10 is very similar to modern Apple and Android mobile technology where the setting is automatically set as you choose and the OS automatically responds and therefore you need not save – the OS does this for you. Very nice I say.

Section 40: Windows 10 Settings for Network and Internet

Go to Start Menu > Settings > Network and Internet ...

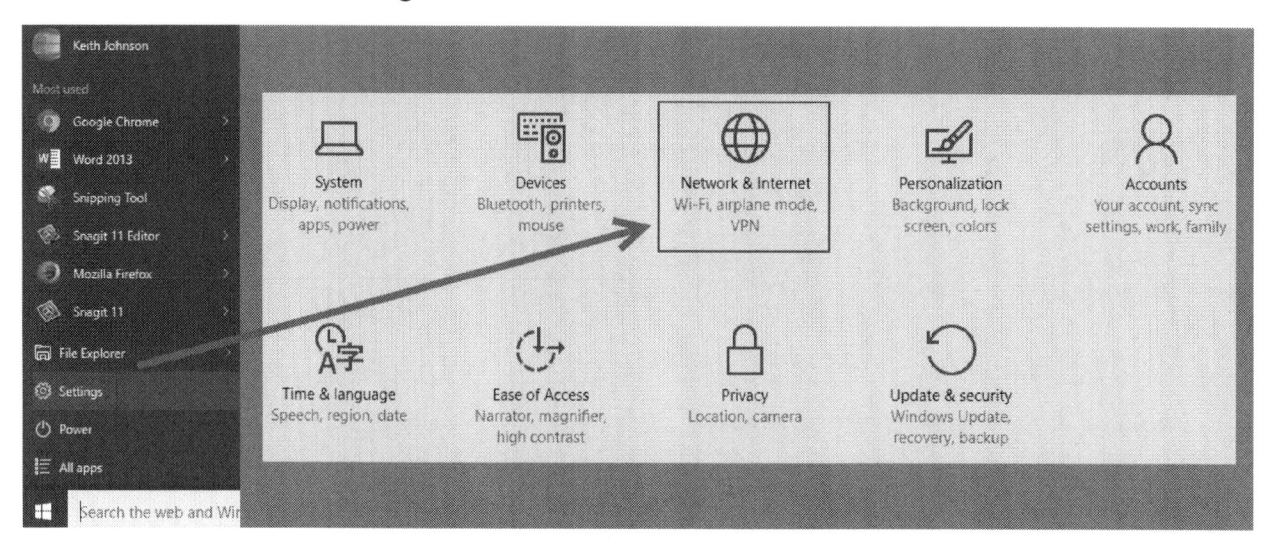

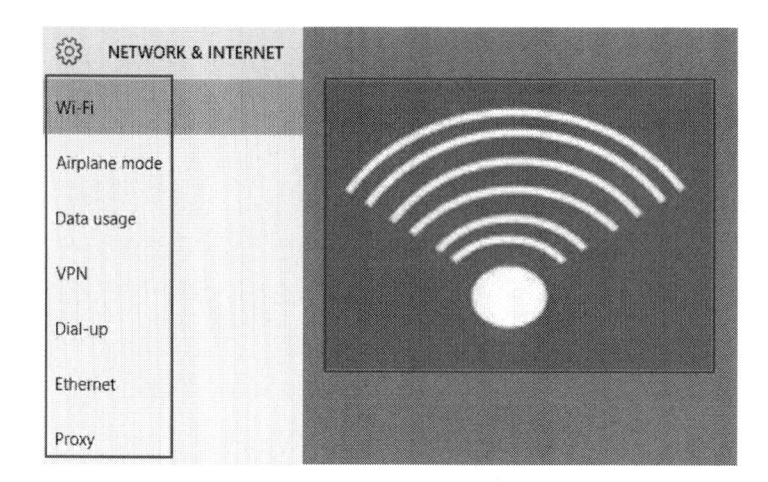

Network and Internet System Settings/Options include Wi-Fi, Airplane Mode, Data Usage, VPN (Virtual Private Network), Dial-Up, Ethernet, and Proxy.

Section 41: Windows 10 Settings for WiFi (Sense)

Go to Start Menu > Settings > Network and Internet > Wi-Fi.

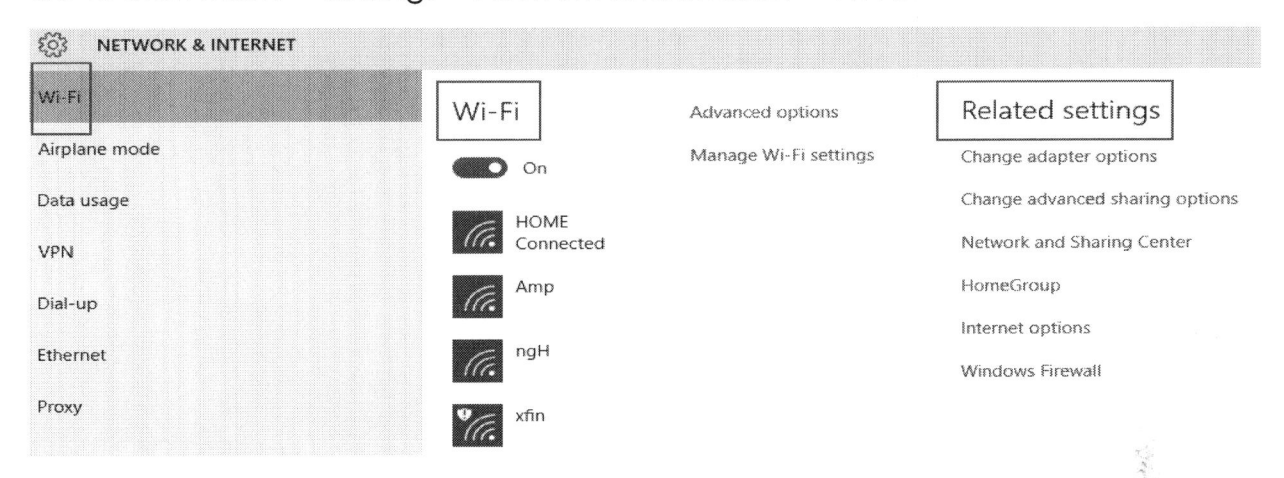

As you can see in the sample screen shot above, Windows 10 has my active Wi-Fi connection listed, but if there was a problem all I have to do is single click on the connection icon, disconnect, and then reconnect.

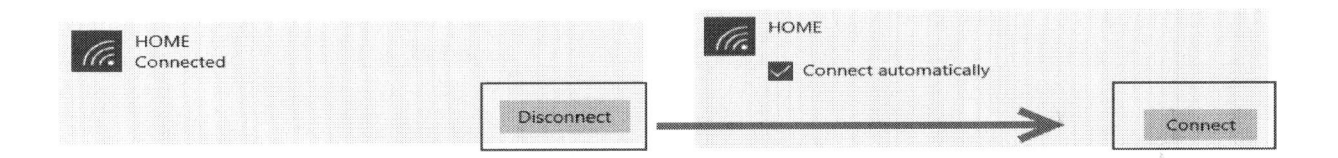

When you select *Advanced Options*, the hardware behind your connection is shown and if necessary you can communicate this information back to your Internet Service Provider (ISP) to ensure a solid connection.

When you select *Manage Wi-Fi Settings*, the following Wi-Fi Sense window is shown. Here is what Microsoft tells us on its windows.microsoft.com Wi-Fi Sense FAQ page.

"Wi-Fi Sense automatically connects you to Wi-Fi, so you can get online quickly in more places. It can connect you to open Wi-Fi hotspots it knows about through crowdsourcing or to Wi-Fi networks your contacts have shared with you by using Wi-Fi Sense. Here are a few things you need to know: (1) you need to be signed in with your Microsoft account to use Wi-Fi Sense, (2) Wi-Fi Sense is available on Windows 10 PCs but not on earlier versions of Windows, and (3) Wi-Fi Sense is not available in all countries or regions."

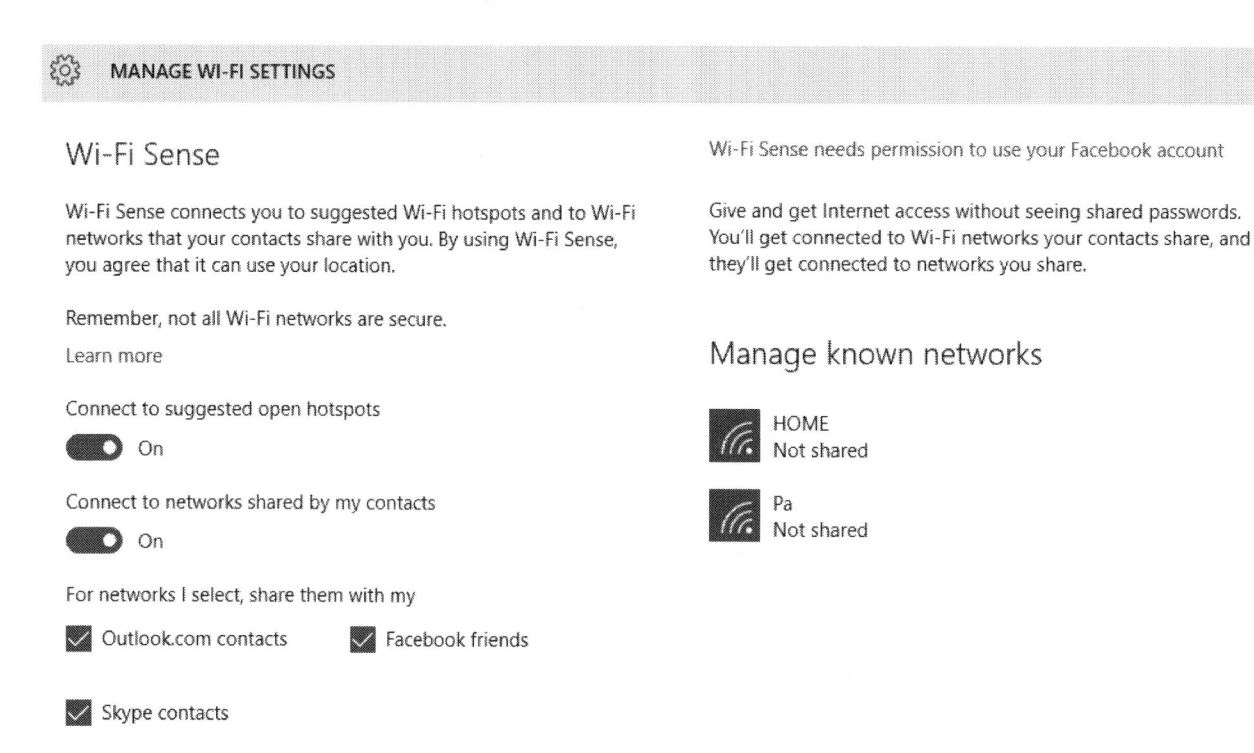

MANAGE WI-FI SETTINGS

Wi-Fi Sense

Wi-Fi Sense connects you to suggested Wi-Fi hotspots and to Wi-Fi networks that your contacts share with you. By using Wi-Fi Sense, you agree that it can use your location.

Remember, not all Wi-Fi networks are secure.

Learn more

Connect to suggested open hotspots
On

Connect to networks shared by my contacts
On

For networks I select, share them with my

☑ Outlook.com contacts   ☑ Facebook friends

☑ Skype contacts

Wi-Fi Sense needs permission to use your Facebook account

Give and get Internet access without seeing shared passwords. You'll get connected to Wi-Fi networks your contacts share, and they'll get connected to networks you share.

Manage known networks

HOME
Not shared

Pa
Not shared

My advice to you as a longstanding Windows user is to be cautious regarding Wi-Fi sense. Wi-Fi is an exceptional technology. Still … Make sure you only connect to the web via truly trustworthy connections. Even if your best friends are using a certain connection hotspot, be cautious so that you don't compromise your data, machine, or otherwise.

Section 42: Windows 10 Settings for Airplane Mode

Go to Start Menu > Settings > Network and Internet > Airplane Mode.

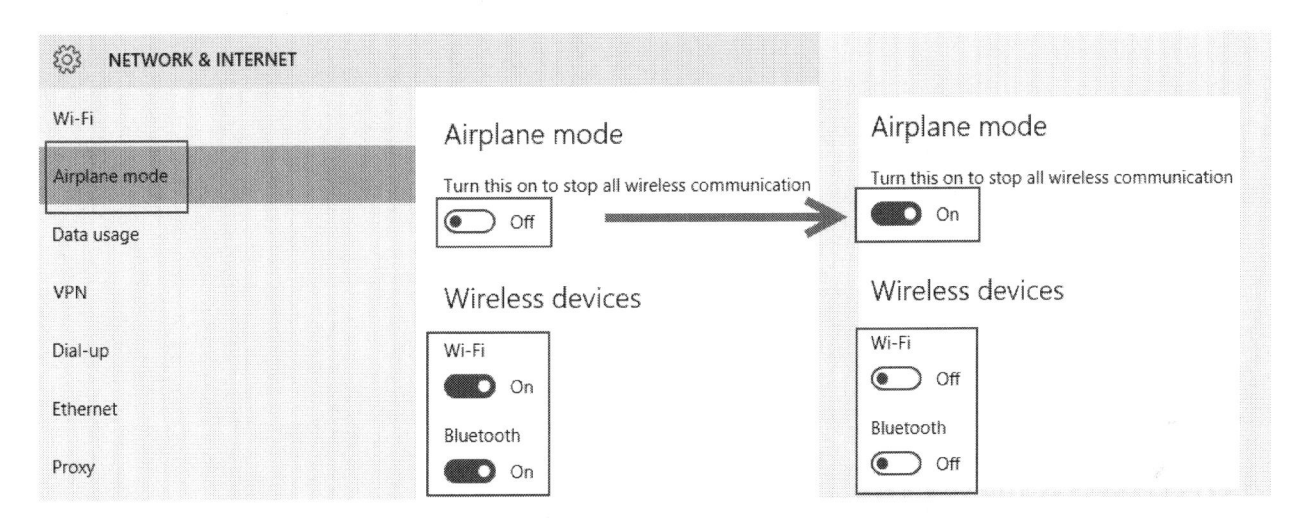

The reason why this connection mode is called "airplane mode" is because when airplanes are about to take off and land, they ask all passengers to turn OFF their mobile devices (phones and phablets), tablets, and computers because there are sensitive connections between a plane and the immediate airport tower that can be affected by devices that are open connection-wise. So, such a setting helps to ensure the safety of the airplane/aircraft during takeoffs and landings.

After turning your device connections OFF using Airplane Mode, you an easily turn connections back ON by turning Airplane Mode to its original OFF setting.

Section 43: Windows 10 Settings for Data Usage

Go to Start Menu > Settings > Network and Internet > Data Usage.

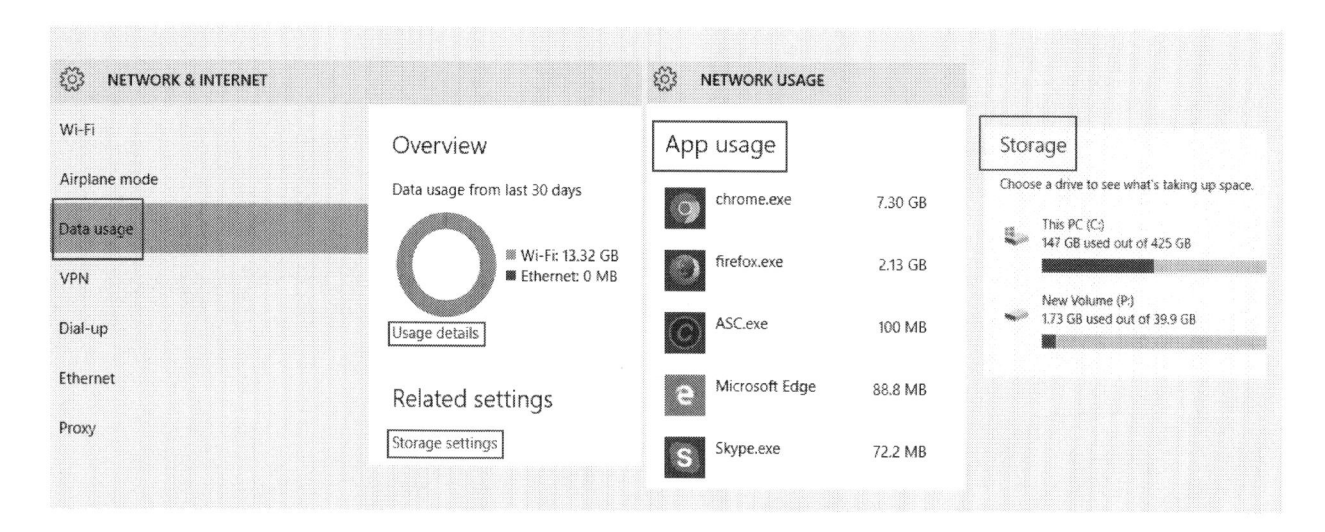

The Data Usage Settings resource enables you to see how your computer is consuming data – in what ways specifically. The Data Usage link shows you an overview and also provides further detail via the Usage Details link and Storage Settings link.

The Usage Details link opens a window showing Apps and the data consumption per App. As you can see in my example above, Google Chrome is my #1 web browser and for that reason it is the top consumer of data.

The Storage Settings link opens a window showing Storage per drive on the computer. As I have mentioned previously in this book, my primary drive (as shown in the screen shot above) is the C drive and my secondary (partitioned) drive of P is used but much less, from the storage vantage point. For those of you with external drives, if you go to Data Usage > Storage Settings with the external drive connected to your USB drive, then you can see all internal and external drives and how they compare, from the data-storage vantage point.

Section 44: Windows 10 Settings for VPN

Go to Start Menu > Settings > Network and Internet > VPN.

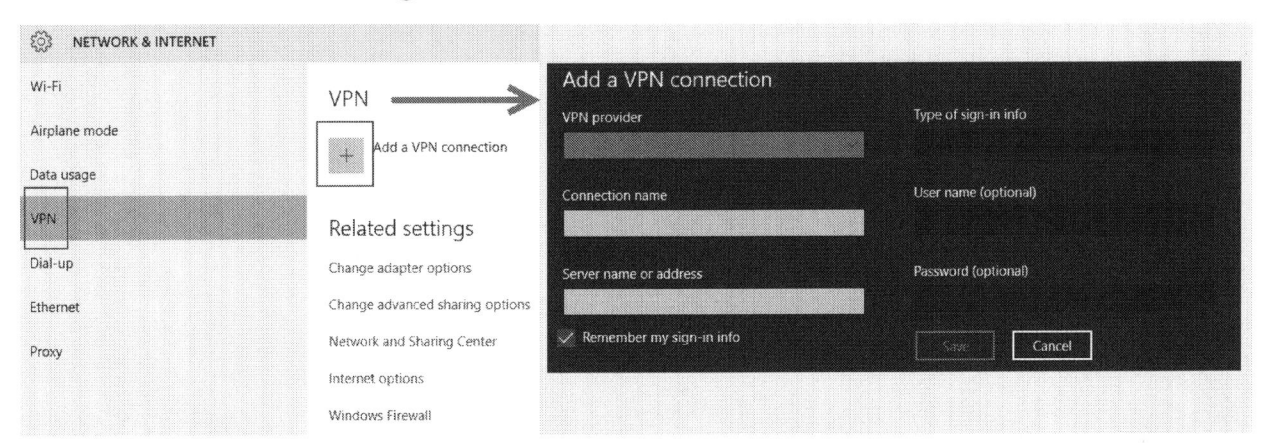

VPN stands for "Virtual Private Network". A VPN is a great way to add a secondary level of security to your Wi-Fi or Landline Connection. VPNs are sophisticated and secure software systems that extend a private network across otherwise public networks. VPNs are established by creating and maintaining the following: a virtual point-to-point connection, virtual tunneling protocols, and traffic (e.g. content and user-identification) encryption.

This option enables you to select a VPN that you have on your machine (if you have one) or to create and establish a VPN if you do not already have one. As you can see in my sample screen shot above, I do not currently have a VPN because I have no need for one with my personal laptop. However, if I was using a corporate account of some kind, I would be mandated to use, for sure, a VPN connection to ensure secure communications thereby maintaining confidential data privacy. To add a VPN in Windows 10 is simple. Click on the + icon (as shown above) and you are directed to a window where you can establish connection details that constitute the VPN that will be listed in Windows 10. You must enter 100% accurate information for all fields requiring completion – VPN Provider, Connection Name, Server Name (or address), Type of Sign-In, User Name, Password, and then Save. When you connect now via the VPN you will be required to login to the VPN and after the login process you will be connected to both the web and your VPN server.

Section 45: Windows 10 Settings for Dialup

Go to Start Menu > Settings > Network and Internet > Dialup.

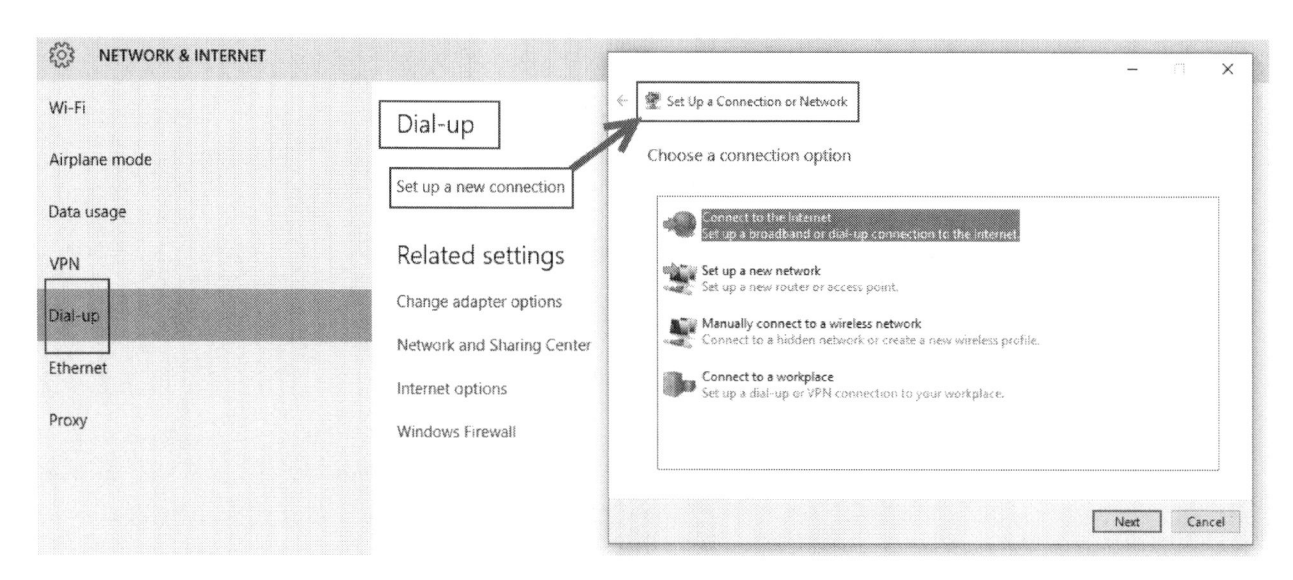

The Dialup option in Settings > Network and Internet, in my humble opinion, is a backup option for those of you without Wi-Fi access to the Internet. Windows 10 is designed to work best with a Wi-Fi connection, however that is not always possible in all situations. In situations where you need to go through a landline connection, you can use this path to get that established. Click on "Setup a new connection" and you are directed to a Connection Wizard which is a set of pop-up windows that take you through the connection process step-by-step. It is a bit like going back into time, for example, when you got your connection CD from AOL or something like that. If you notice in the same screen shot above, there are four major paths here – connect directly to the Internet, set up a new network, manually connect to a wireless network, and connect to a workplace. I recommend you walk through these steps one-by-one with your ISP because there could be backend settings and things they must do on to ensure a complete connection via this path.

Section 46: Windows 10 Settings for Ethernet

Go to Start Menu > Settings > Network and Internet > Ethernet.

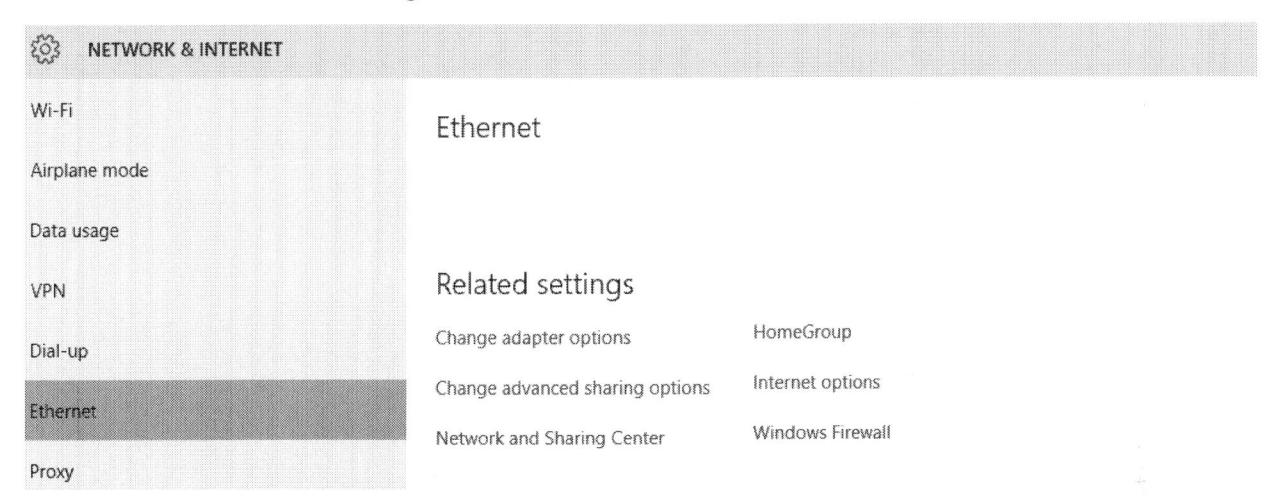

NETWORK & INTERNET		
Wi-Fi	Ethernet	
Airplane mode		
Data usage		
VPN	Related settings	
Dial-up	Change adapter options	HomeGroup
Ethernet	Change advanced sharing options	Internet options
Proxy	Network and Sharing Center	Windows Firewall

Ethernet is a SPECIFIC type of land-line connection where you are connected to the Internet (via your ISP) using an ETHERNET cable. There is a specific port in your computer that is able to accept/receive the ETHERNET cable. The other end must be plugged into the ISP station that is installed at your home or office usually on the wall somewhere. I do not currently have an Ethernet cable connection setup and that is why there is a blank space in the sample screen shot above. Windows 10 is a semi-intelligent OS and so as soon as you plug in the cable to your computer and connect the other end to your ISP (station/line), then Windows 10 will prompt you with the necessary screens to establish your connection. In some cases, ISP can provide you with a CD or DVD or even a downloadable file that can do this for you and all you need to do is complete a few fields in the given wizard.

Section 47: Windows 10 Settings for Proxy

Go to Start Menu > Settings > Network and Internet > Proxy.

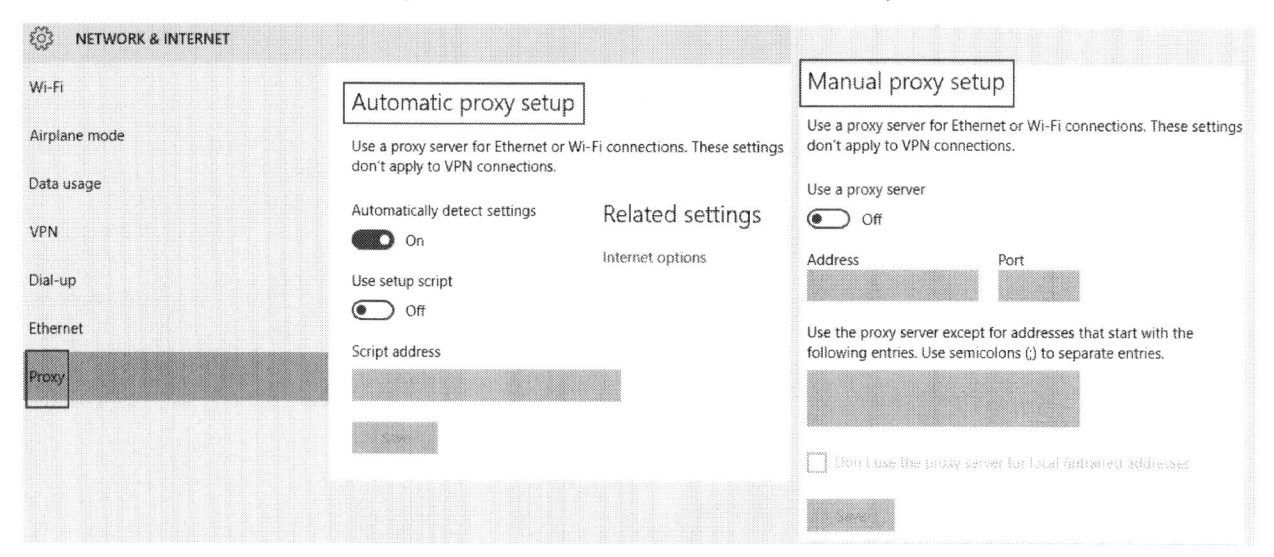

The purpose of a "proxy" is to hide or conceal the IP (Internet Protocol) address of one's computer, thereby maintaining anonymity. There are many reason why people choose to use their computer in this way – they can range from basic security concerns to making a concerted effort not to be tracked by the NSA (the U.S. National Security Agency). Here is a case in point – let us say you are a Nuclear Engineering college student and you are researching the nuts and bolts of atomic energy for school and your classes. You certainly don't want NSA to get the wrong idea especially if they have not seen via your academic enrollment that you are a legitimate engineering student. So, you use this option to keep your web surfing and communications (to a great extent) hidden from this governmental entity. You can set up a Proxy in two ways – automatically and manually. Just complete the fields you must for the one you are setting up and Windows 10 walks you through the rest of the process.

Section 48: Windows 10 Settings for Personalization – Overview

Go to Start Menu > Settings > Personalization.

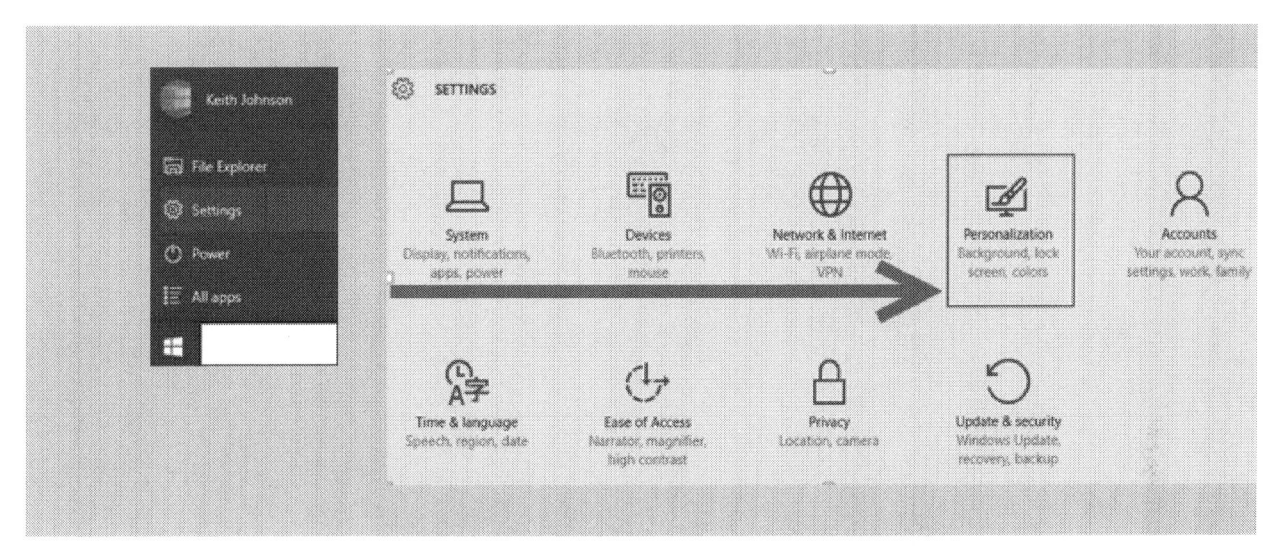

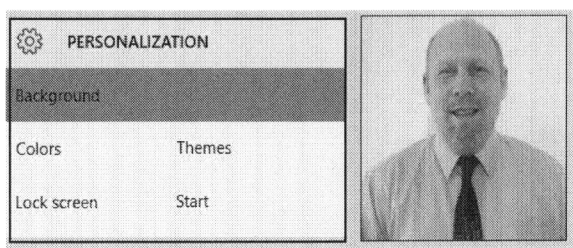

The scope for this "dimension" of Windows 10 Settings includes ... (1) Home Screen, (2) Background, (3) Colors, (4) Lock Screen, (5) Themes and (6) Start.

Section 49: Windows 10 Settings for Background

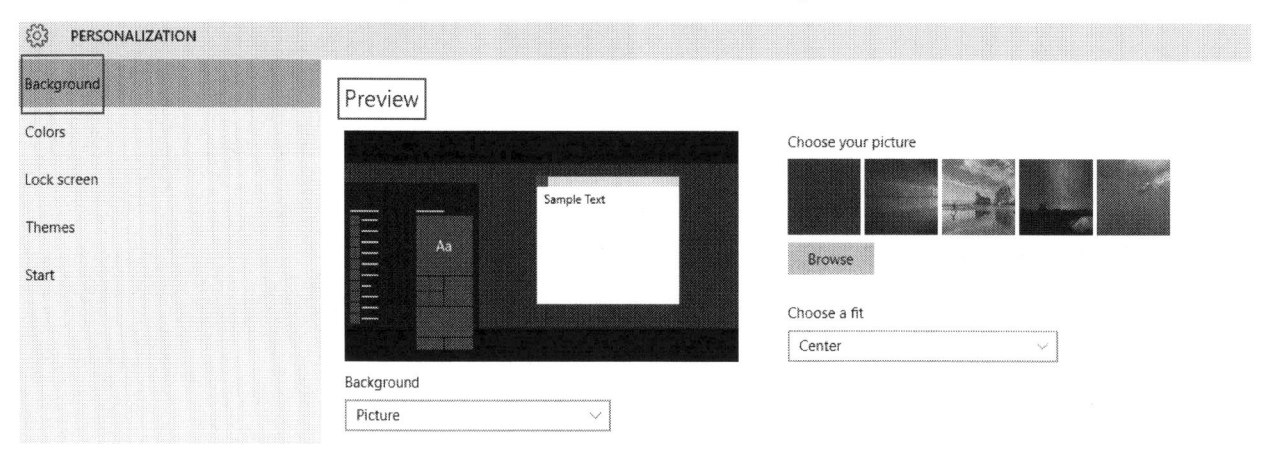

Go to Start Menu > Settings > Personalization > Background.

The Background Settings option enables you to select what you will see as the primary image or color for your Home Screen. The Background drop-down menu lets you select a picture, solid color, or slide show. The other options that are shown are done so in accordance with your choice of background. The sample screen shot above shows your options if Picture is selected. If you select Solid Color, however, then a color palette is shown from which you can choose the color that Windows 10 will display.

Background colors

If you select Slideshow, then the following is shown from which you can display the best possible slideshow: Albums, Change Picture Every (amount of time), and Choose a Fit.

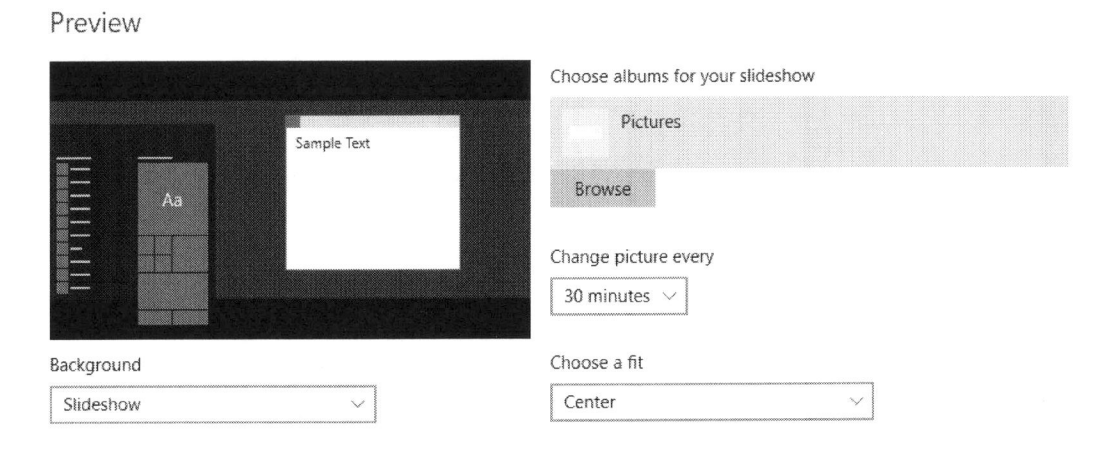

Because I am writing a book about Windows 10, I am, as an example, going to select "Background Color" here and choose the color that most resembles the official color of Windows 10, at least from what I have seen on the Microsoft website. So, here is what my screen looks like after making this selection (for those of you with a paperback, the color here is an aqua-blue).

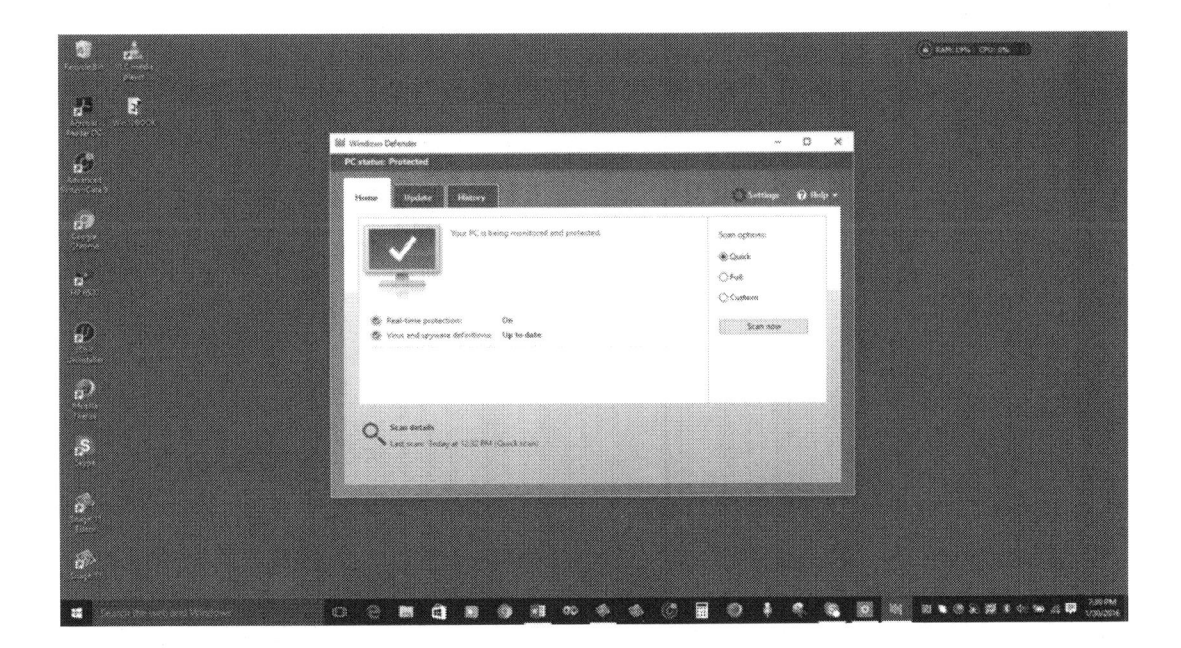

Section 50: Windows 10 Settings for Colors

Go to Start Menu > Settings > Personalization > Colors.

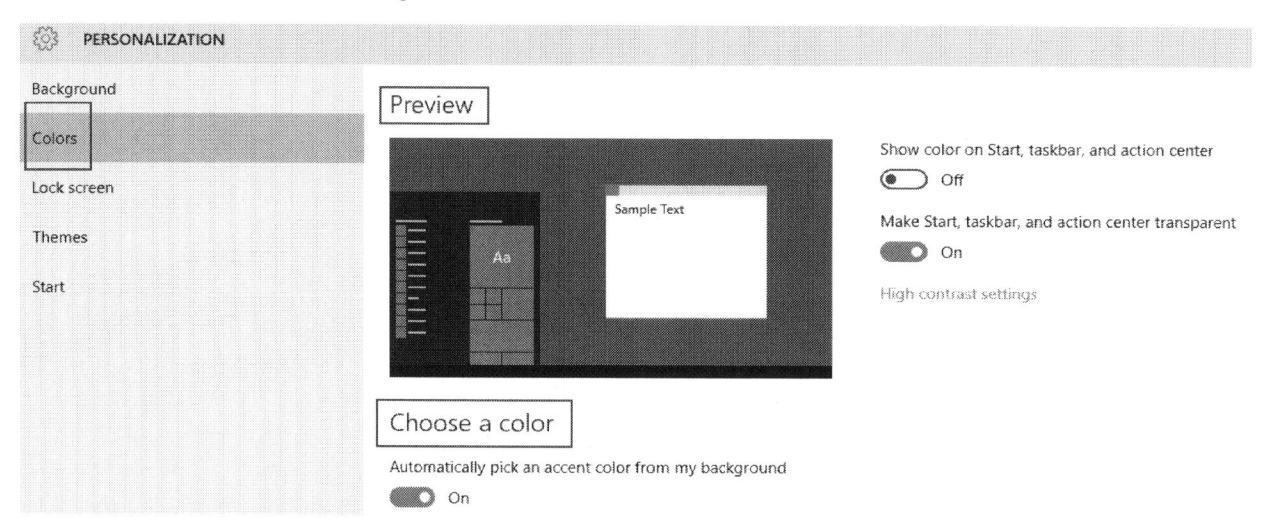

The default setting for Colors in Windows 10 is for the OS to automatically pick an accent color (that works with color from the chosen background). For the blue color I chose as my background color (in the previous section), Windows has chosen a dark gray color as the accent. Let us change this by turning this setting OFF. Now, a palette of colors is shown. To illustrate this, I am going to choose Orange as the accent color, and then you can see the accents that are shown. To make this totally obvious, I am also going to turn "Show color on Start, taskbar, and Action center" and "Make Start, taskbar, and Action Center Transparent". Here is how Windows presents the colors now.

Section 51: Windows 10 Settings for Lock Screen

Go to Start Menu > Settings > Personalization > Lock Screen.

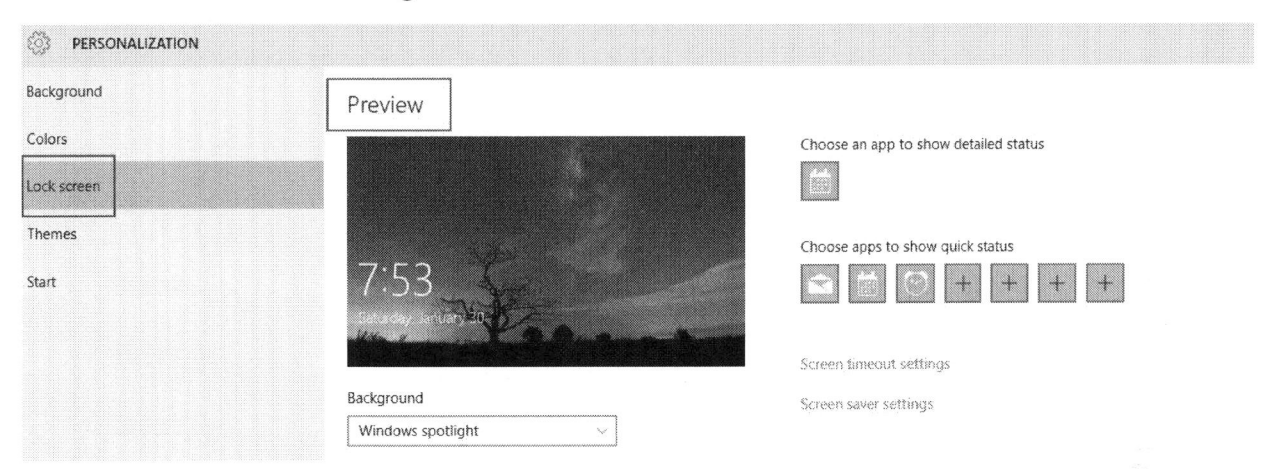

First, for those of you who have a smartphone – iOS, Android, or even Windows as the OS – the true default screen is your lock screen. So, in this spirit of "lock screen customization" Windows 10 - like the other major Operating Systems lets you choose exactly what is to be shown – you can choose the Background via the available drop-down menu – Windows Spotlight, Picture, or Slideshow. The other options available via this Setting are shown in relation to this Background choice.

Second, you can choose an app to show detailed status – e.g. your Calendar.

Third, you can choose apps to show a quick status – currently I have chosen the following apps: Mail (e.g. Outlook), Calendar, and Alarms/Clock.

If necessary, you can click on the link to "Screen timeout settings". This is the same as going through *Settings > System > Power and Sleep*.

If necessary, you can click on the link to "Screen Saver settings". This is like going to *Control Panel >Screen Saver Settings*.

Section 52: Windows 10 Settings for Themes

Go to Start Menu > Settings > Personalization > Themes.

Then, click on the Theme Settings link. The Control Panel > Appearances and Personalization > Personalization window is shown where you can make your selection.

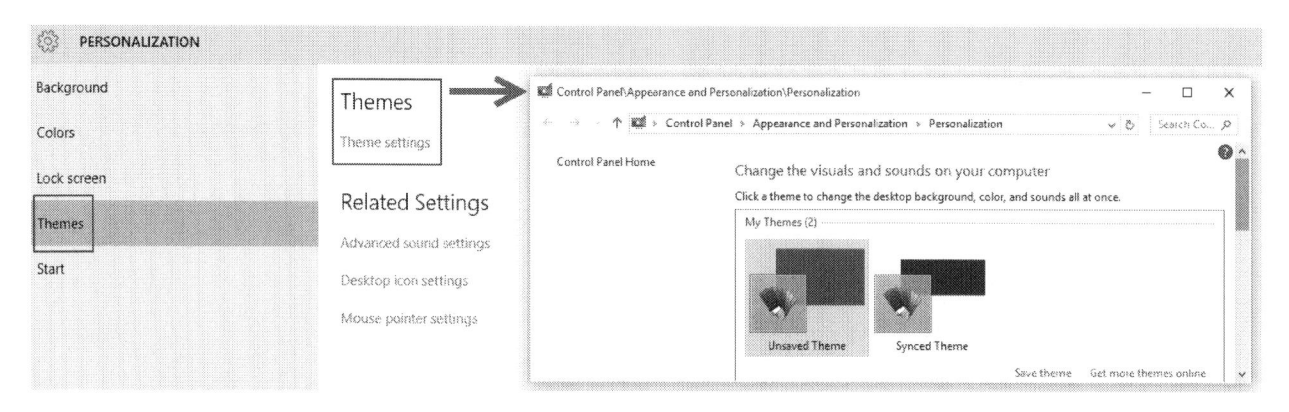

You can choose between "My Themes", "Windows Default Themes", and "High Contrast Themes". There are three Related Settings links – each one also accesses a Control Panel app/resource to fine tune your Windows experience (Sound Settings, Desktop Icon Settings, Mouse Pointer Settings). Choose what is best for you.

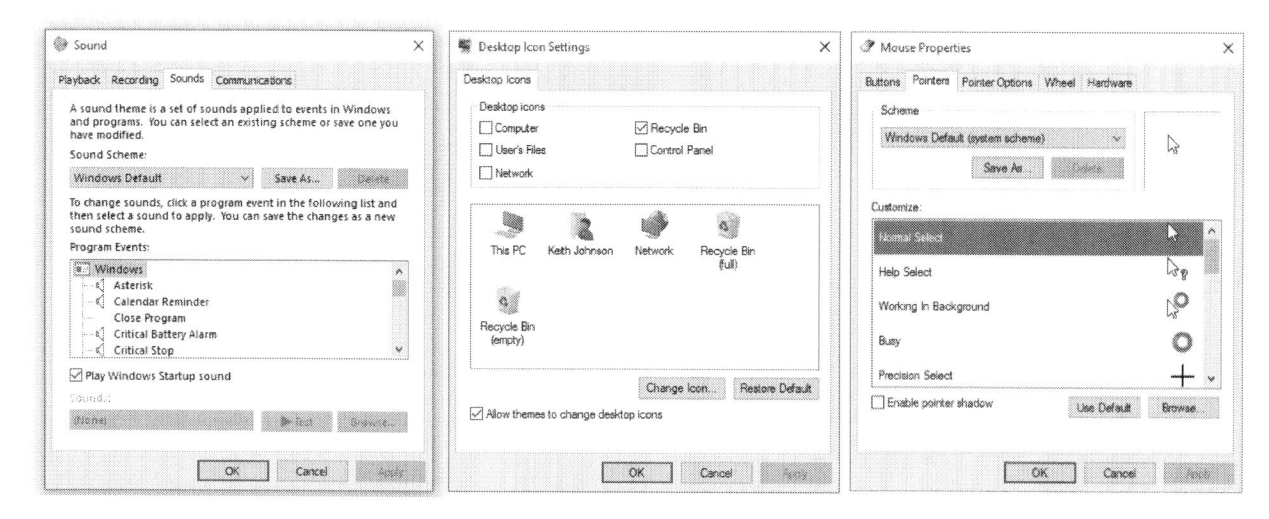

Section 53: Windows 10 Settings for Start

Go to Start Menu > Settings > Personalization > Start.

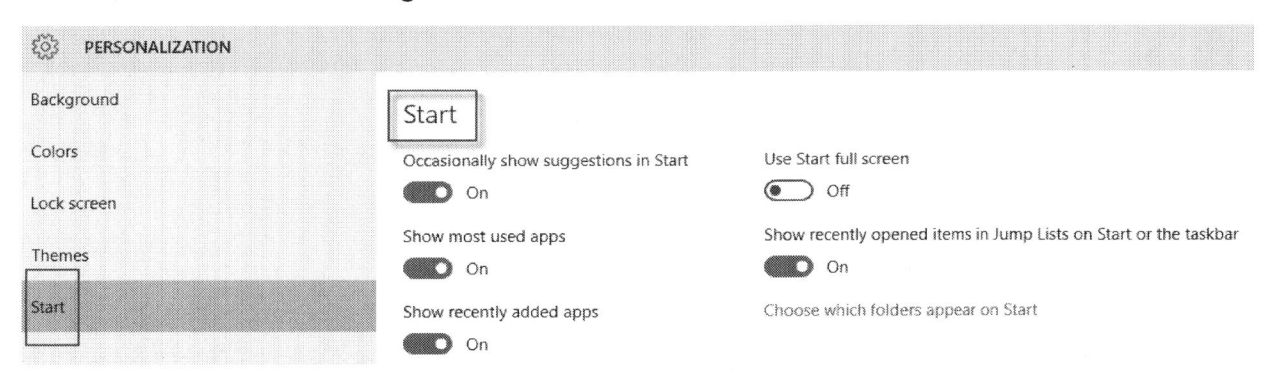

Not only has Microsoft brought back its famous Start Menu from Windows 7 to now "star" in Windows 10, but it has customizations which make it simply fantastic. Here are your options to make the Start Menu a fantastic experience every single time you use it.

1. Occasionally show suggestions in Start (Menu) – keep this setting ON.

2. Show most used apps in Start (Menu) – keep this setting ON.

3. Show recently added apps in Start (Menu) – keep this setting ON.

4. Use Start (Menu) using the full screen – I personally prefer to leave this OFF.

5. Show recently opened items in Jump Lists on Start (Menu) – keep this ON.

6. Choose which folders appear on the Start Menu – click on this link to open the Settings Window where you can choose Folders to be displayed ...

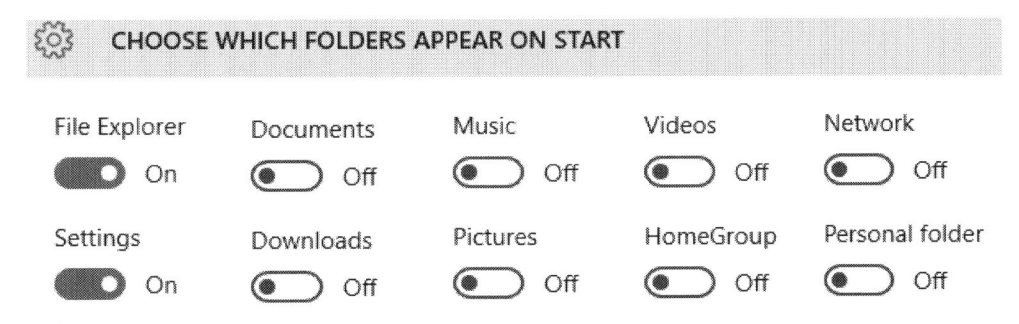

Section 54: Windows 10 Settings for Accounts – Overview

Go to Start Menu > Settings > Accounts.

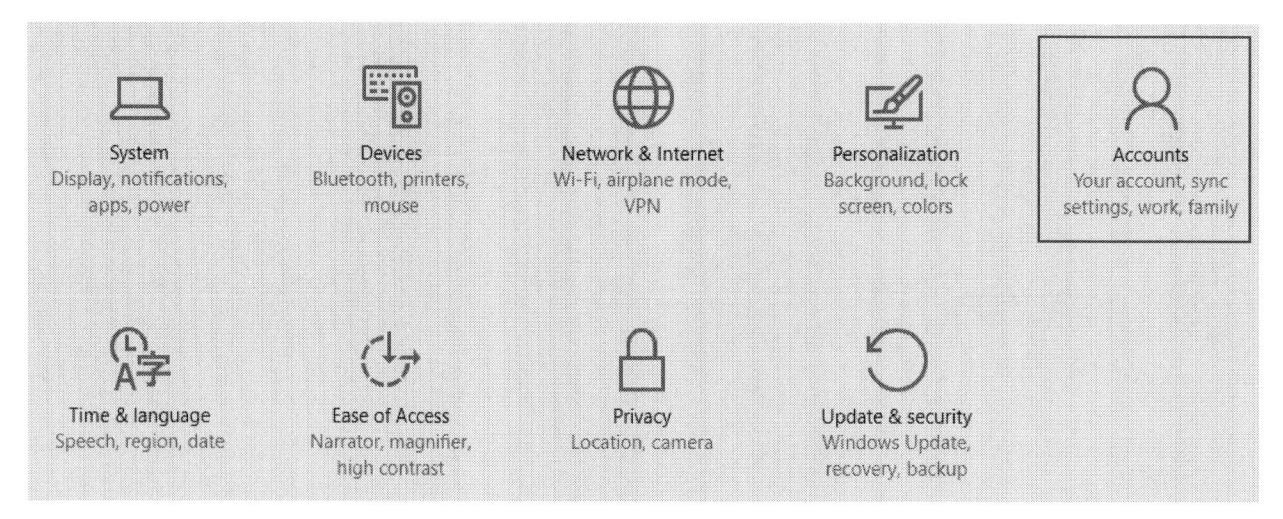

Here are the Account Settings you can manage here ...

1. Your Account

2. Sign-In Options

3. Work Access

4. Family and Other Users

5. Sync Your Settings

Section 55: Windows 10 Settings for Your Account

Go to Start Menu > Settings > Accounts > Your Account.

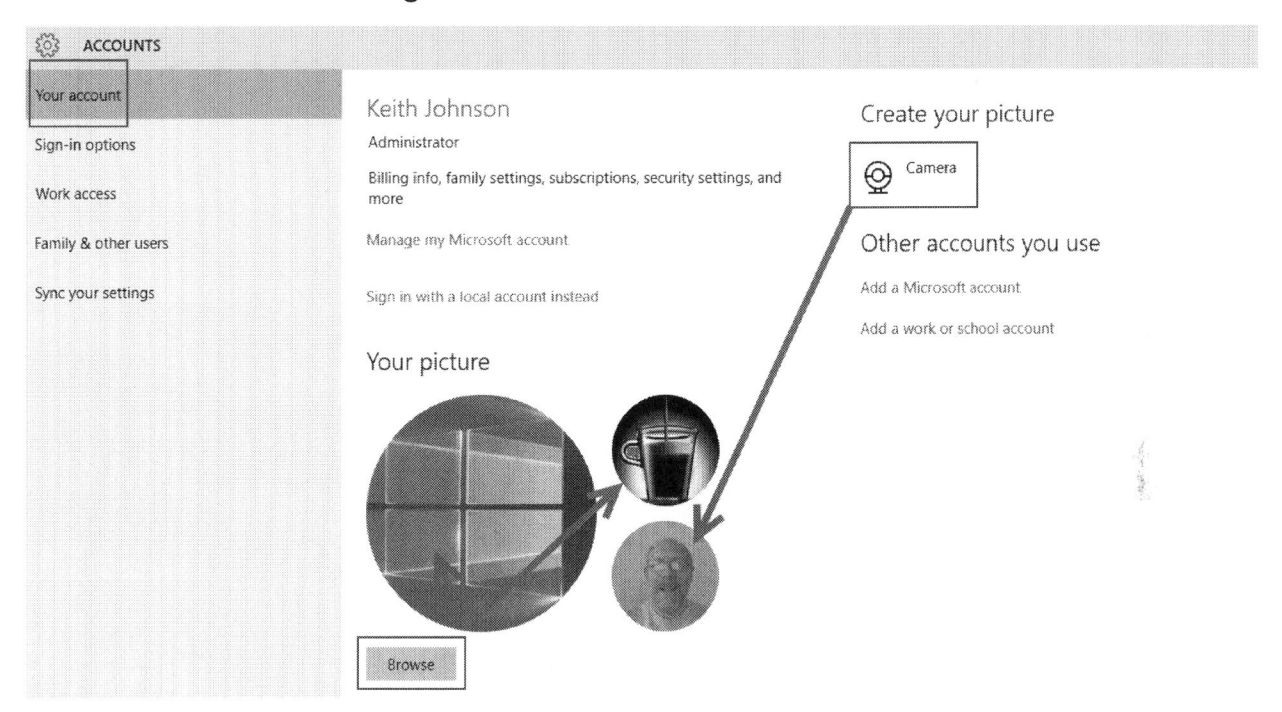

This is the Settings "place" in Windows 10 where you establish your definitive user credentials - e-mail, password, and more but directly via your Microsoft (Outlook/E-mail) account. You can click on the "Manage my Microsoft account" to do this. If you want to use Windows 10 but while you are not connected to your Microsoft account, then you can click on "Sign in with a local account instead". In this way, Microsoft can, in some way, associate the machine with a user of some kind.

To add a picture to your account, you can do this through the Browser button (for images already on one of your drives) or the Camera app - which is listed under the "Create your picture" section of this Settings window. If you click on the Camera, it will activate and a pop-up window will show where the picture is taken. Just click on the picture (and not the video) icon to take your picture via Windows 10 and your camera.

Section 56: Windows 10 Settings for Sign-In Options

Go to Start Menu > Settings > Accounts > Sign-In Options.

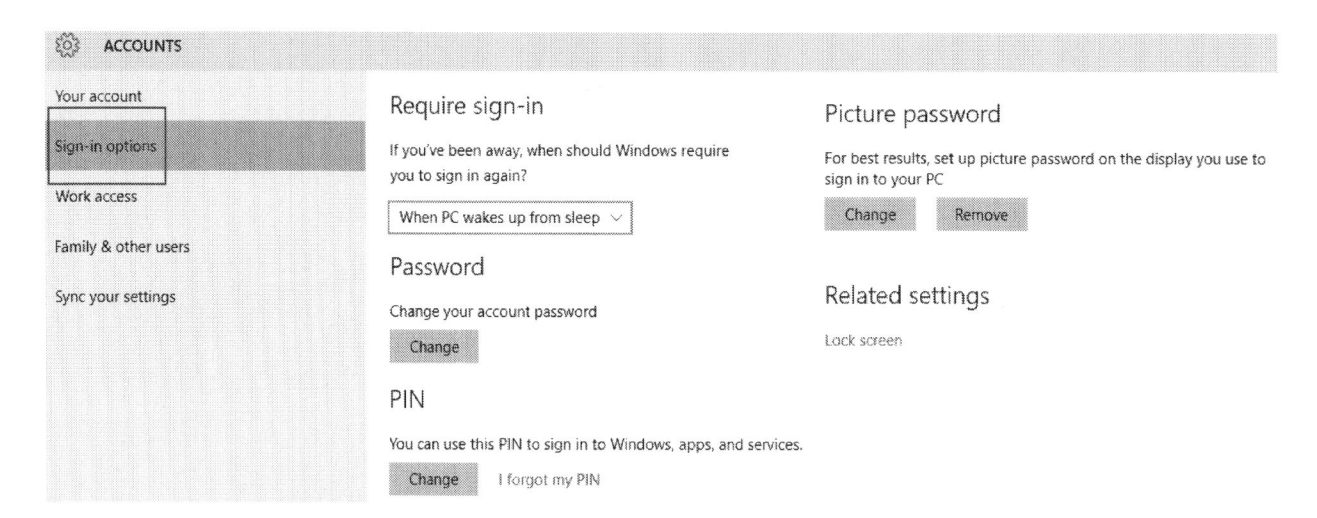

This Settings option is designed to help you manage the actual Windows 10 login or access process. The default set-up from when you establish Windows 10 as your Operating System is the traditional user name (e.g. your Microsoft Outlook e-mail address) and password. However, you can set up a PIN if you wish and depending on the microphone and/or camera of your computer, you can establish a biometrically-secure using either a retina scan (via the camera) or voice-login using the microphone. My computer does not have either of these and for that reason these options are not shown in this same screen. However, when your machine is capable of the biometrically-secure login processes featured in Windows 10 – those options are shown. The Picture password is a login path where a picture is shown instead of your Microsoft e-mail address but you still have to enter either a login PIN or a series of gestures that you setup if you are using a touch-screen device like a Surface Pro.

Section 57: Windows 10 Settings for Work Access

Go to Start Menu > Settings > Accounts > Work Access.

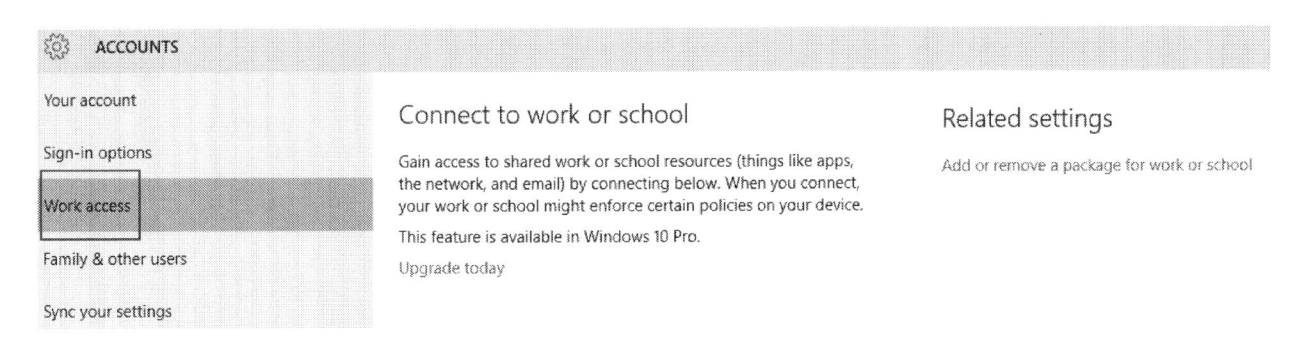

As Microsoft tells us here directly in this Settings option, this resource is to "connect to work or school" where you can "gain access to shared work or school resources – things like apps, the network, and e-mail – by connecting below (you need to click on the Upgrade today link)". Also, "when you connect, your work or school might enforce certain policies on your device. This feature is available in Windows 10 Pro." Mind you, for this to happen, schools will most likely be using Windows 10 Education and businesses will most likely be using Windows 10 Enterprise. But, to connect from your client side that requires Windows 10 Pro.

You can of course upgrade to Windows 10 Pro without having to connect to an outside organization using Windows 10 in any way. Windows 10 Pro is merely a more advanced version of Windows 10 Home that is designed for enhanced business and personal productivity.

Section 58: Windows 10 Settings for Family

Go to Start Menu > Settings > Accounts > Family and Other Users.

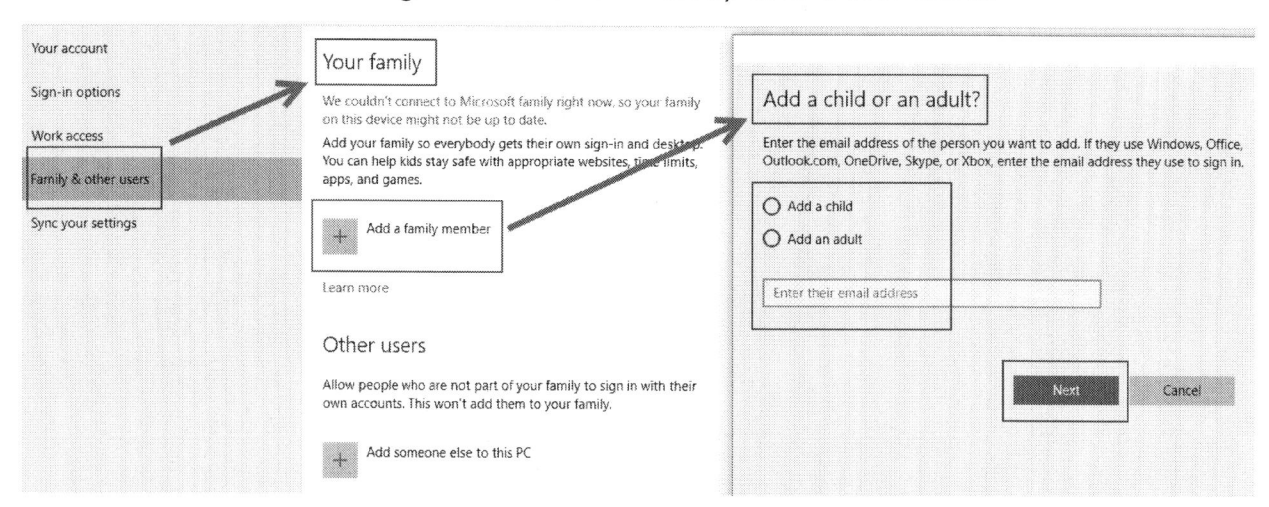

The Family and Other Users Settings Option enables you to manage Windows 10 users beside yourself and categorize them in TWO major ways – family and non-family. Both options are similar in that they ask you to go through a formal "add" process (where you are creating a profile here in Windows 10). A pop-up window is shown and this is where you enter information like if it is a child or adult along with that person's e-mail). Windows 10 handles this in exactly the same way it handles your Account and Login data – so that it can facilitate the person's access to the computer and also via Windows 10 as the OS. When the "Add" process is complete then the new user will receive an e-mail notification that he or she must accept for Windows 10 (on your machine here) to add that name to its definitive list of recognized users.

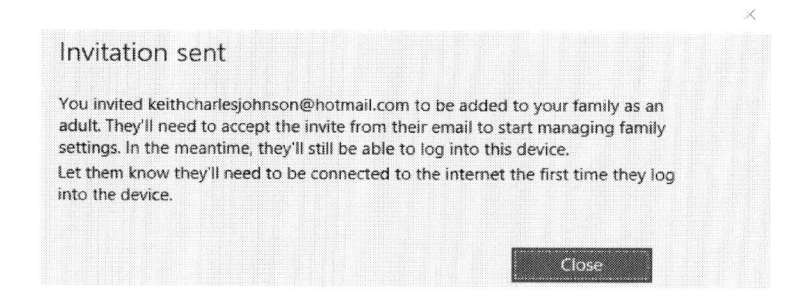

Section 59: Windows 10 Settings to Sync Devices

Go to Start Menu > Settings > Accounts > Sync Your Settings.

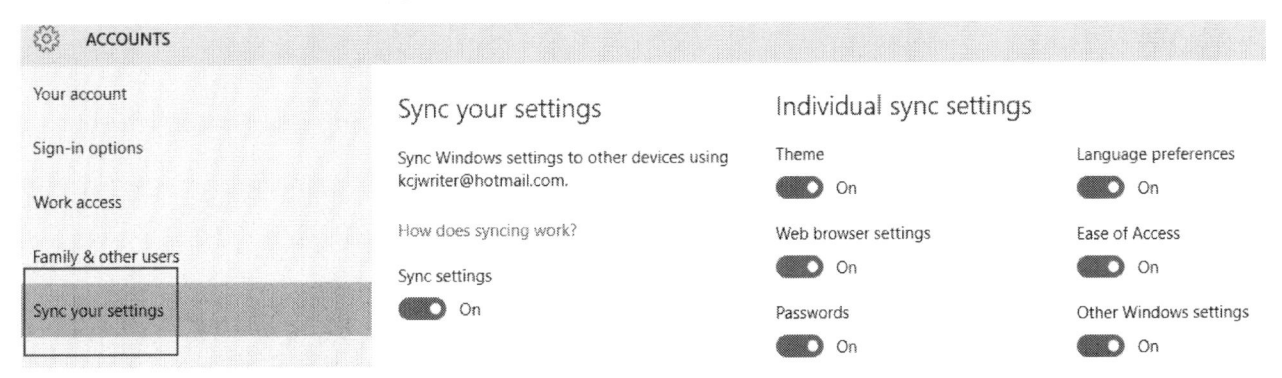

For those of you familiar with Apple and iOS technology, this setting is exactly the same here. What you are doing is working with Windows 10 as more than just an OS for your computer – you are recognizing Windows 10 as the prevailing OS for your Cloud Account and other devices too. In this way, Windows 10 becomes the medium through which functionality and apps can be realized not just on your computer but also on other devices like a Windows Phone (e.g. like a Lumia) or Microsoft Surface Pro or a Windows tablet. For this to happen successfully, the "sync settings" option must be ON. From there, you can choose individual settings to sync to your computer (via Windows 10) – such as Theme, Web Browser settings, Passwords, Language preferences, Ease of Access, and other Windows settings.

If you are still unsure about this Settings option, then click on the "how does syncing work?" link for more information. I personally believe that what you see here is the future of computing – where there is a massive sync via the Cloud and in this way all of your devices will be able to work with a massive array of apps and data – so in this way it does not matter the device you are using. You can easily then switch between your Windows phone, Windows tablet, and/or Windows computer as you need and all data and app functionality/integrity is there, and on top of that, in a secure way. The more I write about Windows 10, the more I want to give up my iPhone and get a Windows phone just to be able to do all of these things I am writing about here ... very exciting indeed.

Section 60: Windows 10 Settings for Time/Language – Overview

Go to Start Menu > Settings > Time and Language.

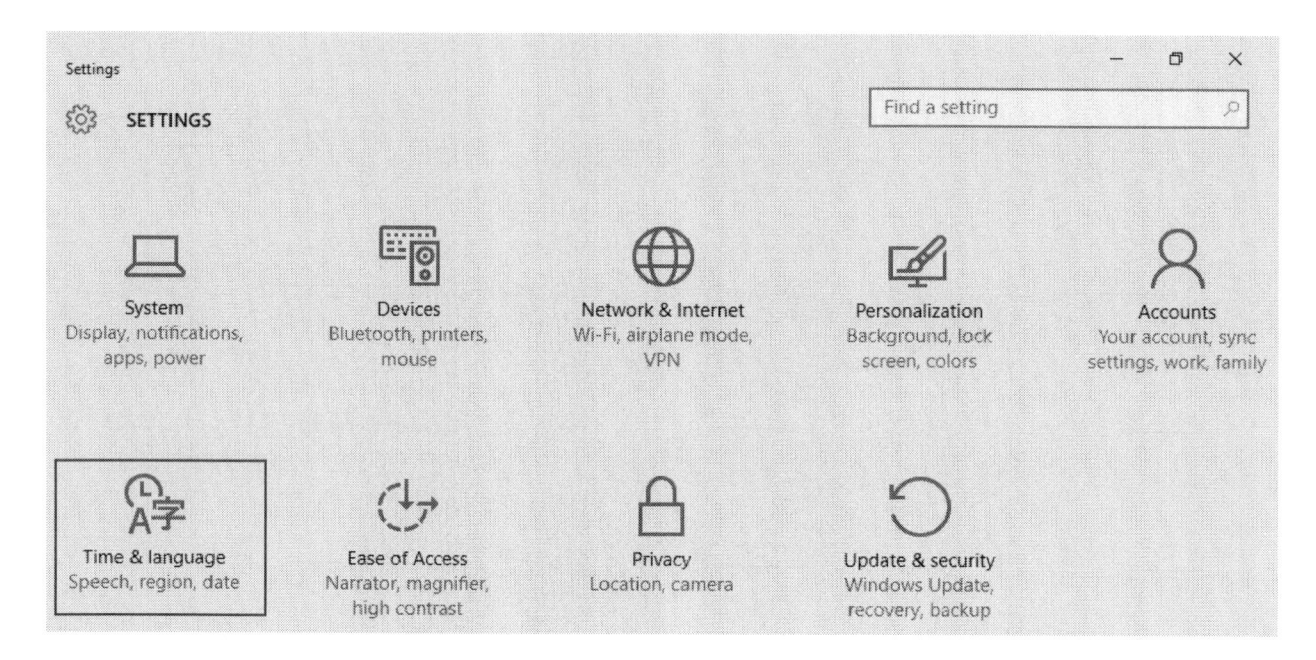

The three major Settings options here are ...

1. **Date and Time**

2. **Region and Language**

3. **Speech**

Section 61: Windows 10 Settings for Date/Time

Go to Start Menu > Settings > Time and Language > Date and Time.

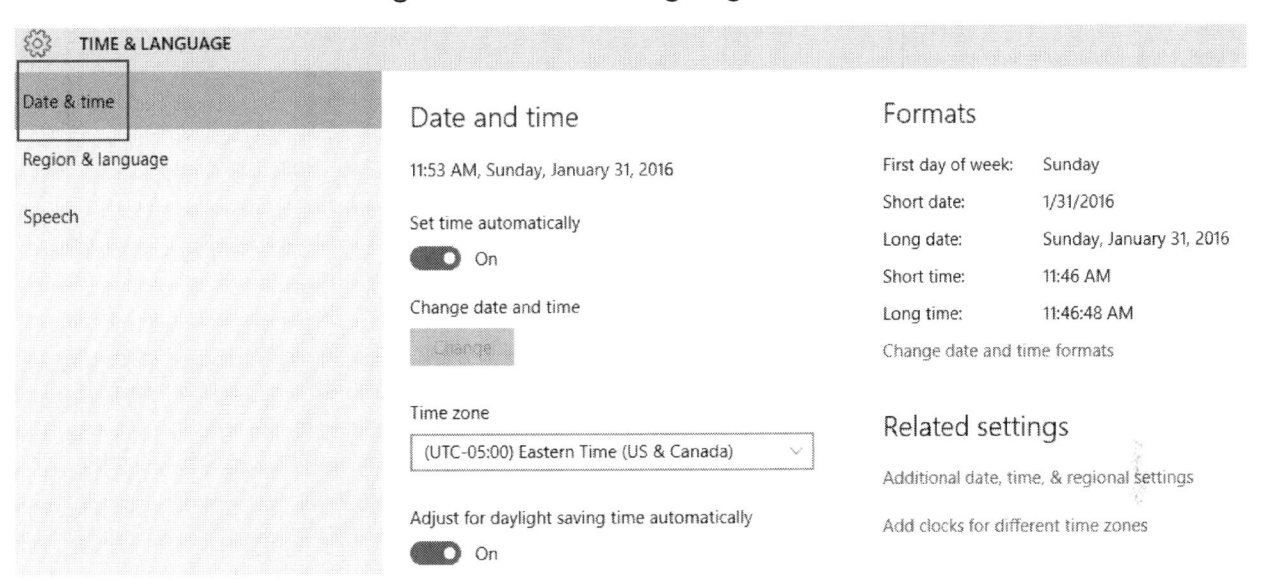

This Settings option is here to help you manage the visual aspect of your Windows 10 experience – and more specifically Date and Time settings as your Windows 10 clock presents such information and also data that is loaded from Windows 10 into apps that utilize such information like your Calendar. I personally recommend you select ON to set the System/OS time automatically, but if you wish to do this manually you can – just turn "set time automatically" to OFF and then click on the button that says "Change Date and Time". You can also select your time zone and change the date and time formats (presentation) if you must by clicking on this link that you see in the sample screen shot above.

I personally recommend that you let Windows 10 adjust for daylight saving time automatically – just leave this setting ON. Windows 10 is much more than an Operating System underlying your apps – it is a great provider of official data that Microsoft can send your machine through its syncing with the World Clock and other official standards services from its end. You get this benefit each time Windows 10 sends updates to your machine.

Section 62: Windows 10 Settings for Region/Language

Go to Start Menu > Settings > Time and Language > Region and Language.

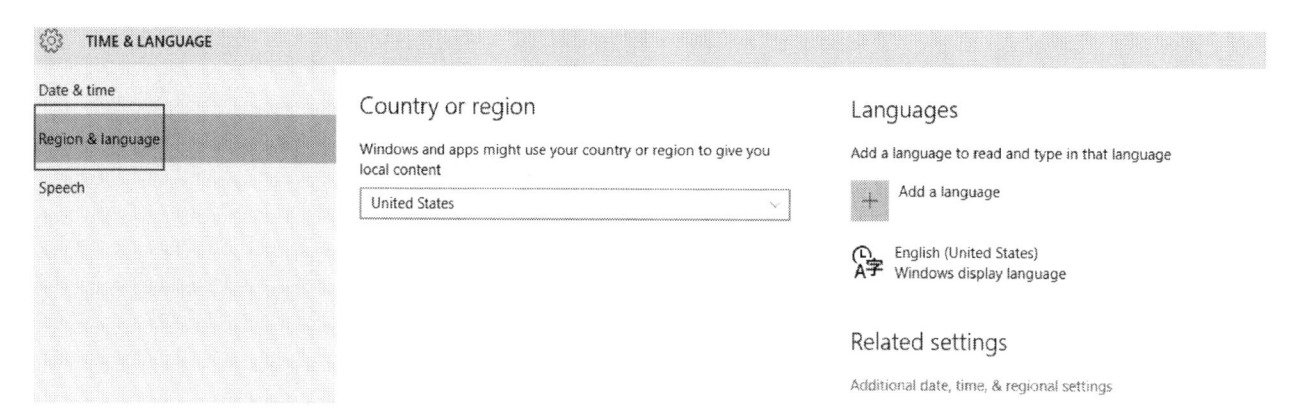

This Settings option enables you to manage a very important visual aspect of your Windows 10 experience – the language presented as well as the specific country or region so that Microsoft can modify what is presented so that you have a better experience, for example, when you go to your Start Menu and see Content through your Microsoft account – local and national news that you might want to see will be presented in the Outlook or MSN tile. To modify the Country or Region, click on the arrow for this drop-down menu and make your selection. Windows 10 is updated automatically. To modify your language or add a language, click on the "Add a Language" + icon and a pop-up window is shown (as you see below) with languages from which you may choose. Make your selection and again Windows 10 updates itself in terms of its presentation to you now that you have made this choice/inclusion.

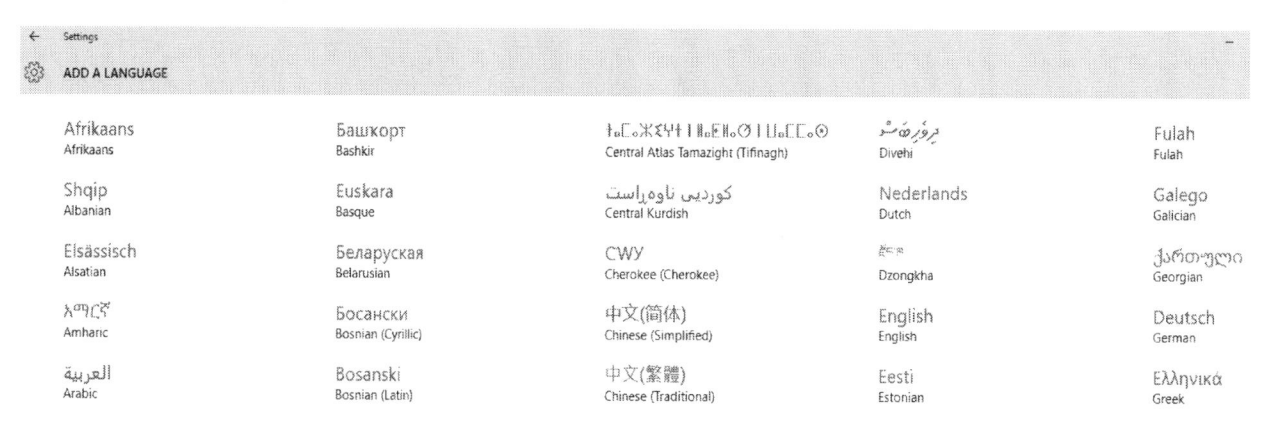

Section 63: Windows 10 Settings for Speech

Go to Start Menu > Settings > Time and Language > Speech.

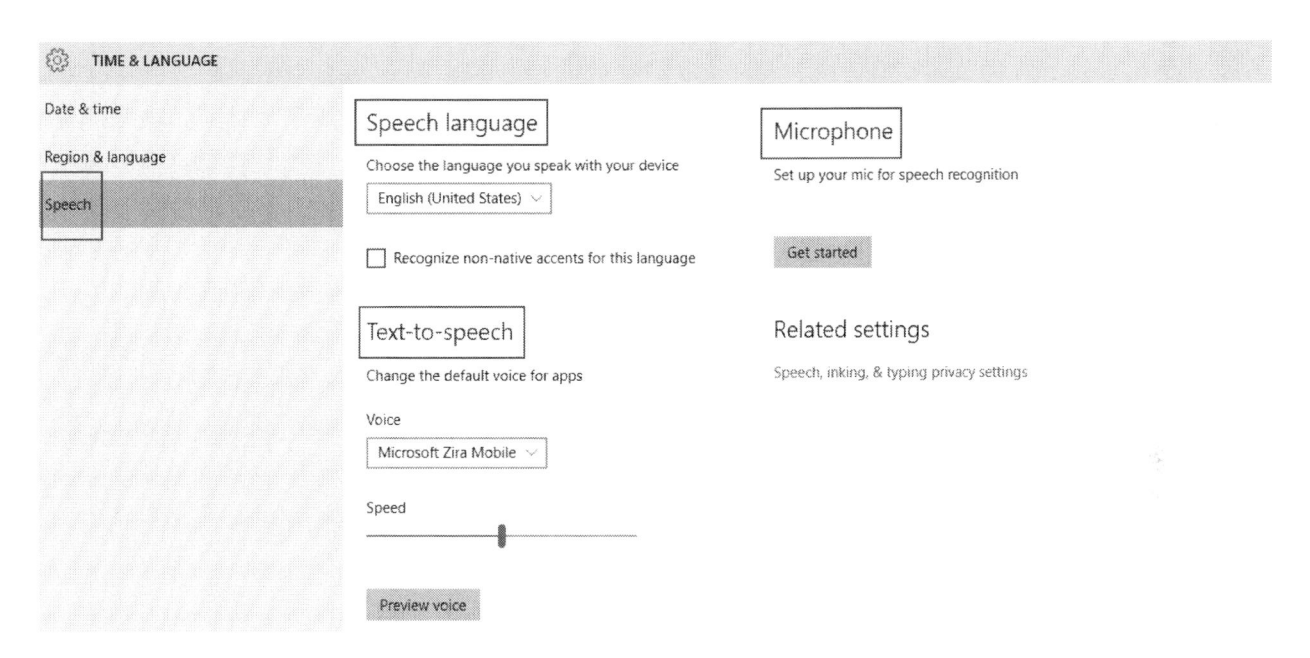

The Speech Settings option is here for those of you who plan to use speech as a driving force behind your Windows 10 OS and Windows 10 app experiences. For Windows 10, of course, you can use your voice to guide Cortana and provide this Digital Assistant with input information as you search or perform tasks. There are also apps for typing and other activities that can work directly with voice input and so it is here that you can get yourself configured voice-wise so that Windows 10 recognizes you and your specific voice tone. The three major areas you can setup here are Speech Language, Text-To-Speech, and Microphone. Most people today use their keyboard and/or mouse (or touchpad) as data input methods while working with Windows 10 and apps. But there are some of you – either by choice or necessity – who will benefit by getting Speech setup via this option. Follow the options per each choice as you need and Microsoft will direct you accordingly to what you must do next, especially the wizard for the Microphone option.

Section 64: Windows 10 Settings for Ease of Access

Go to Start Menu > Settings > Ease of Access.

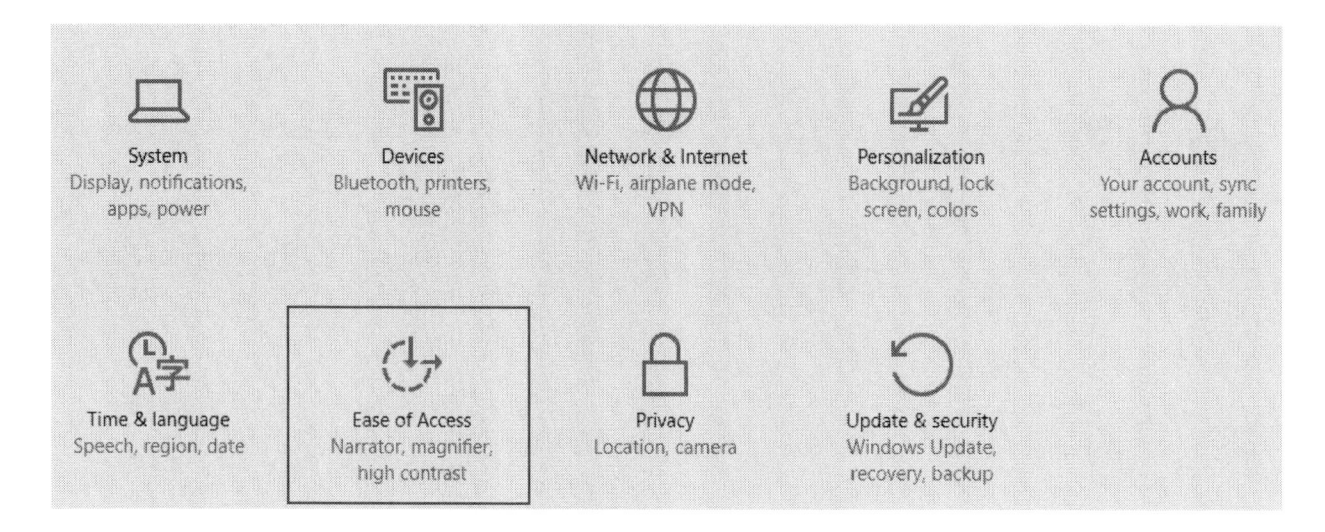

System Display, notifications, apps, power	**Devices** Bluetooth, printers, mouse	**Network & Internet** Wi-Fi, airplane mode, VPN	**Personalization** Background, lock screen, colors	**Accounts** Your account, sync settings, work, family
Time & language Speech, region, date	**Ease of Access** Narrator, magnifier, high contrast	**Privacy** Location, camera	**Update & security** Windows Update, recovery, backup	

The Settings options for Easy of Access include Narrator, Magnifier, High Contrast, Closed Captions, Keyboard, Mouse, and Other Options.

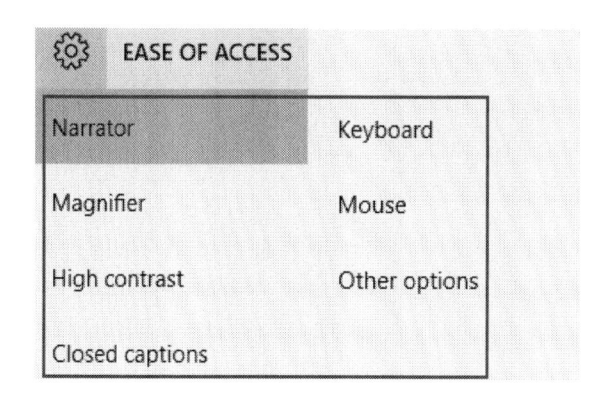

EASE OF ACCESS

Narrator	Keyboard
Magnifier	Mouse
High contrast	Other options
Closed captions	

Section 65: Windows 10 Settings for Narrator

Go to Start Menu > Settings > Ease of Access > Narrator. The Narrator Settings option enables you to hear (audibly) what is presented on your screen. If the Narrator is turned OFF as in the sample screen shot below, then this resource is deactivated and this is what your screen should look like.

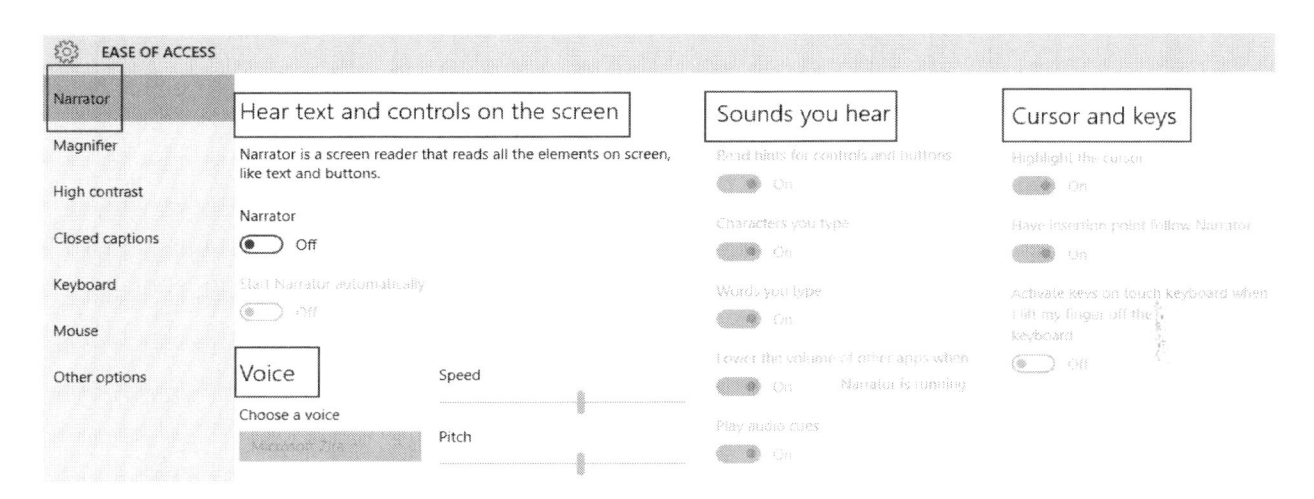

If the Narrator is turned ON and you also decide to start the Narrator automatically, then this is what your Settings screen should look like. You will hear from Windows 10 (audibly) what is presented on the screen and also what you select with your cursor/mouse.

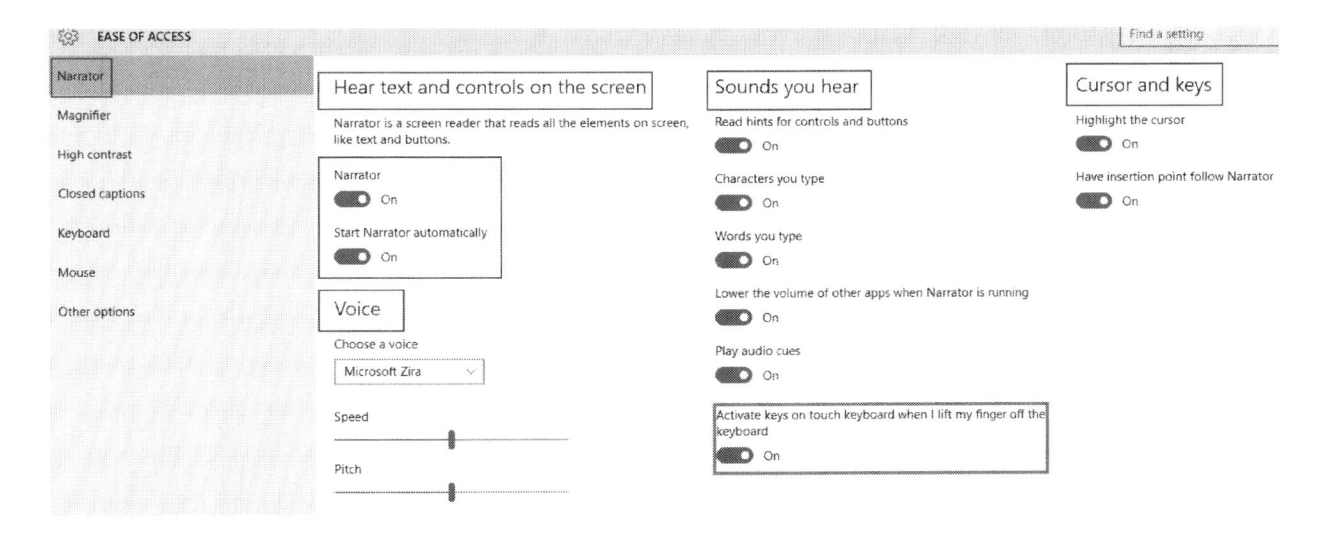

Section 66: Windows 10 Settings for Magnifier

Go to Start Menu > Settings > Ease of Access > Magnifier.

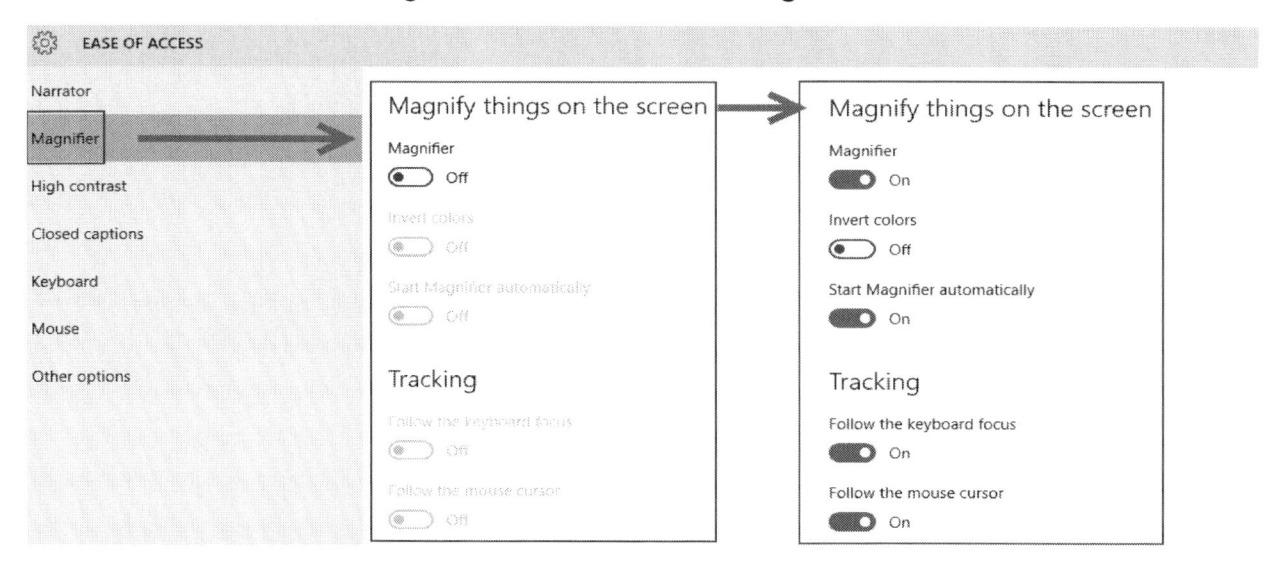

The Magnifier Settings option enables you to manage the use of the Magnifier as well as related options that are available when the Magnifier is turned on. As you can see in the sample screen shot above, when the Magnifier is turned OFF, then none of the other Settings options are available. However, once the Magnifier is turned ON, then other options become available for use. Here they are ...

1. Invert Colors – this flips your User Interface where lights become darks and darks become lights. So, for example, the background of your screen is black instead of white. You need to turn this ON to take effect.

2. Start Magnifier Automatically – turning this settings option ON means you are giving Windows 10 control over the Magnifier and how/when it is started.

3. Tracking – Following the Keyboard focus – if you choose to turn this settings option ON then as the Magnifier is used, Windows 10 can and will follow your keyboard focus.

4. Tracking – Following the Mouse cursor – if you choose to turn this settings option ON then as the Mouse is used, Windows 10 can and will follow your Mouse cursor and where you move it.

Section 67: Windows 10 Settings for High Contrast

Go to Start Menu > Settings > Ease of Access > High Contrast.

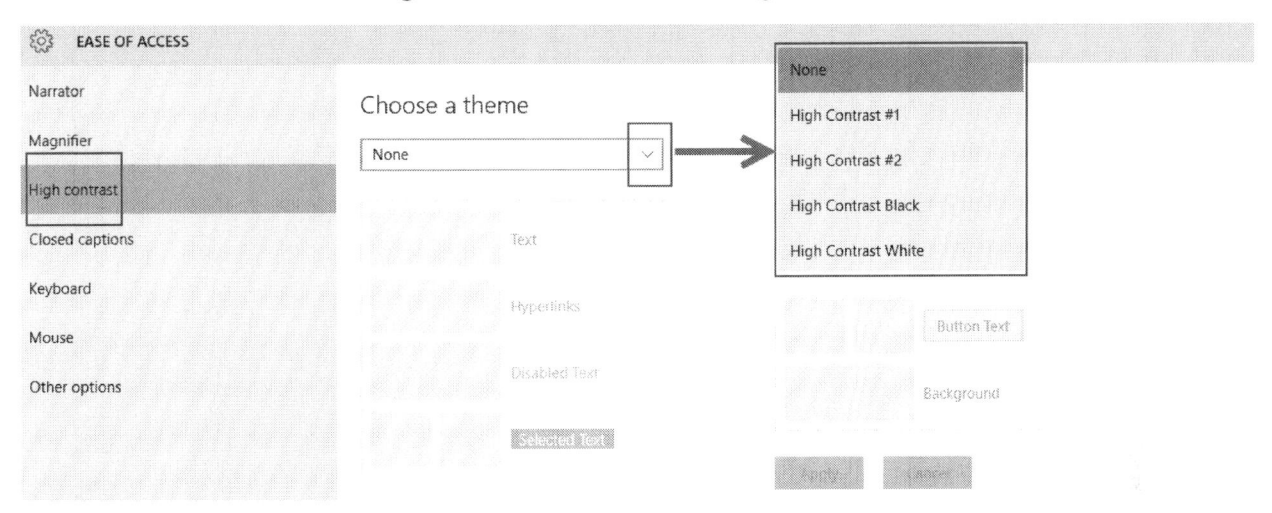

The High Contrast Ease-of-Access Settings option is here to help you manage the visual display of your Windows 10 experience – especially the color contrast combinations available. Right now, there is the default option of "None" (no high contrast) as well as four other options – High Contrast #1, High Contrast #2, High Contrast Black and High Contrast White.

Each of these Contrast options features a unique combination of Text, Hyperlinks, Disabled Text, Selected Text, Button Text, and Background colors.

If you decide to move from the default of "None" to one of these four or alternate between them or even move back to the default of "None", select "Apply" to activate your choice.

This option is great on two ends – (1) for those of you who enjoy the high-contrast display as well as (2) those of you who can actually benefit from the high-contrast display due to eye-vision limitations.

Section 68: Windows 10 Settings for Closed Captions

Go to Start Menu > Settings > Ease of Access > Closed Captions.

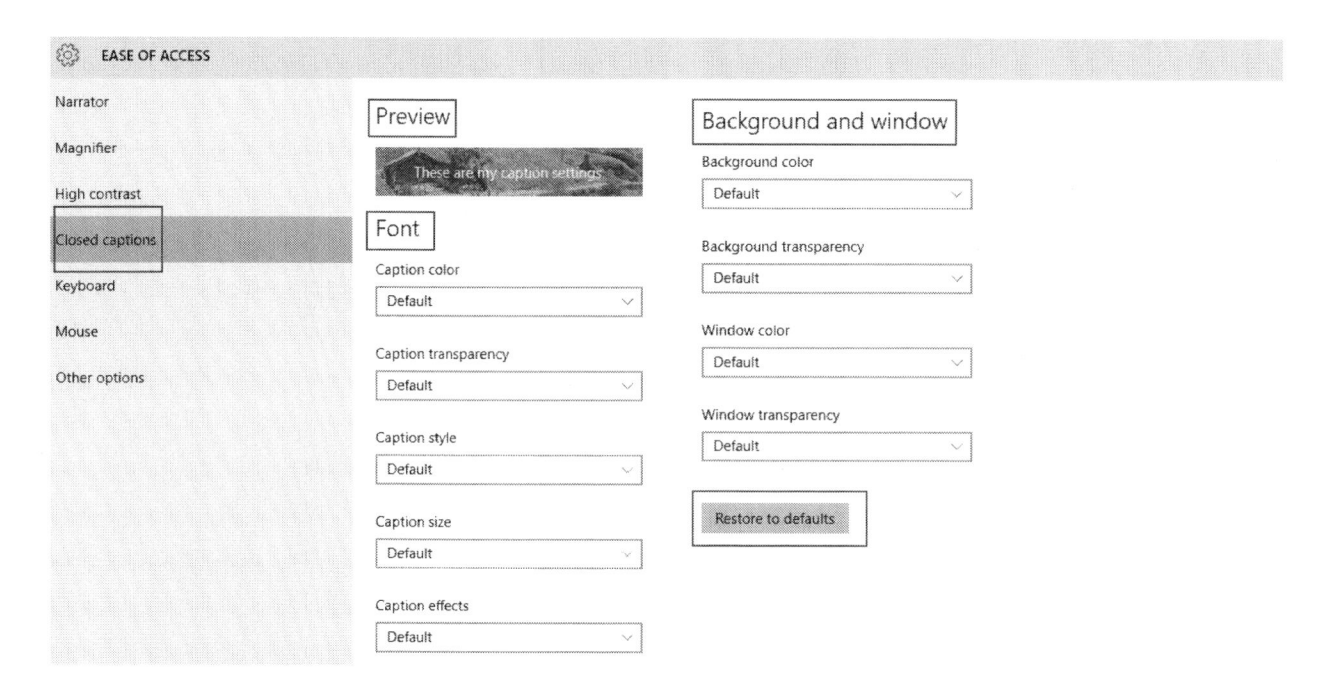

The Closed Captions Settings option empowers you to manage both captions and their backgrounds. Here are your options and what they can do for you (above and beyond the default setting).

FONT

Caption Color – White, Black, Red, Green, Blue, Yellow, Magenta, Cyan.

Caption Transparency – Opaque, Translucent, Semitransparent, Transparent.

Caption Style – Mono Serif, Proportional Serif, Mono Sans Serif, Proportional Sans Serif, Casual, Cursive, Small Caps.

Caption Size – 50%, 100%, 150%, 200%.

Caption Effects – None, Raised, Depressed, Uniform, Drop Shadow.

BACKGROUND AND WINDOW

Background Color - White, Black, Red, Green, Blue, Yellow, Magenta, Cyan.

Background Transparency - Opaque, Translucent, Semitransparent, Transparent.

Window Color - White, Black, Red, Green, Blue, Yellow, Magenta, Cyan.

Window Transparency – Opaque, Translucent, Semitransparent, Transparent.

[Restore to defaults]

Use the Restore to defaults button to allow Windows 10 to reset the Closed Captions aspect of its User Interface (UI) according to default settings.

Section 69: Windows 10 Settings for Keyboard

Go to Start Menu > Settings > Ease of Access > Keyboard.

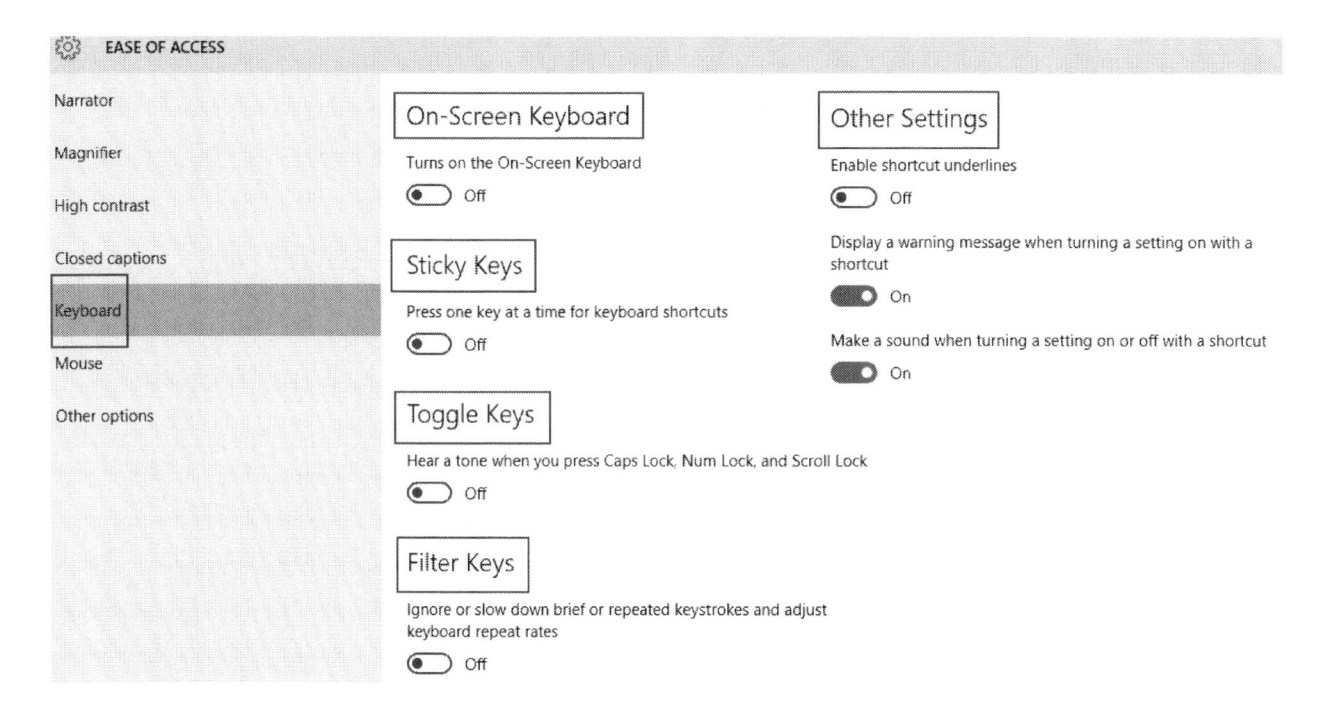

This Settings option (for keyboard use) is self-explanatory. Observe the option available and turn it ON or OFF according to your needs. These options are as follows:

1. On-Screen Keyboard

2. Sticky Keys (e.g. press one key at a time for shortcuts)

3. Toggle Keys

4. Filter Keys

5. Other Settings - which include (a) enable shortcut underlines, (b) display a warning message when turning a setting on with a shortcut, and (c) make a sound when turning a setting on or off with a shortcut.

Section 70: Windows 10 Settings for Mouse

Go to Start Menu > Settings > Ease of Access > Mouse.

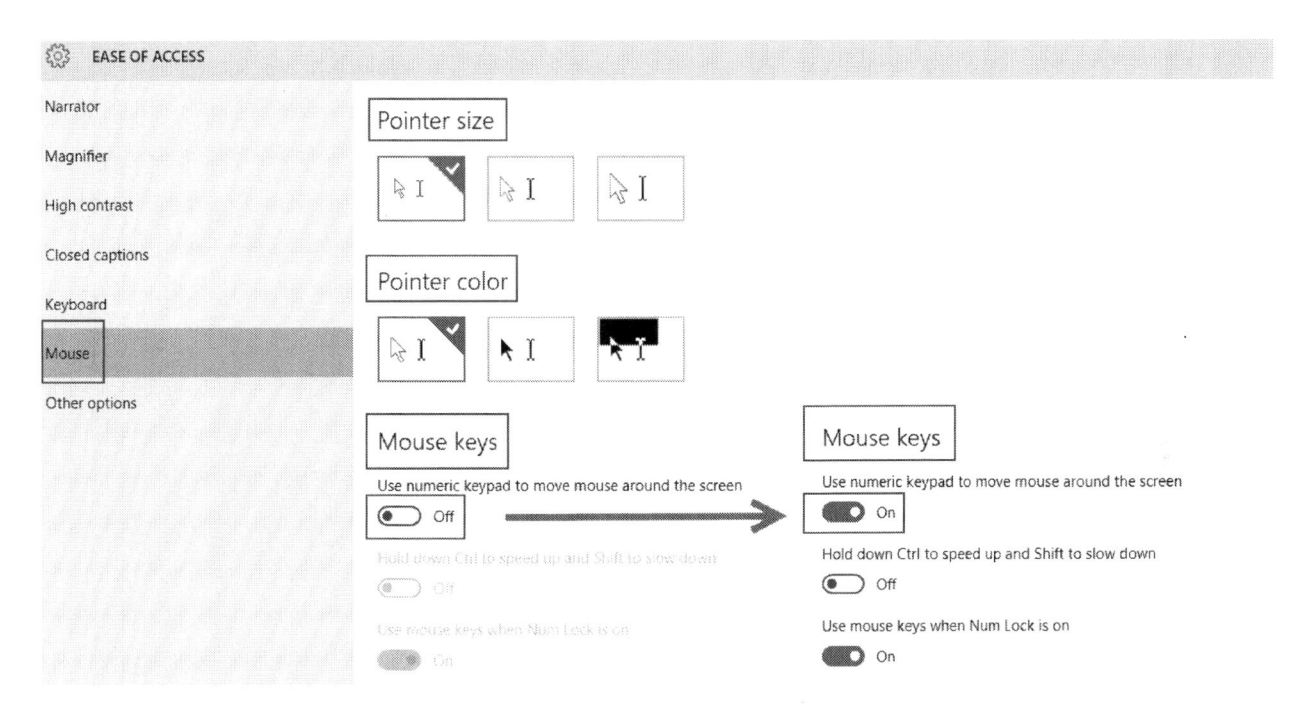

This Settings option enables you to manage the following aspects of your Mouse (if you are using a mouse) – Pointer Size, Pointer Color, and Mouse Keys.

The sample screen shot above shows the Mouse Keys (e.g. use numeric keyboard to move mouse around the screen) OFF as well as ON. When this setting is ON, then the setting for using the mouse keys when the Num Lock is on is automatically turned ON but the Hold down Ctrl key to speed up and Shift key to slow down is not turned on – you need to do this manually.

Section 71: Windows 10 Settings for Other Devices

Go to Start Menu > Settings > Ease of Access > Other Devices.

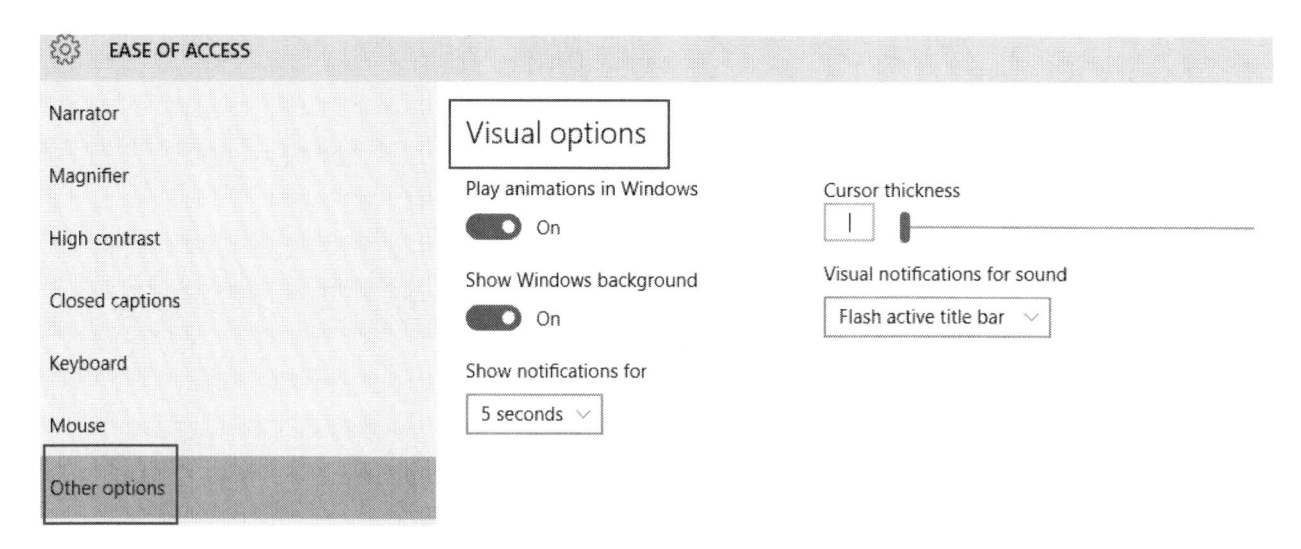

This Windows 10 Setting of "Other Options" is for Visual Options. You can turn two individual settings ON or OFF according to your need.

1. Play Animations in Windows

2. Show Windows Background

In this Setting, you can choose the show notifications duration using the available drop-down menu.

In this Setting, you can choose the thickness of the cursor using the drag-and-drop lateral bar (left for very thin and right for very thick).

Finally, in this Setting, you can choose from drop-down menu options regarding the visual notification process for sound. Choose according to your needs.

Section 72: Windows 10 Settings for Privacy

Go to Start Menu > Settings > Privacy.

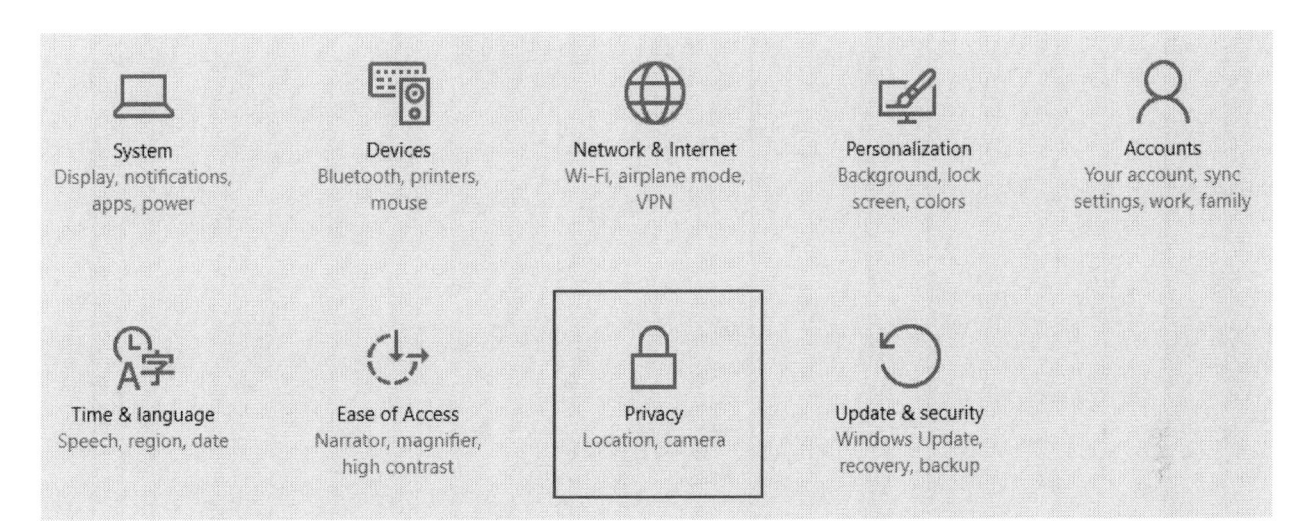

Your options for the Privacy Settings option include the following:

1. General
2. Location
3. Camera
4. Microphone
5. Speech, Inking, Typing
6. Account Information
7. Contacts
8. Calendar
9. Messaging
10. Radios
11. Other Devices
12. Feedback and Diagnostics
13. Background Apps

Section 73: Windows 10 Settings for General Privacy

Go to Start Menu > Settings > Privacy > General.

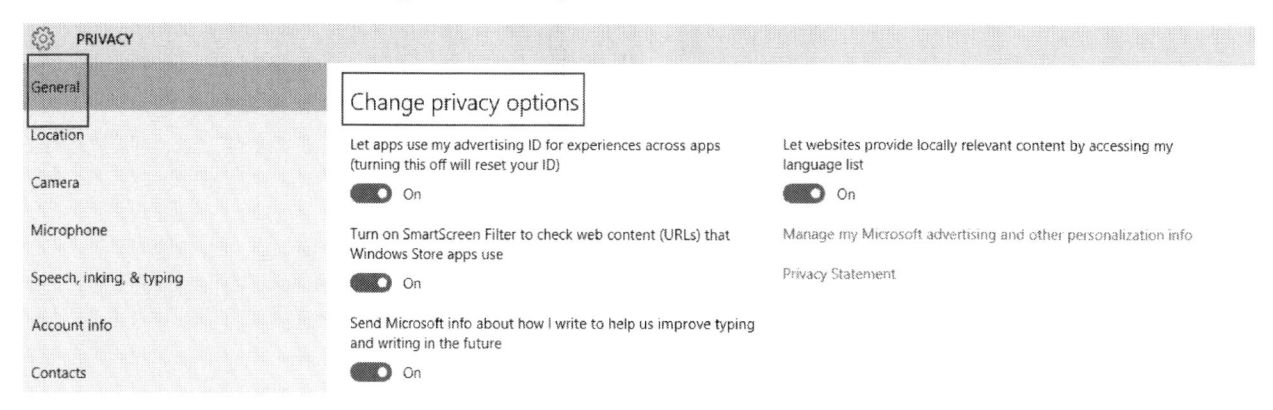

Privacy is a VERY important topic among Windows 10 users. In this particular Settings option you can turn the following Privacy Options ON or OFF depending upon your user interests.

1. Let apps (applications) use my advertising ID for experiences across apps (note that turning this option OFF will reset your ID).

2. Turn on SmartScreen Filter to check web content (URLs) that the Windows Store apps use.

3. Send Microsoft information about how I write to help us (Microsoft) improve typing and writing in the future.

Note: This is essentially a key-logger program so Microsoft is recording keyboard activity and even though it says that it is just gathering information for writing research, it has your passwords and things like this. Definitely turn this one OFF.

4. Let websites provide locally relevant content by accessing my language list.

Note: Here, Microsoft is "profiling" you via your language setting so only let this stay ON if this does not bother you. Otherwise, turn this OFF for language privacy.

Section 74: Windows 10 Settings for Location

Go to Start Menu > Settings > Privacy > Location.

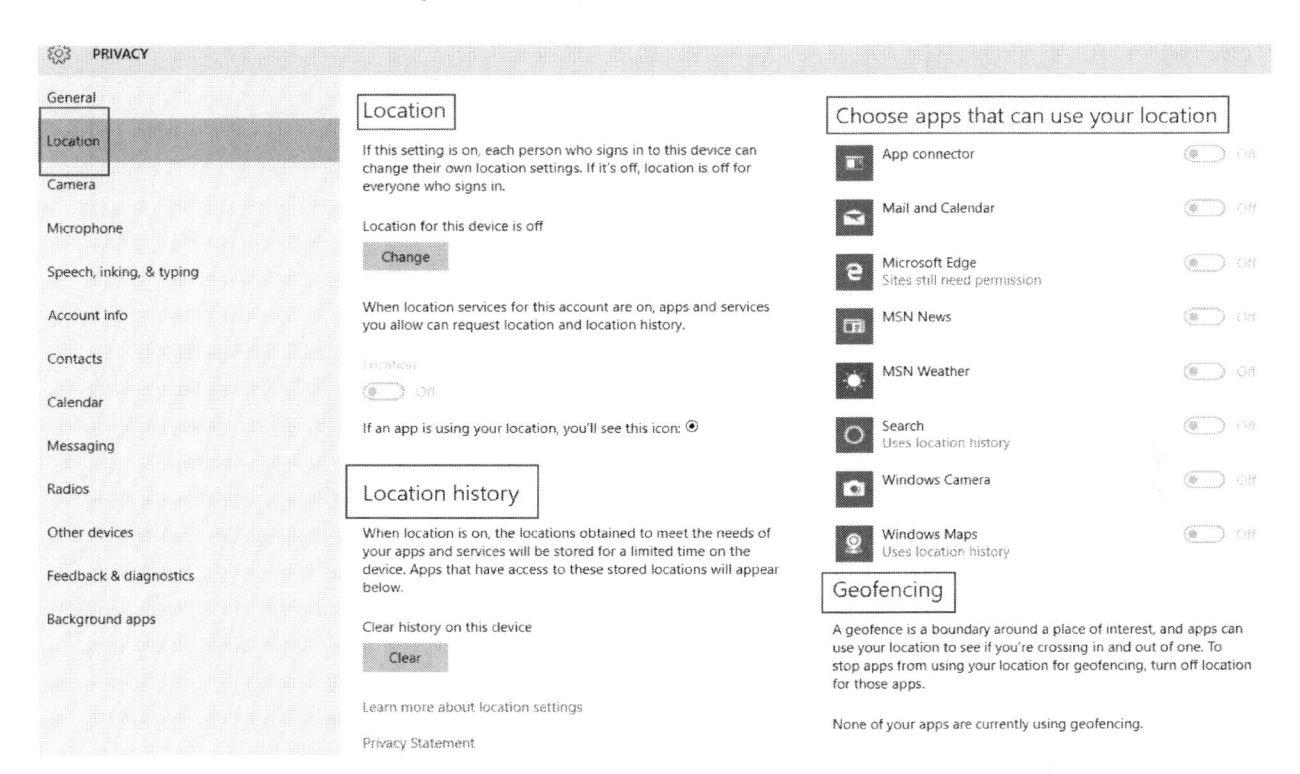

The Location Privacy Settings option has four major parts. First, if you choose Location to be ON then apps and services can request location and location history from your machine. If this option is OFF, then no apps or services can get such information from your machine. Second, you can clear Location history as many times as you want. So, if you decide to turn Location ON, then there is no location history for apps or services to gain from your machine. Third, if your Location option is ON then you can choose the apps that are allowed to use your location. You will see a sample list of apps in the same screen shot above. You can turn these ON or OFF as you need. Finally, and fourth, be aware of something called GEOFENCING. This is a setting that is automatically activated when your Location setting is ON. Geofencing enables apps to set up, according to their own specs, "boundaries" which help them measure location activity (e.g. in and out of the fence/border-defined area). This gives apps a new angle on your user history from the location angle.

Section 75: Windows 10 Settings for Camera

Go to Start Menu > Settings > Privacy > Camera.

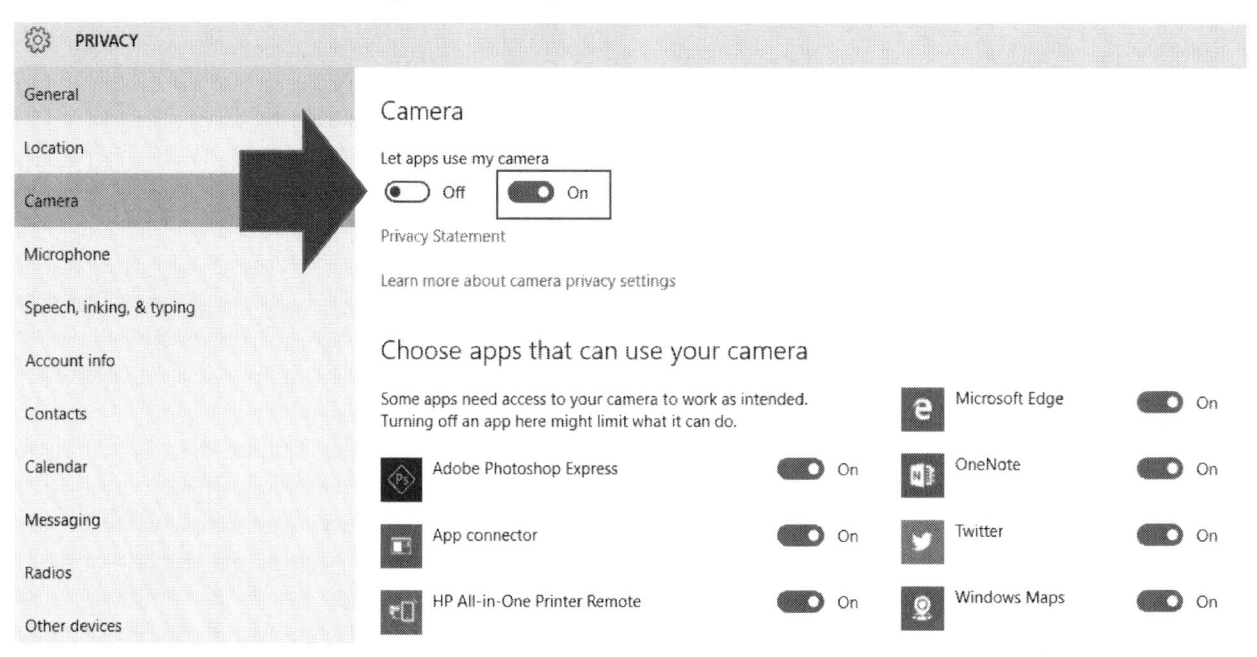

The Camera Privacy Settings option is one that I would be especially mindful of. Here is why. If you leave the Camera setting ON then all the companies that are behind these products can potentially eavesdrop on your activities even without you knowing or without the camera even lighting up as it should. I would only turn this on TEMPORARILY to protect myself. It is OK to turn the Camera setting ON when you know specifically that you are going to use the camera. Go ahead, use the camera, and then turn this option OFF for your true safety and security. When it is OFF, even if the apps are listed as ON, you are safe. You can, however, leave apps that you want to use with the camera ON so that when you do select Camera as ON, then you can use them immediately. If you click on the link "Learn more about camera privacy settings", then Microsoft directs you to its Windows 10 Camera and Privacy FAQ webpage.

http://windows.microsoft.com/en-us/windows-10/camera-privacy-faq

Section 76: Windows 10 Settings for Microphone

Go to Start Menu > Settings > Privacy > Microphone.

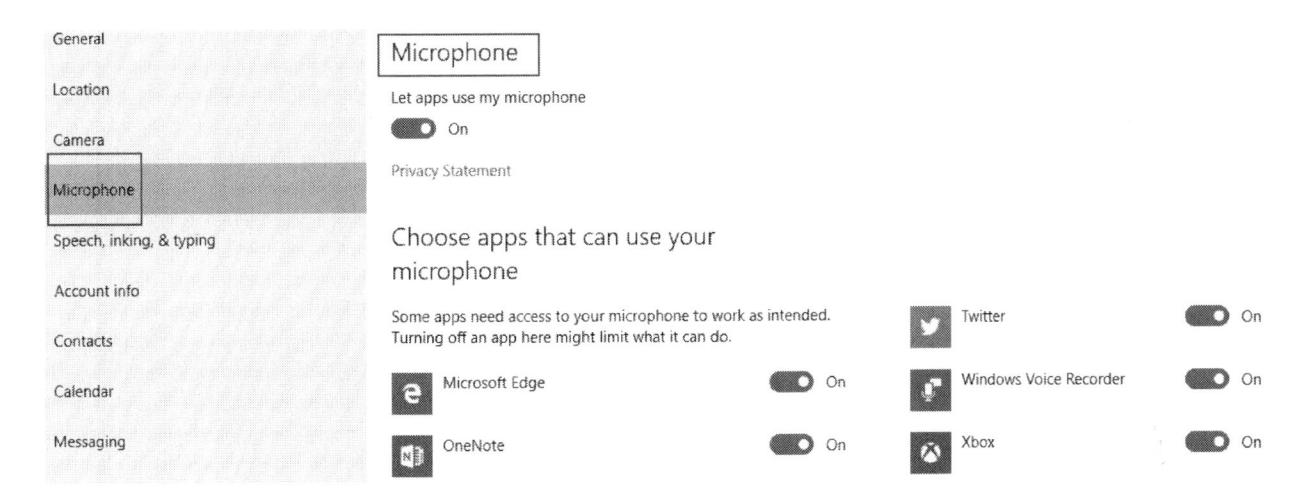

The Privacy setting for the Microphone acts in a similar way to the privacy setting of the Camera.

What you can do is leave the apps ON (the apps that can use and access your microphone) however, only turn the Microphone ON itself when you are going to use it. Otherwise, leave it OFF for your own safety and security and privacy.

If you click on the Privacy Statement link (as shown above), then Microsoft directs you to the following webpage.

https://www.microsoft.com/en-us/privacystatement/default.aspx

Section 77: Windows 10 Settings for Speech/Inking/Typing

Go to Start Menu > Settings > Privacy > Speech, Inking & Typing.

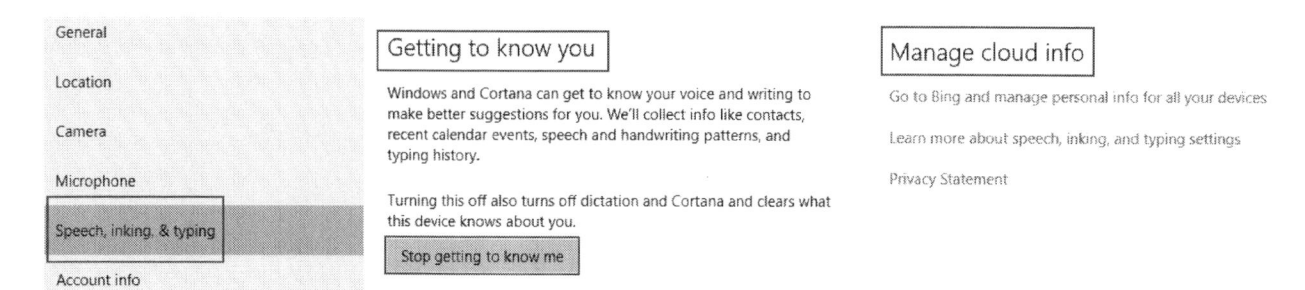

This Speech/Inking/Typing Privacy Settings option is the essential ON/OFF switch that enables or disables Windows 10 from tracking/following your keyboard inputs and voice inputs. To disable this functionality, click on the "Stop getting to know me" button. The following pop-up window is shown ... click "Turn off". Now Windows 10 is not following your voice and/or typing inputs.

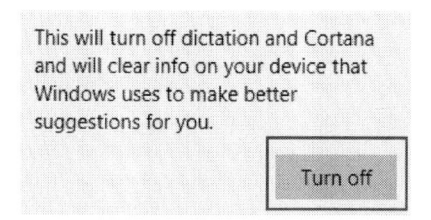

To reactivate this functionality of Windows 10, the button to be clicked will say "Get to know me". Click on this and a pop-up window is shown - click the "Turn on" button and Windows 10 will again work with your inputs from both microphone (voice) and keyboard (typing). Clicking on the "Go to Bing and manage personal info for all your devices" link takes you to a webpage where you can login with your Microsoft account and clear personal data. Clicking on the "Learn more about speech, inking, and typing settings" link takes you to this Microsoft FAQ webpage ...

http://windows.microsoft.com/en-us/windows-10/speech-inking-typing-privacy-faq

Section 78: Windows 10 Settings for Account Information

Go to Start Menu > Settings > Privacy > Account Info.

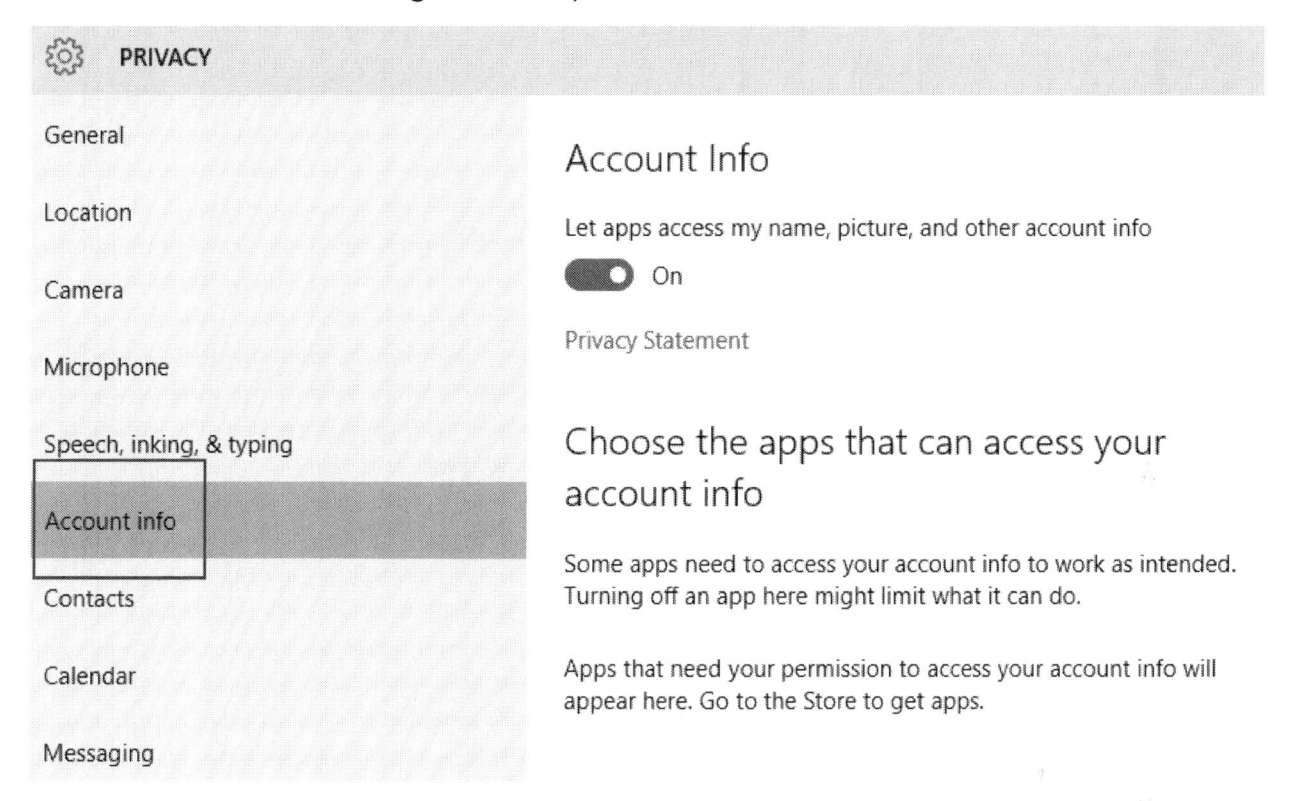

PRIVACY	
General	**Account Info**
Location	Let apps access my name, picture, and other account info
Camera	●○ On
Microphone	Privacy Statement
Speech, inking, & typing	**Choose the apps that can access your account info**
Account info	
Contacts	Some apps need to access your account info to work as intended. Turning off an app here might limit what it can do.
Calendar	Apps that need your permission to access your account info will appear here. Go to the Store to get apps.
Messaging	

This Privacy Settings option (Account Info) enables you to grant permission to apps to access your information – like name, picture, and other miscellaneous account data. If this setting is ON, then apps can access your Microsoft Account Information. If this setting is OFF, then apps cannot do this.

There are also apps which require your explicit permission in order to work with your Microsoft Account Information. If you have such apps on your computer, they would be listed in this Settings area. As you can see in the sample screen shot above, I currently do not have any such apps on my computer.

Section 79: Windows 10 Settings for Contacts

Go to Start Menu > Settings > Privacy > Contacts.

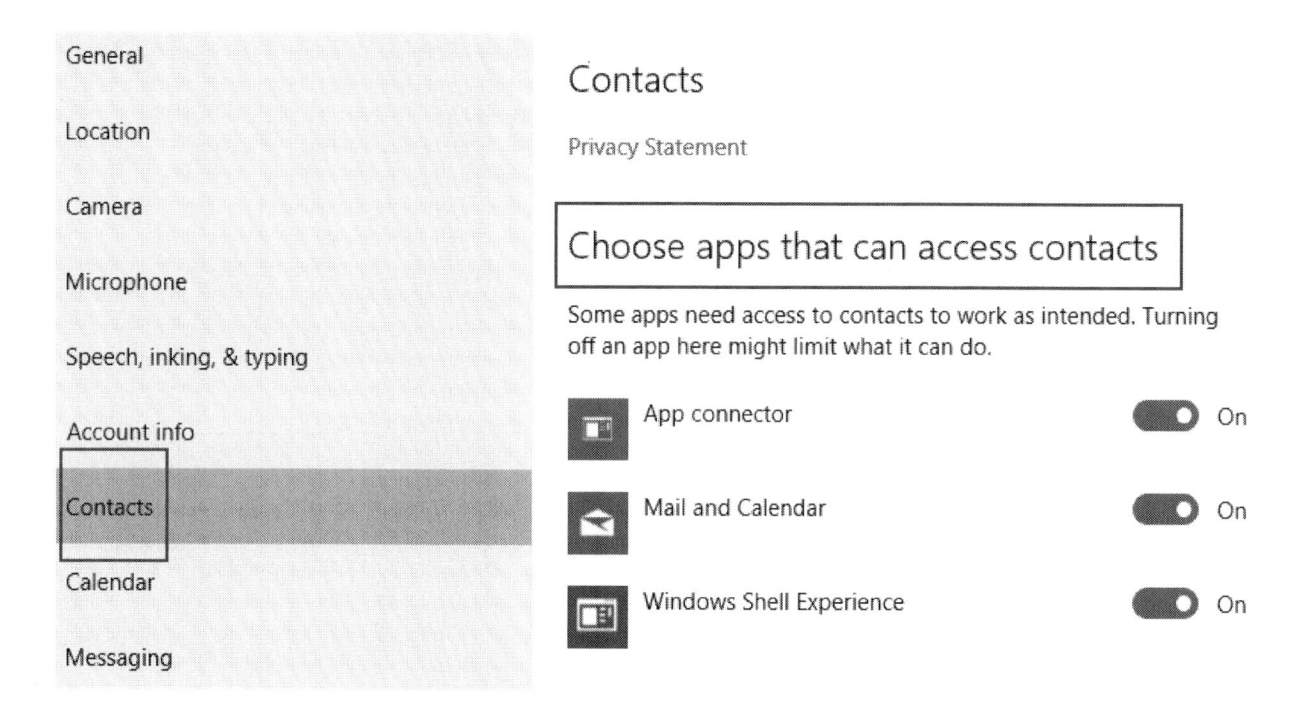

General	Contacts
Location	Privacy Statement
Camera	
Microphone	Choose apps that can access contacts
Speech, inking, & typing	Some apps need access to contacts to work as intended. Turning off an app here might limit what it can do.
Account info	App connector — On
Contacts	Mail and Calendar — On
Calendar	Windows Shell Experience — On
Messaging	

This Privacy Settings option (Contacts) enables you to determine which apps are allowed to access your Contacts information. Contacts normally come from your e-mail account but in the case of a Windows phone (just as an example here) contacts could be your actual phone contacts listing. As you can see in the sample screen shot above from my computer, there are three apps which I allow to work with my Contacts list – App Connector, Mail and Calendar, and the Windows Shell Experience. At any time, I can turn each app OFF, then ON again, then OFF, as I need. The same is true for your experience in this part of Settings.

Section 80: Windows 10 Settings for Calendar

Go to Start Menu > Settings > Privacy > Calendar.

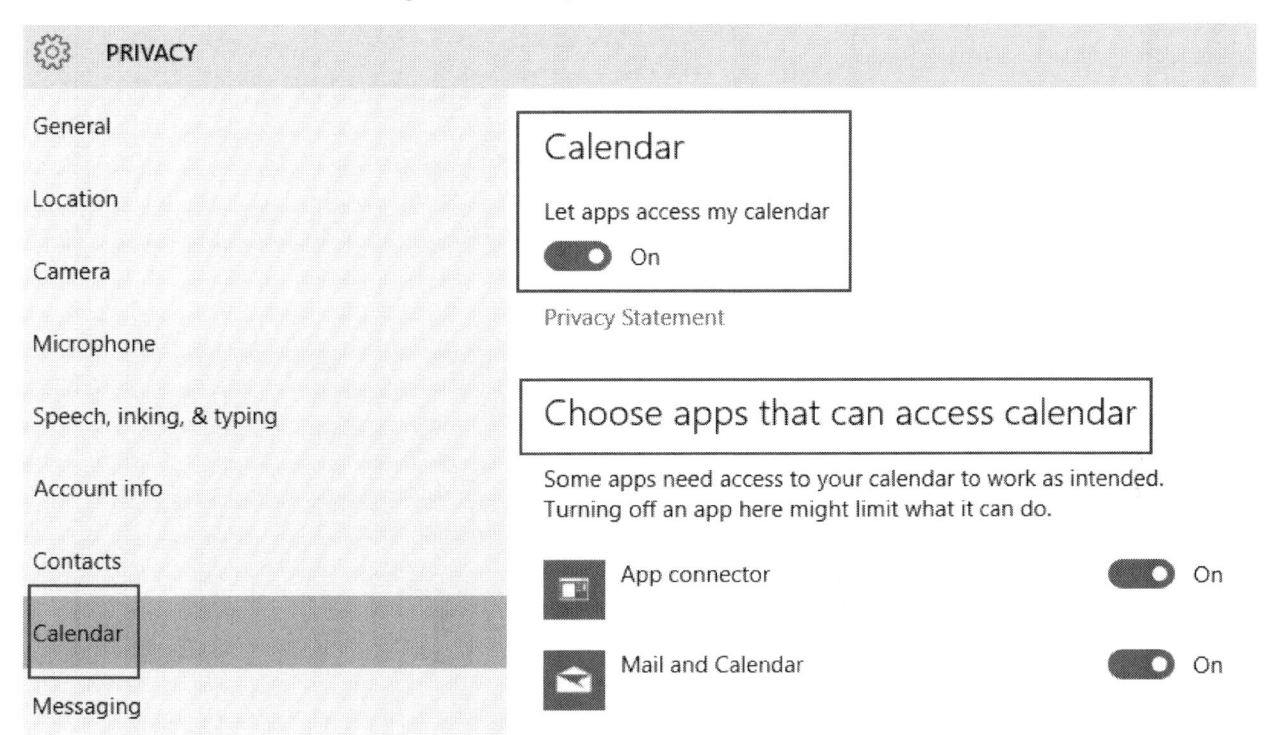

PRIVACY	
General	**Calendar**
Location	Let apps access my calendar
Camera	● On
Microphone	Privacy Statement
Speech, inking, & typing	**Choose apps that can access calendar**
Account info	Some apps need access to your calendar to work as intended. Turning off an app here might limit what it can do.
Contacts	App connector — On
Calendar	Mail and Calendar — On
Messaging	

This Privacy Settings option (Calendar) enables you to determine which apps are allowed to access your Calendar information data. As you can see in the sample screen shot above from my computer, I have this Setting ON because I want the two listed apps to be able to read data from my Calendar – App Connector and Mail and Calendar. Like Contacts, this Setting can be turned ON and OFF as you need. As I am writing this book, there was an article on the web saying that just now Cortana has the new ability to work with Calendar data. So, perhaps at some future point you will see Cortana (the app) also in this listing of apps that can potentially work with Calendar information.

Section 81: Windows 10 Settings for Messaging

Go to Start Menu > Settings > Privacy > Messaging.

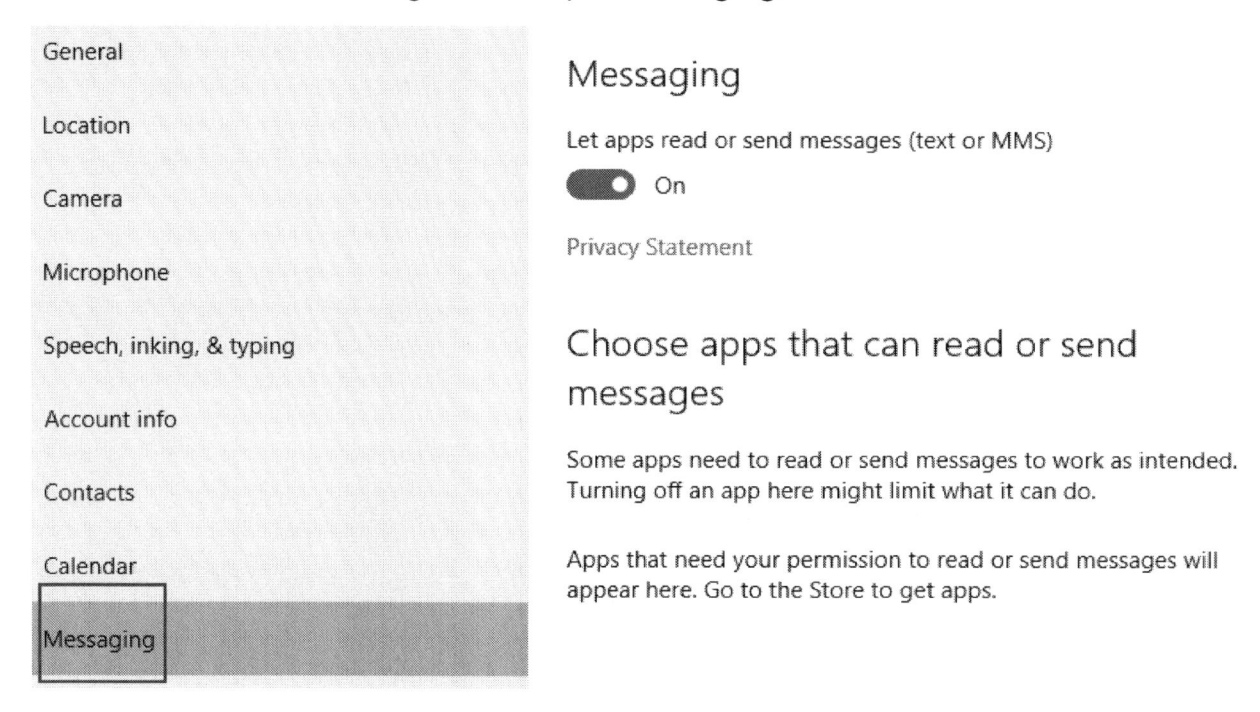

General

Location

Camera

Microphone

Speech, inking, & typing

Account info

Contacts

Calendar

Messaging

Messaging

Let apps read or send messages (text or MMS)

On

Privacy Statement

Choose apps that can read or send messages

Some apps need to read or send messages to work as intended. Turning off an app here might limit what it can do.

Apps that need your permission to read or send messages will appear here. Go to the Store to get apps.

This Privacy Settings option (Messaging) enables you to determine which apps are allowed to access your message data. This setting must be ON for the apps can gain permission and access. I currently do not have any apps that can work with messaging data but if I did then they would be listed in the sample screen shot above. You can turn this setting ON and OFF as you need and in this way you can do your part to ensure messaging privacy on your computer.

Section 82: Windows 10 Settings for Radios

Go to Start Menu > Settings > Privacy > Radios.

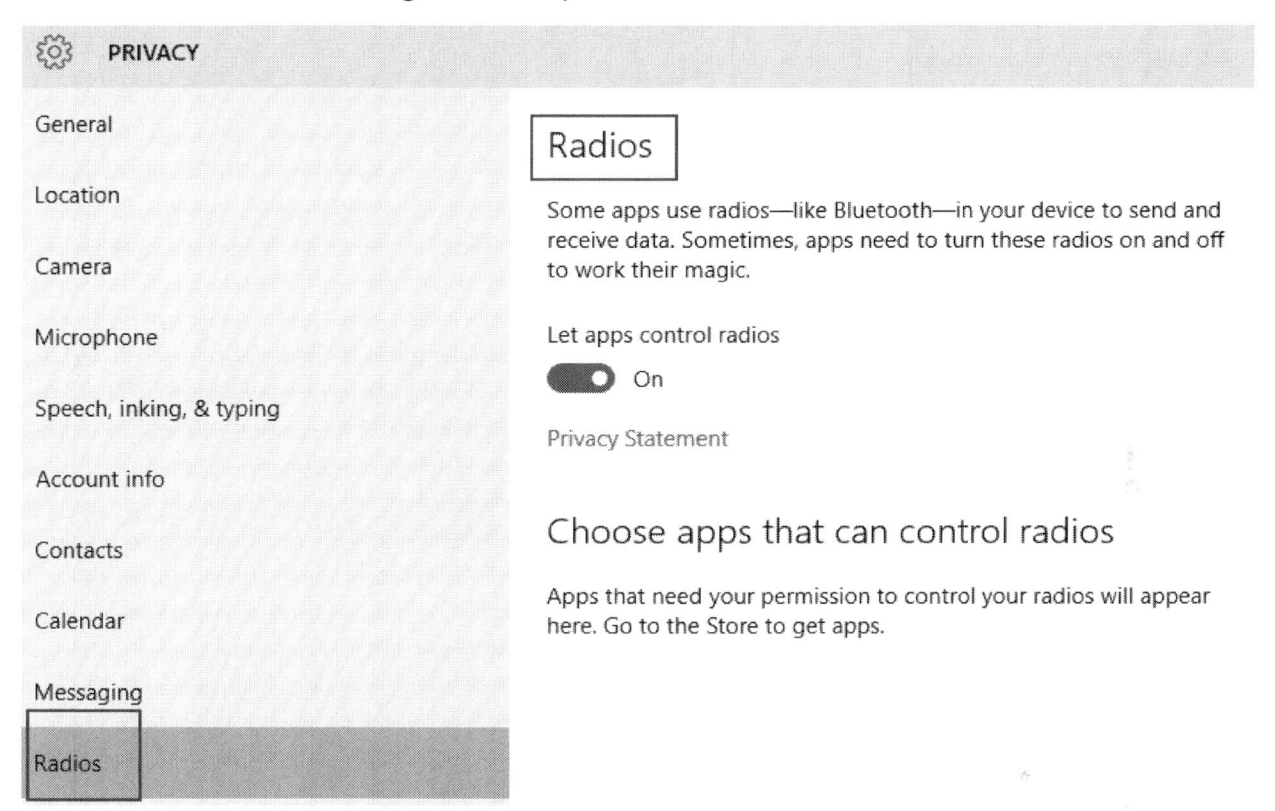

PRIVACY	
General	**Radios**
Location	Some apps use radios—like Bluetooth—in your device to send and receive data. Sometimes, apps need to turn these radios on and off to work their magic.
Camera	
Microphone	Let apps control radios
	On
Speech, inking, & typing	Privacy Statement
Account info	
Contacts	**Choose apps that can control radios**
Calendar	Apps that need your permission to control your radios will appear here. Go to the Store to get apps.
Messaging	
Radios	

This Privacy Settings option (Radios) enables you to determine which apps are allowed to access your radio(s) and turn them on or off to be able to work. In the sample screen shot above, you can see I have allowed such apps permission (via the ON setting) to turn such a radio on so that the app can work with the radio device, but currently do not have any apps of this nature on my machine.

Section 83: Windows 10 Settings for Other Devices

Go to Start Menu > Settings > Privacy > Other Devices.

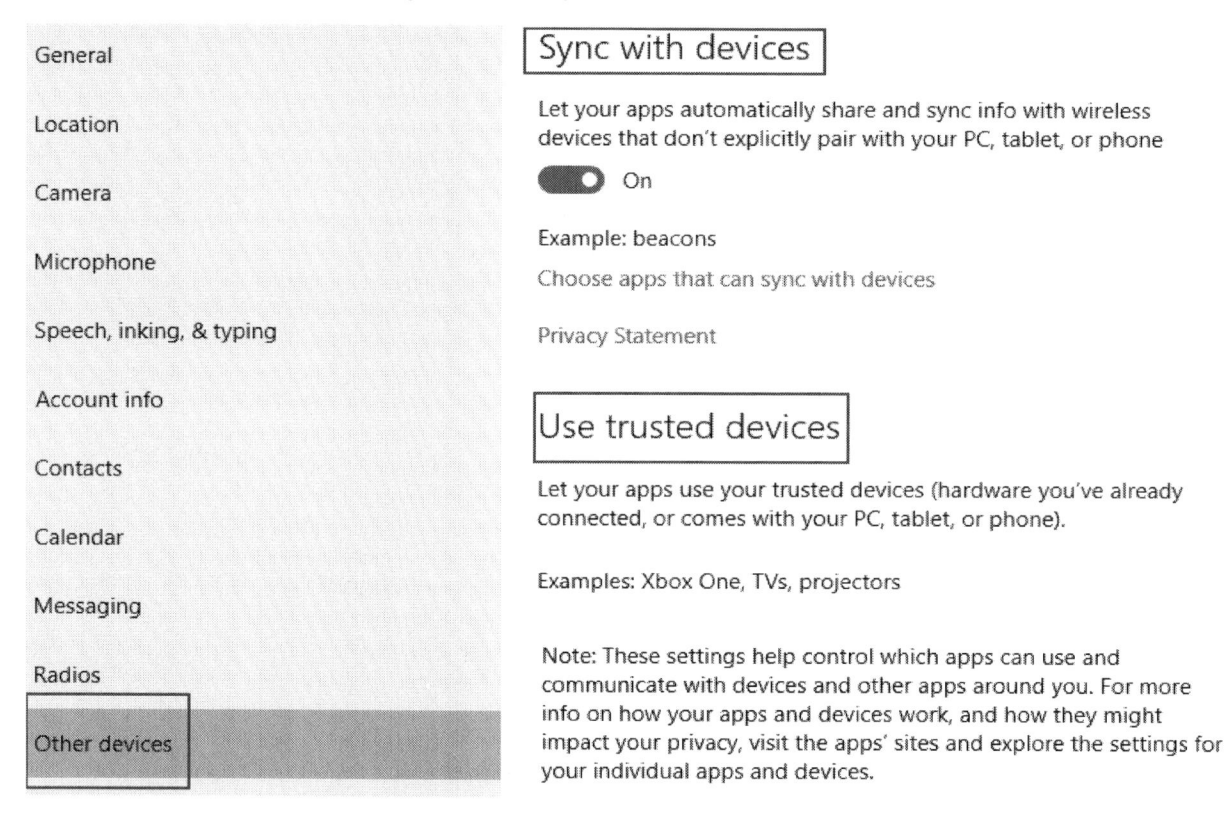

General

Location

Camera

Microphone

Speech, inking, & typing

Account info

Contacts

Calendar

Messaging

Radios

Other devices

Sync with devices

Let your apps automatically share and sync info with wireless devices that don't explicitly pair with your PC, tablet, or phone

On

Example: beacons

Choose apps that can sync with devices

Privacy Statement

Use trusted devices

Let your apps use your trusted devices (hardware you've already connected, or comes with your PC, tablet, or phone).

Examples: Xbox One, TVs, projectors

Note: These settings help control which apps can use and communicate with devices and other apps around you. For more info on how your apps and devices work, and how they might impact your privacy, visit the apps' sites and explore the settings for your individual apps and devices.

This Privacy Settings option (other devices) enables you to allow apps to sync with wireless devices that don't explicitly pair with one's PC, tablet, or phone. You can download such apps from the Microsoft Store and if you have recently used "trusted" devices - perhaps that have connected wirelessly or via a USB port, for example, to your computer, then Windows 10 will show them in the "Trusted Devices" section of this Settings option.

Section 84: Windows 10 Settings for Feedback & Diagnostics

Go to Start Menu > Settings > Privacy > Feedback and Diagnostics.

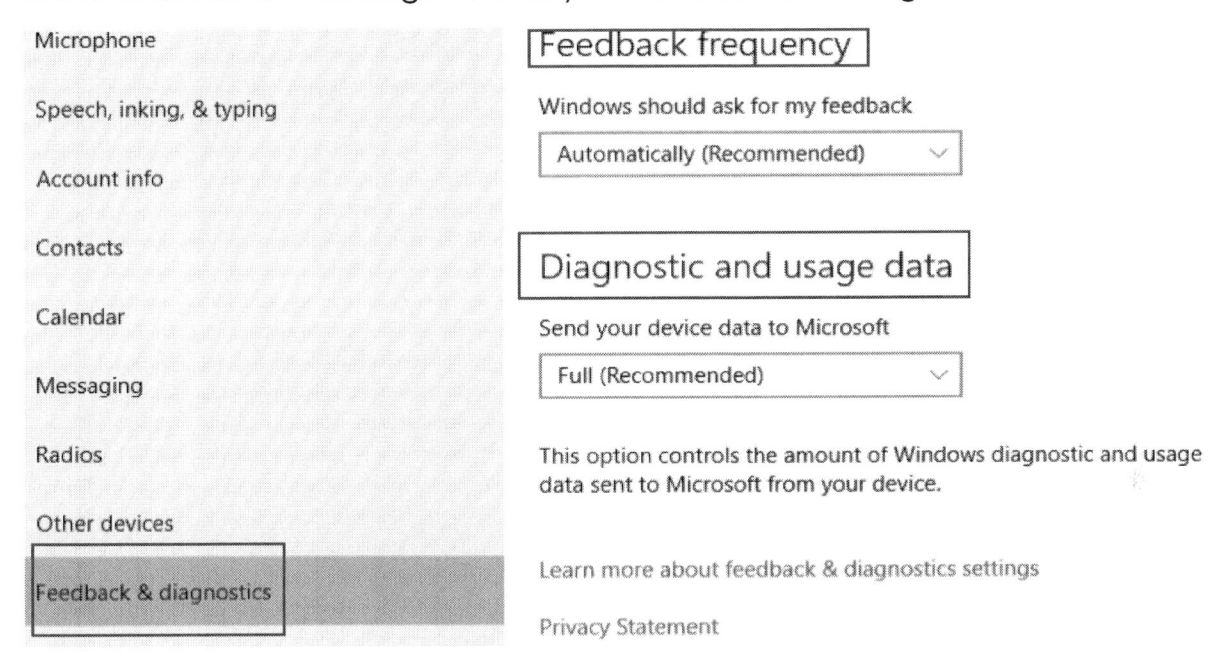

Microphone	**Feedback frequency**
Speech, inking, & typing	Windows should ask for my feedback
Account info	Automatically (Recommended)
Contacts	**Diagnostic and usage data**
Calendar	Send your device data to Microsoft
Messaging	Full (Recommended)
Radios	This option controls the amount of Windows diagnostic and usage data sent to Microsoft from your device.
Other devices	
Feedback & diagnostics	Learn more about feedback & diagnostics settings
	Privacy Statement

This Privacy Settings option (feedback and diagnostics) enables you to choose the frequency and depth of "user feedback" information that is reported back to Microsoft from your computer. If you click on the drop-down menu for Feedback Frequency you can make your selection there. If you click on the drop-down menu for Diagnostic and Usage Data, you can make your selection there as well.

Section 85: Windows 10 Settings for Background Apps

Go to Start Menu > Settings > Privacy > Background Apps.

General	**Let apps run in the background**	
Location	Choose which apps can receive info, send notifications, and stay up-to-date, even when you're not using them. Turning background apps off can help conserve power.	
Camera		
Microphone	Privacy Statement	
Speech, inking, & typing	Alarms & Clock — On	People — On
Account info	Calendar — On	Phone Companion — On
Contacts	Get Office — On	Photos — On
Calendar	Groove Music — On	Settings — On
Messaging	HP AiO Printer Remote — On	Store — On
Radios	Maps — On	Twitter — On
Other devices	Microsoft Edge — On	Voice Recorder — On
Feedback & diagnostics	OneNote — On	Xbox — On
Background apps		

This Privacy Settings option (background apps) enables you to choose which apps can receive information, send notifications, and stay up-to-date when you are not using them (that is why they are called background apps here). Please note that turning such "background apps" off can indeed help the computer conserve energy especially if it is running on battery power.

Section 86: Windows 10 Settings for Updates/Security

Go to Start Menu > Settings > Updates and Security.

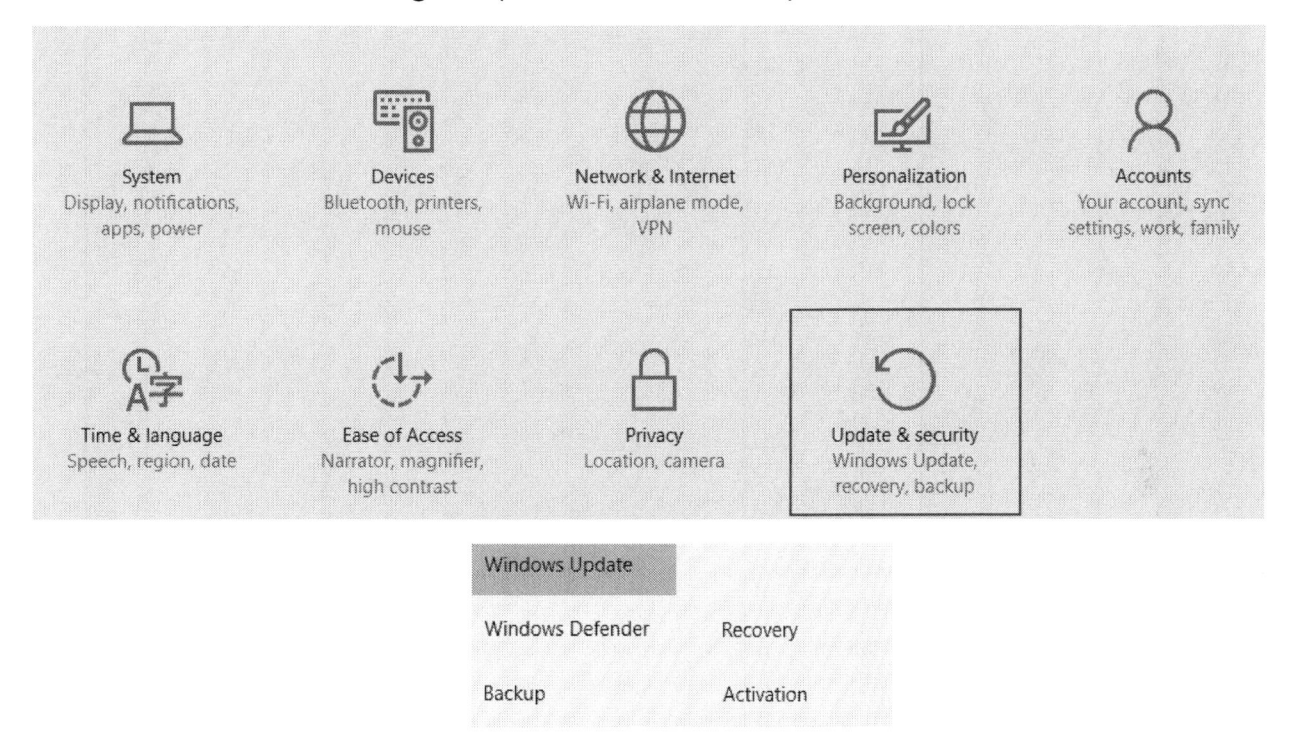

The Settings options available under the *Update and Security* category:

1. Windows Update

2. Windows Defender

3. Backup

4. Recovery

5. Activation

Note: Because this user guide is not intended for Windows 10 developers or Windows 10 system administrators, I have decided not to include the last Settings Update and Security option called "for developers". My intention here is to keep the number of total book pages under 250 to keep the book's price as cheap as possible. Thanks for your understanding.

Section 87: Windows 10 Settings for Windows Update

Go to Start Menu > Settings > Updates and Security > Windows Update.

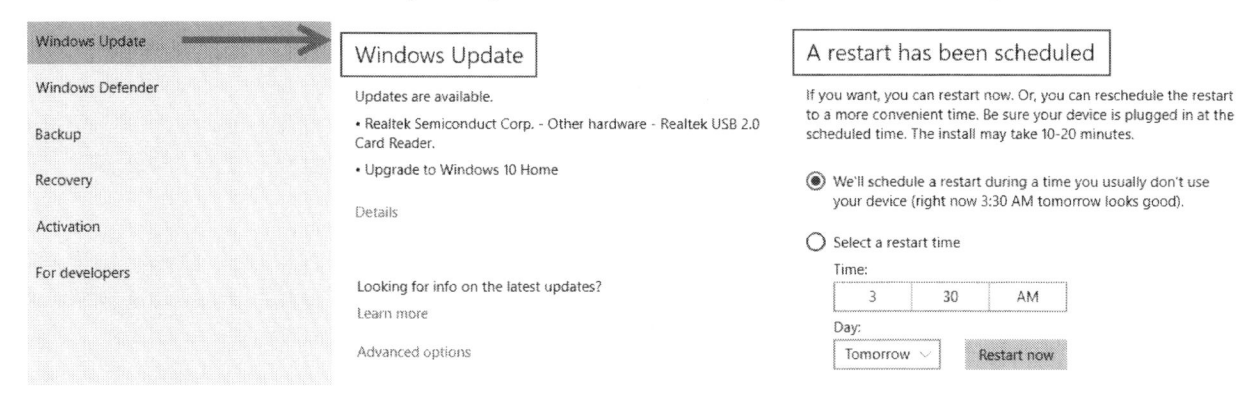

If you go onto the web and read blog posts about Windows 10, you will quickly see that the most controversial part of Windows 10 is the _process_ by which the OS remains both _up-to-date_ and _secure_. This is the _Windows 10 Update process_.

Some Windows 10 users *do not* like to get their OS updated. The price you pay for this mindset is this "increased vulnerability" … the OS becomes more and more vulnerable over time to hacking, especially as hackers figure out ways to manipulate the Windows 10 source code. So, while you might think you are playing it safe by not updating your OS, you could be weakening your defense against a system attack because the longer hackers can study your release of Windows 10, the greater the chance they can do something potentially harmful.

On the flip side, as you update your Windows 10 OS especially through the regular and systematic "Microsoft Update" process – which is when Microsoft reaches out to your machine from its servers and installs files, patches and things like that – you are gaining the very "latest and greatest" in tested Windows 10 code which necessarily means Microsoft has resolved issues and improved overall source code performance. This means your computer has become more secure. Why is this so? The answer is simple – **Microsoft values its customers and especially your patronage**. A bad OS experience on your part creates unfathomable damage to the Microsoft brand name. Your secure Windows 10 experience is as important as the general functionality of any Windows 10 app. With that said, let's look at how this two-step Update process works (first downloading of the Update and then as the machine is restarted, the Update is applied to Windows 10).

The default setting for Microsoft 10 update is what you see in the sample screen shot on the previous page. Microsoft wants to send you its latest release but at a time that is most likely convenient for you and that will not get in the way of your day to day activities. So the radio button for "we'll schedule a restart during a time you usually don't use your device (right now 3:30am tomorrow looks good). Mind you it is through the restart process that Microsoft is able to connect to your machine and download Windows 10 updates via your Internet connection. Essentially this is a transfer of files from a Microsoft server to your local machine. You can of course select a better restart time if the default time is not convenient for you. Just click on the radio button for "select a restart time" and specify the time and day that is best for you.

A restart has been scheduled

If you want, you can restart now. Or, you can reschedule the restart to a more convenient time. Be sure your device is plugged in at the scheduled time. The install may take 10-20 minutes.

○ We'll schedule a restart during a time you usually don't use your device (right now 3:30 AM tomorrow looks good).

⦿ Select a restart time
  Time:
  | 4 | 00 | AM |
  Day:
  Tomorrow ˅

This addresses weekly updates. You can also at any time click on the Restart Now button to initiate an instant restart on the fly.

Restart now

There are two links at the very bottom of the Windows Update page - Learn More and Advanced Options. "Learn more" takes you to a web page that offers a monthly summary of updates for that month. So, if I am in the month of February 2016, then the top link listed by Bing or my default search engine will feature Microsoft Updates for February 2016, according to the edition of Windows 10. The "Advanced Options" link gets into the how of the Updates process.

Here is the Settings page displayed via this link.

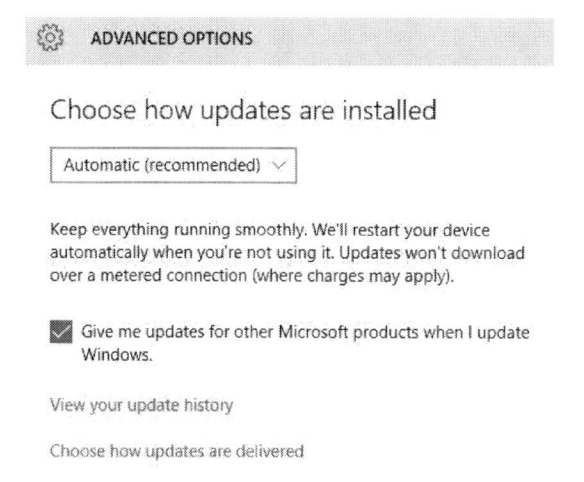

ADVANCED OPTIONS

Choose how updates are installed

[Automatic (recommended) ⌄]

Keep everything running smoothly. We'll restart your device automatically when you're not using it. Updates won't download over a metered connection (where charges may apply).

☑ Give me updates for other Microsoft products when I update Windows.

View your update history

Choose how updates are delivered

There are two major options at the top of this page. You can allow Microsoft to update your Windows 10 automatically or (via the drop-down menu) you can choose to control the update process – by choosing "notify to schedule restart". What this means is that if the former is chosen (automatic updates), then will in fact take place even if you are using your machine. The latter means that you will get a notification that an update process is about to begin. So, this way, if you want, you can save and backup your work before the updates process begins.

There is a link to "view your update history" on this page. Through this link you are brought to a page that shows a historical (most recent and as you go down, to previous updates) listing of Windows 10 updates. You can review them but also if you need you can undo an update through the "uninstall updates" link at the top of the page.

VIEW YOUR UPDATE HISTORY

Uninstall updates

Uninstall latest preview build

Update history

Definition Update for Windows Defender - KB2267602 (Definition 1.213.5341.0)
Successfully installed on 2/3/2016

Definition Update for Windows Defender - KB2267602 (Definition 1.213.5231.0)
Successfully installed on 2/2/2016

Definition Update for Windows Defender - KB2267602 (Definition 1.213.5133.0)
Successfully installed on 2/1/2016

Note: The link of "uninstall latest preview build" is for those of you who have joined the Windows Insider program. However, the Windows Insider program is a whole book topic unto itself, so I will not be discussing this.

Also on the "Choose How Updates are Installed" Settings page is a link called "Choose how updates are delivered". This takes you to the following Settings page.

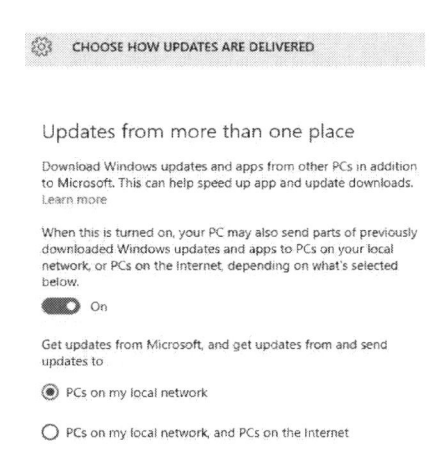

CHOOSE HOW UPDATES ARE DELIVERED

Updates from more than one place

Download Windows updates and apps from other PCs in addition to Microsoft. This can help speed up app and update downloads.
Learn more

When this is turned on, your PC may also send parts of previously downloaded Windows updates and apps to PCs on your local network, or PCs on the Internet, depending on what's selected below.

On

Get updates from Microsoft, and get updates from and send updates to

⦿ PCs on my local network

○ PCs on my local network, and PCs on the Internet

To learn more about the actual Update that Microsoft has prepared to send to your machine, click on the "Details" link under the Windows Update header you see at the top of the Settings window. As an example, here is what my machine is awaiting from Microsoft.

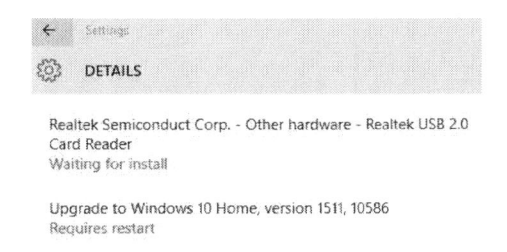

← Settings

DETAILS

Realtek Semiconduct Corp. - Other hardware - Realtek USB 2.0 Card Reader
Waiting for install

Upgrade to Windows 10 Home, version 1511, 10586
Requires restart

In summary, *Windows 10 Updates* keep your machine at top performance and secure. You can control the *how and when* of the Update process, but please do not get left behind by not allowing Windows 10 to send updates to your PC.

Section 88: Windows 10 Settings for Windows Defender

Go to Start Menu > Settings > Updates and Security > Windows Defender.

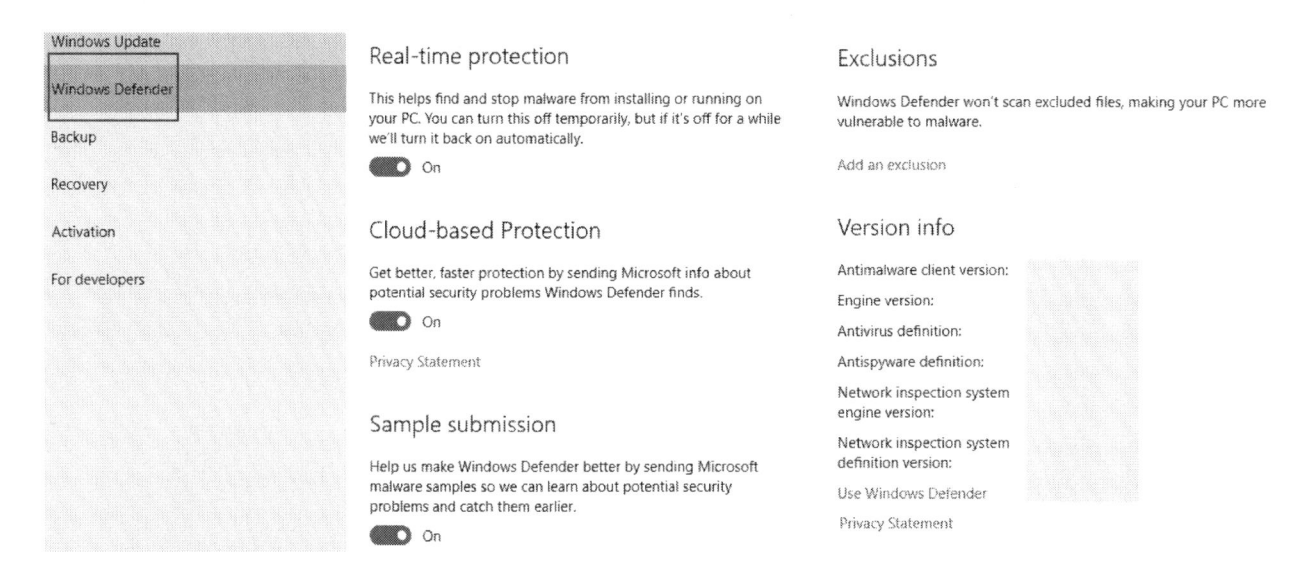

This Settings Update and Security option is very important because Windows Defender is the primary Windows 10 resource that keeps your machine safe and secure. As Defender keeps your machine bloatware-free and malware-free, it should empower your machine toward optimal performance – speed and otherwise.

There are five major sections for the Windows Defender Settings option. First, there is **"Real-Time" protection**. Windows Defender watches your activity and especially online activity. So, if Windows Defender sees a file that seems like a threat, then it will take preventive action and quarantine the file. I recommend you leave this Setting ON.

Second, there is **"Cloud-Based" protection**. Here, when the Setting is ON, then you are giving Microsoft permission to collect data from Defender and bring that information back to the Microsoft Cloud for processing and review. Again, I would leave this Setting ON at all times. Eventually, you are the one who benefits from this dialogue between your machine and the Microsoft Windows 10 Team.

Third, the Setting of **"Sample Submission"** is similar to the second setting but rather than just informing Microsoft of potential security problems, you allow your machine to report back actual samples (if they exist) of malware encountered.

Leaving this Setting ON helps Microsoft to battle the latest in malware.

Fourth, there is a Setting called **"Exclusion"** where you can click on the "Add an Exclusion" link to create an exclusion to the Defender defense system. In other words, maybe Windows Defender sees a file as malware but you know better so create the exclusion so that Microsoft Windows 10 does not quarantine or delete the file. That is fine – but please do make sure you know what you are doing. If the file turns out to be harmful, this could prove to be a bad action. Use this particular setting with extreme caution.

Fifth, there information given about the **Version of Windows Defender** running within your copy of Windows 10. This is good to know because perhaps there might be an issue with a specific release of Windows Defender. If this is the case, you can take action to make sure you have the latest version and help to ensure the safety and security of your machine, data, and Windows 10 overall.

To use Windows Defender, simply click on the link that says "Use Windows Defender". The first and default tab shown is "Home".

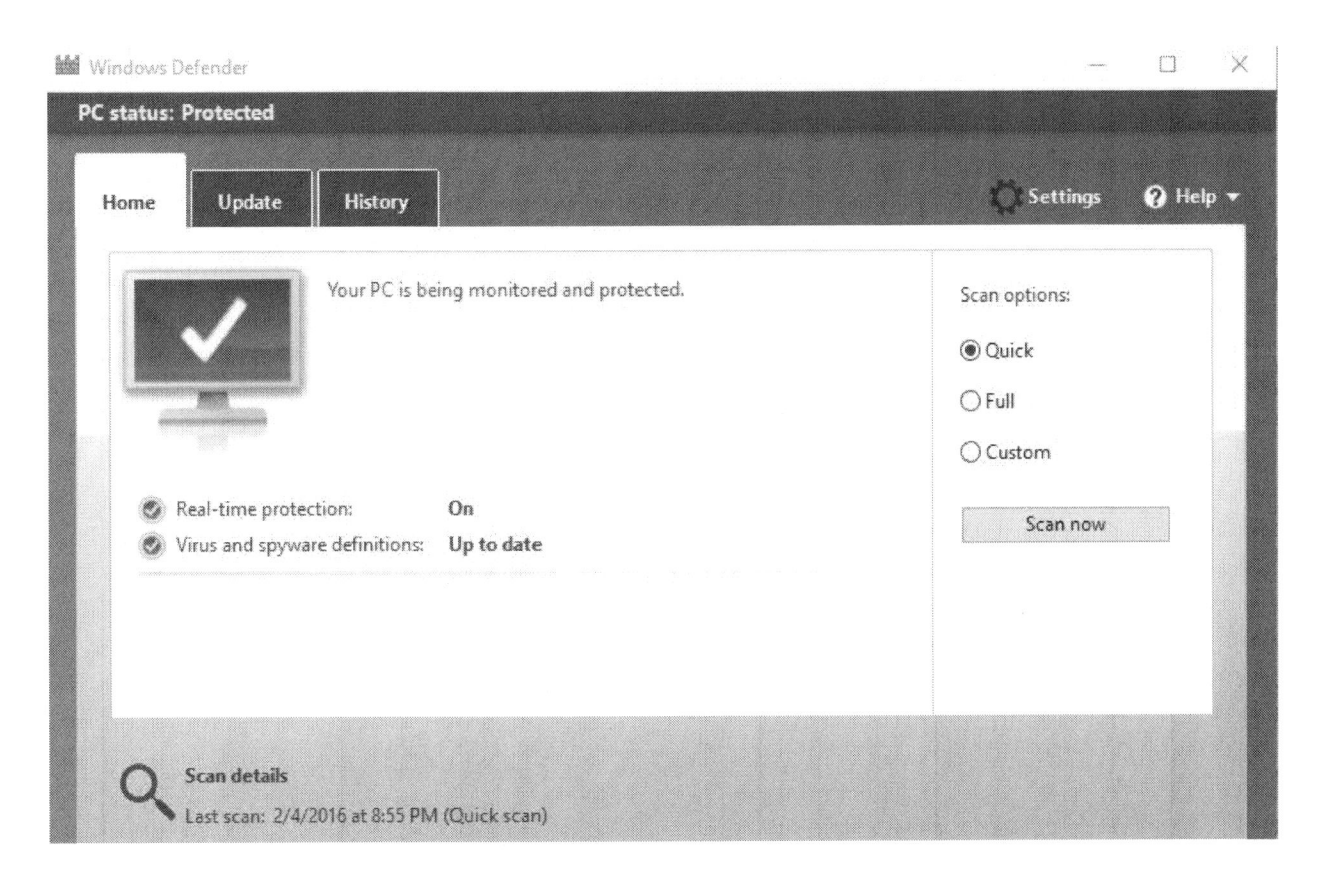

The "Home" tab is where you can select the Scan option that you want to use – Quick, Full, or Custom. Clicking on the "Scan now" button executes this decision.

The second tab of Windows Defender is "Update". Here, you can check to see if your app is up-to-date.

As you can see in the sample screen shot below, my machine and copy of Windows 10 is up-to-date. But of course if that was not the case, I can click on the "Update" button to download the latest and greatest for Microsoft Windows Defender, thereby making its status "up-to-date".

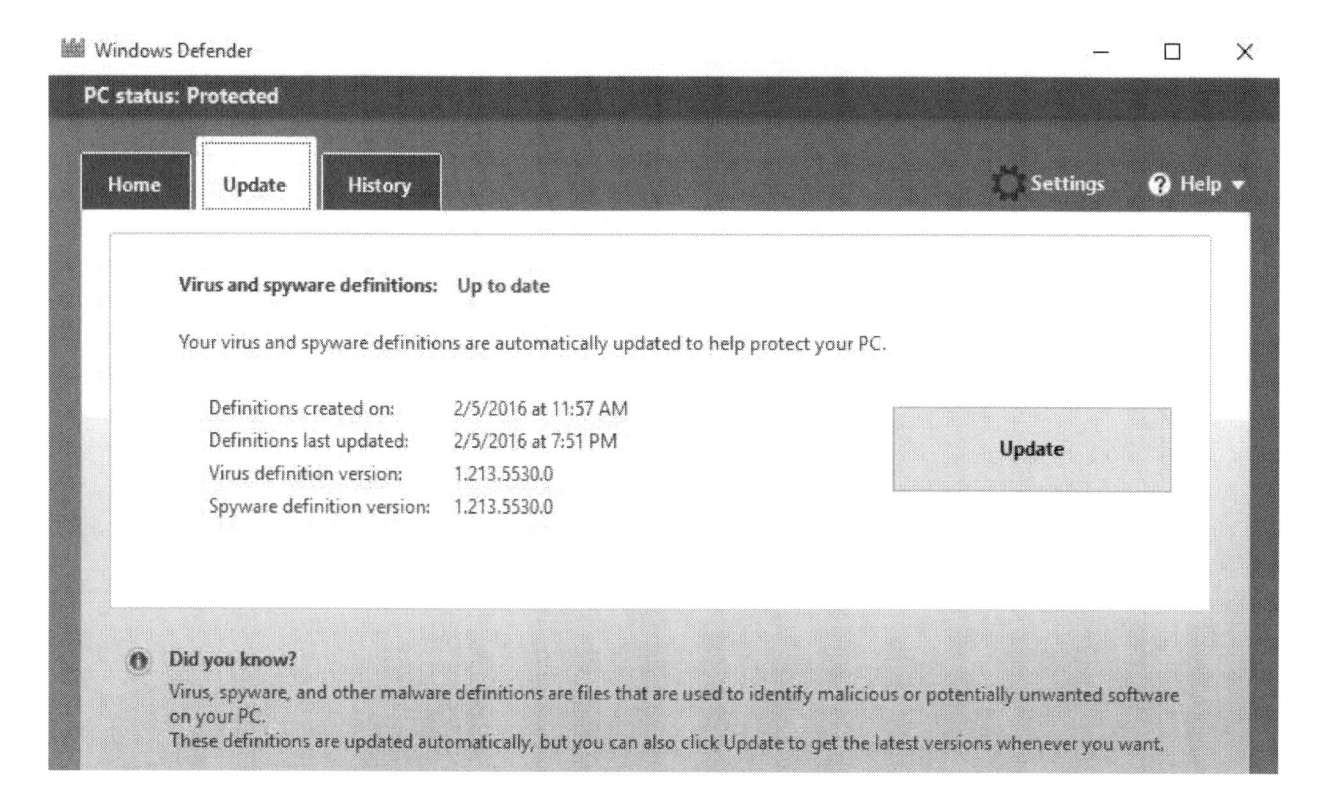

![Windows Defender Update tab screenshot showing PC status: Protected, Virus and spyware definitions: Up to date, Definitions created on: 2/5/2016 at 11:57 AM, Definitions last updated: 2/5/2016 at 7:51 PM, Virus definition version: 1.213.5530.0, Spyware definition version: 1.213.5530.0]

The third tab of Windows Defender is "History".

Here, you can see items that "were detected as potentially harmful and the actions that you took". The three radio buttons and respective options here are Quarantined items, Allowed items, and All Detected Items.

What you can do here is select the radio button for the option then click on the "View Details" button to see such file details.

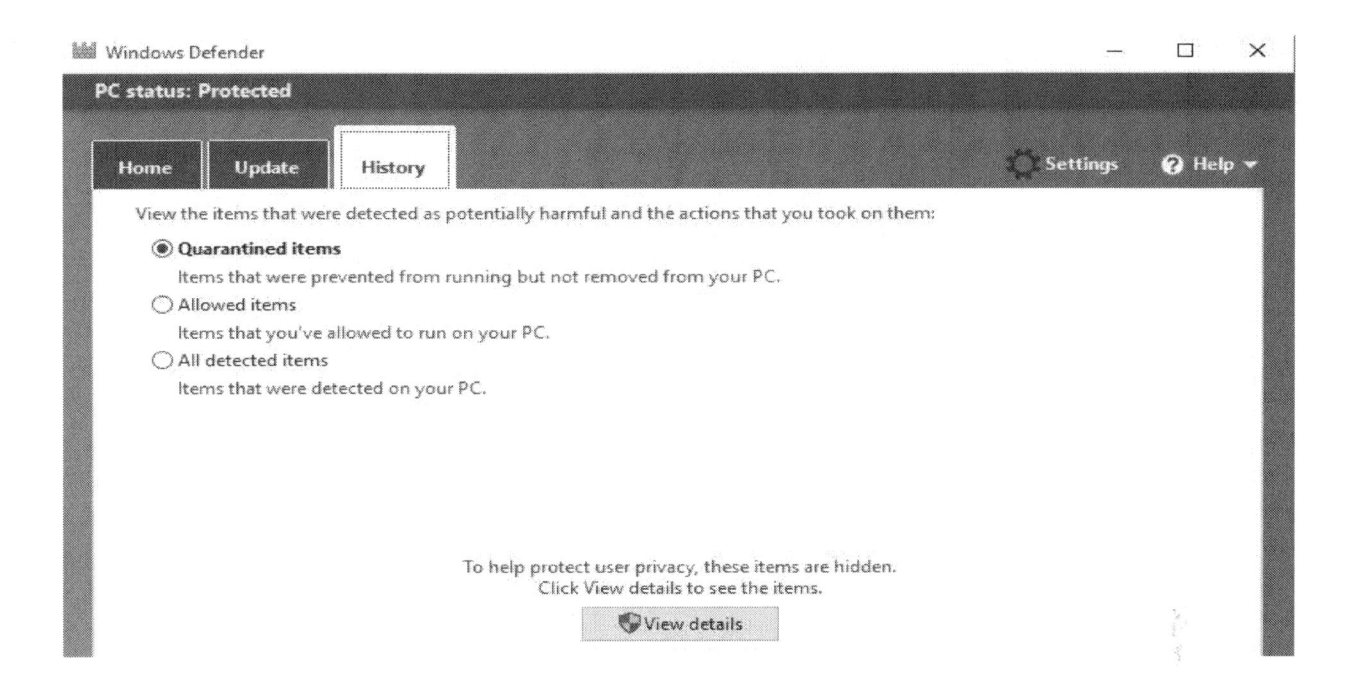

What happens next is the Windows Defender app refreshes and shows you a listing of items that are in question. You can choose one or more and then respectively select Remove All, Remove, or Restore according to what you believe and know to be the best path of action.

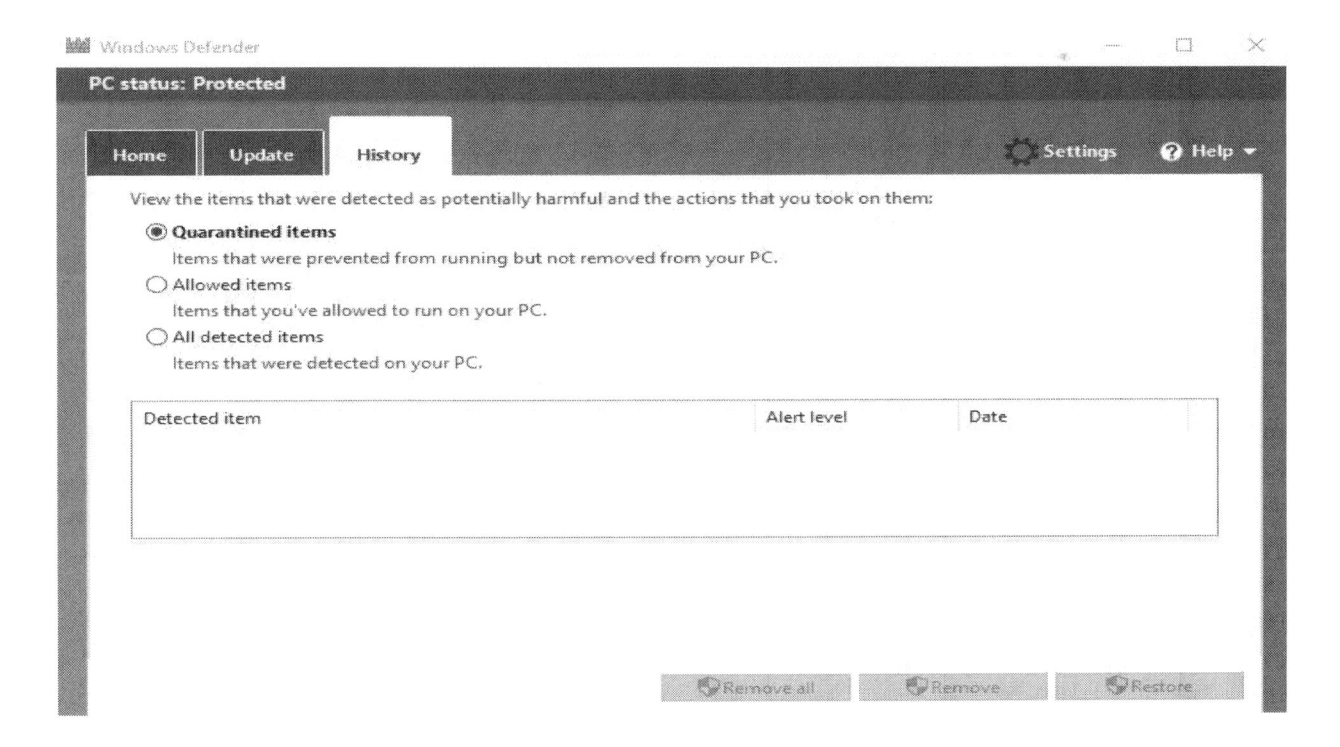

In addition to Windows Defender, there are two other apps that can help to keep your PC safe and secure. They are *Advanced System Care by iObit* and *Hopla! By Wistiki*. Let me say a few words about each.

Advanced System Care is a free computer-care resource I have been using for almost ten years and it inspects your system in the following ways: spyware threats, registry errors, privacy issues, junk files, internet problems, shortcut errors, registry fragments, performance issues, browser security issues, disk errors, security holes, and disk optimization issues. After Advanced System Care scans your machine, you can either choose to have the software automatically repair issues it has found or you can make this request manually.

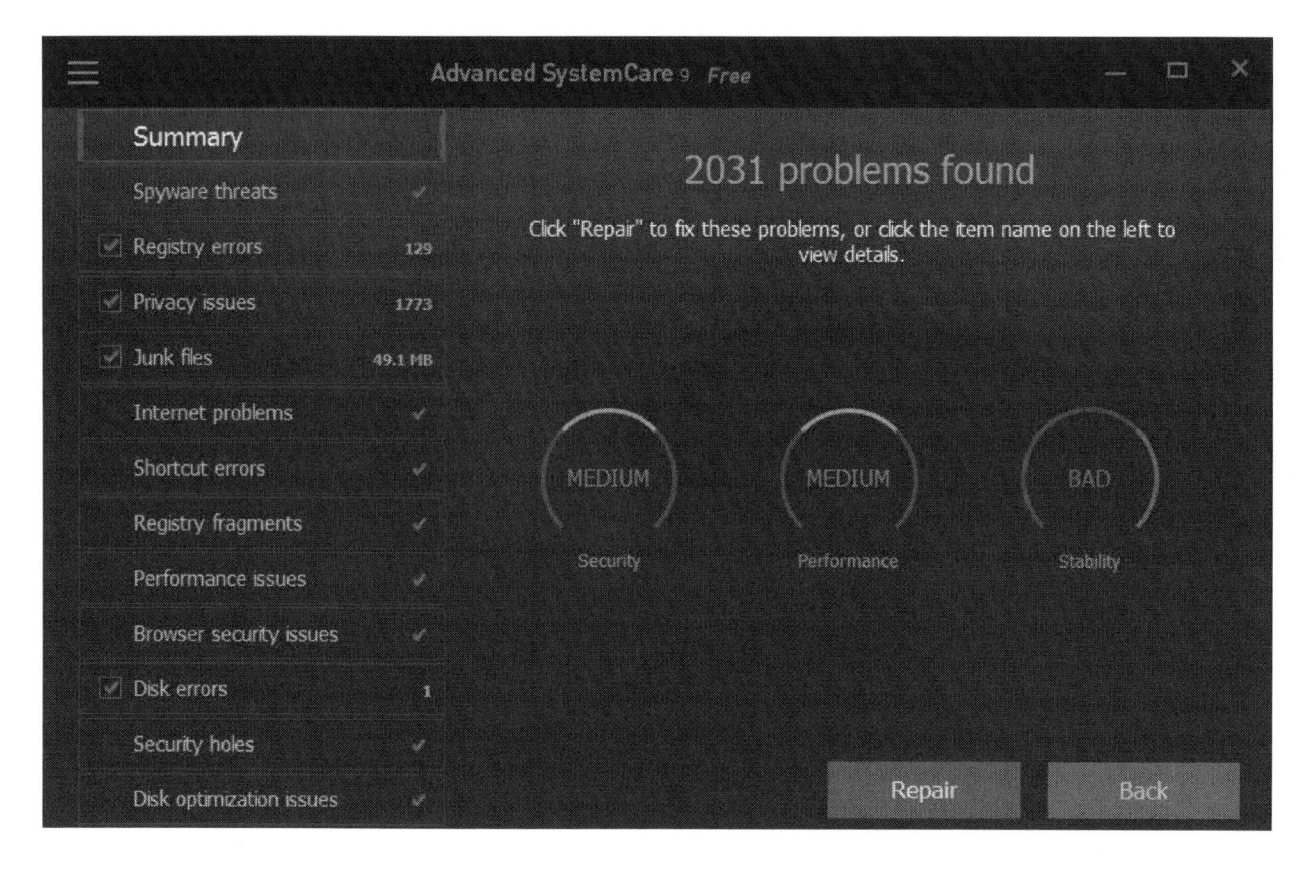

Click on the Repair button to fix and repair problems that the software has identified and that will restore full speed and functionality to your machine. Advanced System Care then refreshes this display window with updated information showing that your machine is in great shape and ready to go.

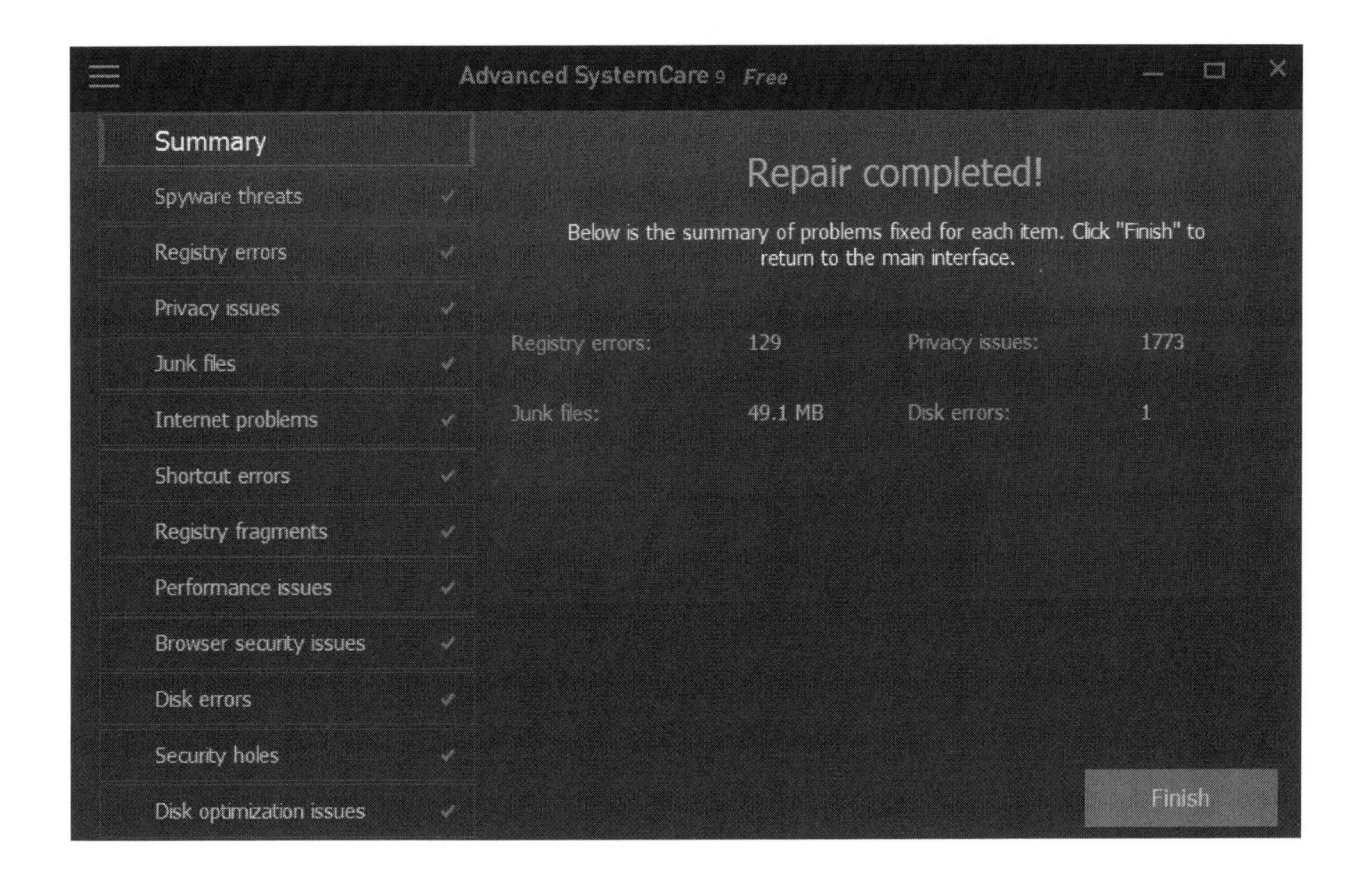

Click on the Finish button to close Advanced System Care. You might be prompted with a message in this window that says "you are not currently protected with a third party antivirus software. Click here to download Advanced System Care Pro". This is optional only and you are under no obligation to do this. However, if you want to spend a few dollars for the premium version of this software, it is excellent and definitely not a waste of money. To download Advanced System Care, go to the following website and download the installation file from there: http://www.iobit.com.

As a Technical Writer, my computer is a way of life and a professional platform so I need to have my machine bug-free; therefore I always have the latest versions of both Windows 10 Defender and Advanced System Care from iObit.

One final resource that will add to the overall security of your computer is a product called "Hopla!" made by a company named Wistiki. Wistiki products carry an RFID chip that enables you, via a smartphone app, to locate your computer, tablet, or phone or even wallet if misplaced. You can use the app to initiate a sound from the attached card on your device and then you can locate it easily. Wistiki products also use product crowdsourcing where if another person is close by your computer or tablet then that app is used to relay a message to the Wistiki server and back to your smartphone helping you to locate your misplaced computer or tablet or phone. You can learn more by visiting this company's website at this URL: http://www.wistiki.com.

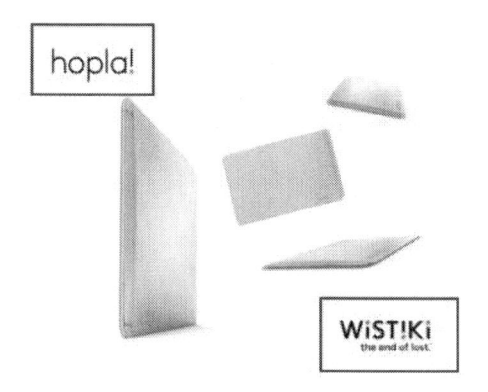

Here is the URL of an article I wrote on **LinkedIn Pulse** back in December of 2015 for Wistiki. They were also a leading-recognized company at the recent Consumer Electronics Show (CES) in Las Vegas, Nevada for their accomplishments in the area of technology security.

https://www.linkedin.com/pulse/let-wistiki-help-you-find-important-items-keith-johnson

Here is an article I wrote about Wistiki on my Tech Writing blog, showcasing all of the company's major products (a bit more in-depth than the LinkedIn article).

http://www.techwriterguy.com/2015/12/wistiki-end-of-lost.html

So, in conclusion the way I keep my Windows 10 computer safe and secure is by (1) working with the Microsoft Updates process on a regular basis, (2) using Windows 10 Defender on a regular basis, (3) using Advanced System Care on a weekly basis, and (4) attaching a Wistiki RFID-enabled card to my PC in case I misplace it and need to locate it quickly.

Section 89: Windows 10 Settings for Computer Backup

Go to Start Menu > Settings > Updates and Security > Backup.

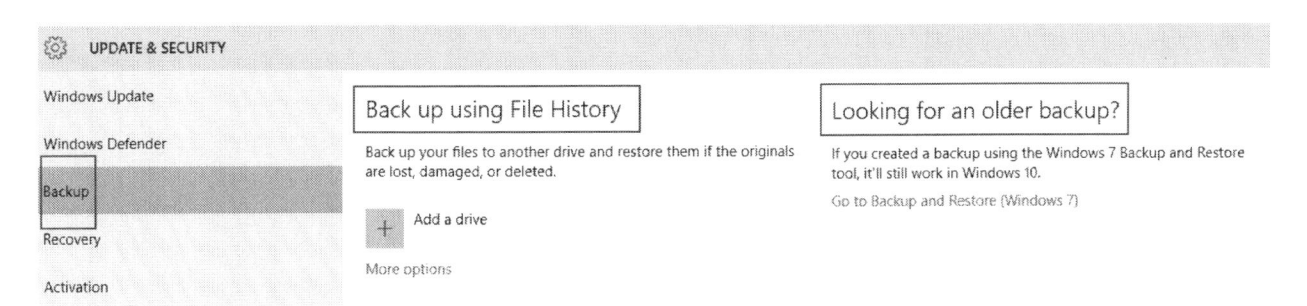

UPDATE & SECURITY		
Windows Update	**Back up using File History**	**Looking for an older backup?**
Windows Defender	Back up your files to another drive and restore them if the originals are lost, damaged, or deleted.	If you created a backup using the Windows 7 Backup and Restore tool, it'll still work in Windows 10.
Backup	+ Add a drive	Go to Backup and Restore (Windows 7)
Recovery	More options	
Activation		

Now that we have addressed 98% of what needs to be covered in this book regarding Windows 10, there three final Settings options I need to address – Backup, Recovery, and Activation. This page deals with Backup. Most importantly, you need to keep a backup of your INSTALLATION file for Windows 10. Depending on how you got Windows 10 onto your machine, you need to have this file backed up for your own good. I personally recommend you have an external drive that you can connect via your USB drive. That is the easiest path in my humble opinion. Next, you need to have backups of your software/apps. Perhaps you have some downloads and some installation DVDs. In the similar spirit, keep backups of these for your own good. Finally, for your data, you can manually copy files to an external drive or to a trustworthy Cloud drive like your Google Drive or Microsoft OneDrive – both are excellent. These are all hands-on manual and human-sides processes. To automate this process, you can use the Backup Settings option that you see in the sample screen shot above.

First, plug in your backup drive to your USB port. I recommend you have an external drive that is at least as big as your primary C: drive. Go to Backup and then click on the + Add a Drive button you see. A popup window is shown where you can select the attached backup drive. In my case here, as an example, I have a Free Agent Flex Drive. Let us select this.

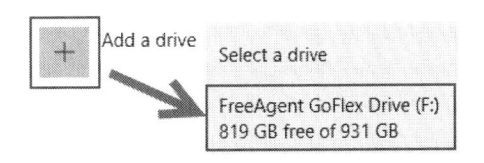

+ Add a drive → Select a drive
FreeAgent GoFlex Drive (F:)
819 GB free of 931 GB

Windows 10 then recommend that you back up your files using a File History method. For this to work, you need to leave the Setting "Automatically back up my files" ON. To learn more about this option, click on the More options link.

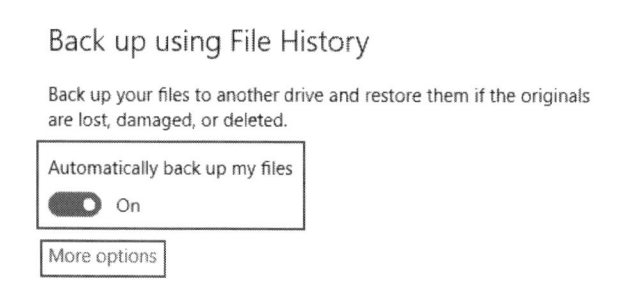

Back up using File History

Back up your files to another drive and restore them if the originals are lost, damaged, or deleted.

Automatically back up my files
On

More options

This is what Settings displays:

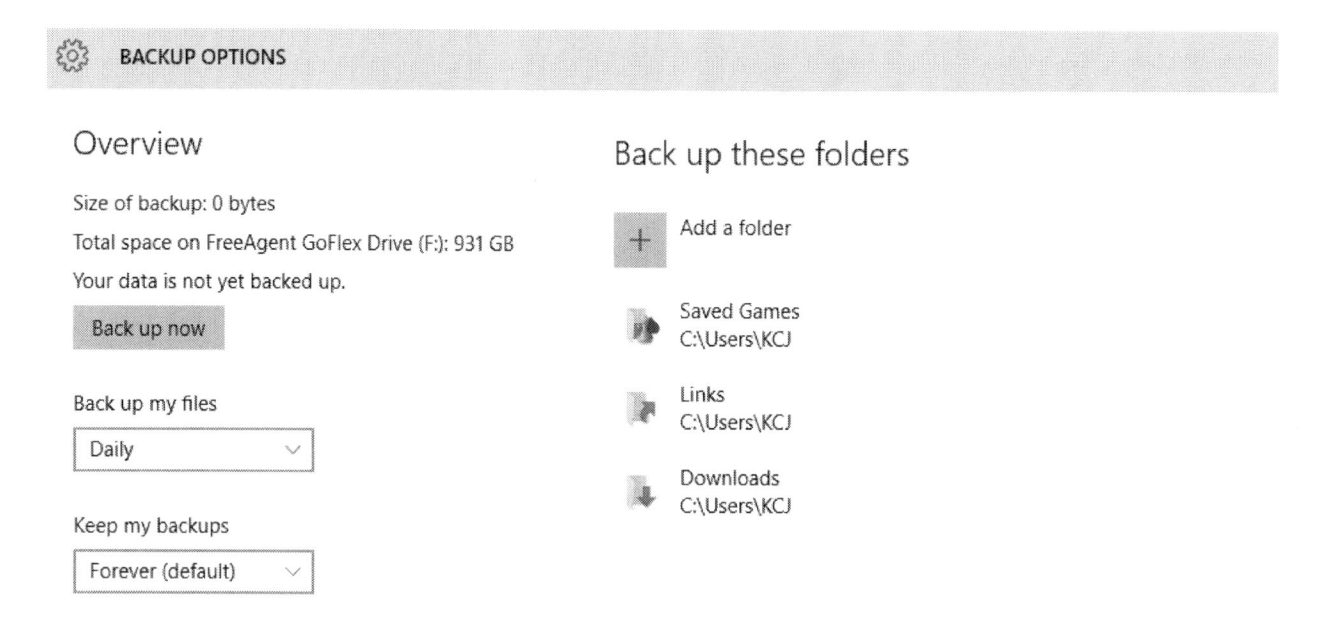

BACKUP OPTIONS

Overview

Size of backup: 0 bytes
Total space on FreeAgent GoFlex Drive (F:): 931 GB
Your data is not yet backed up.

Back up now

Back up my files

Daily

Keep my backups

Forever (default)

Back up these folders

Add a folder

Saved Games
C:\Users\KCJ

Links
C:\Users\KCJ

Downloads
C:\Users\KCJ

You can essentially establish your own "protocol" for backups. I personally need and prefer to back up my files on a daily basis and choose to keep my backups as long as possible. You can choose what is best for you here. Remember that this Windows 10 interface is designed to be user-friendly so as soon as you make a Settings change – that change is instantly implemented and recognized by Windows – three is no need to keep on clicking "Save" button after "Save" button like you had to do with earlier versions of Windows. As soon as you are ready to back up your files, click on the "Back up now" button and just follow Microsoft's lead until this process is finished.

Section 90: Windows 10 Settings for Recovery

Go to Start Menu > Settings > Updates and Security > Recovery.

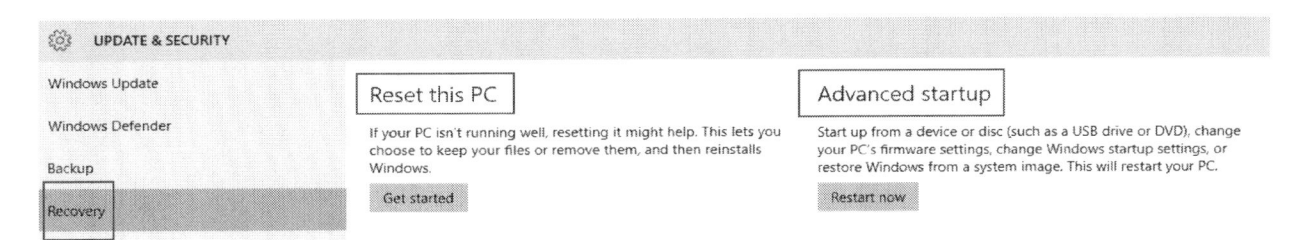

![Update & Security Recovery screen showing Reset this PC and Advanced startup options]

The Recovery Settings option is designed to help you restore your computer to full functionality and operability with Windows 10. There are two important players in this process – the actual hardware of your computer and the release of Windows 10 that you have on your computer. Before using either the "Reset this PC" or "Advanced Startup" options, I *would first consult* with the manufacturer of your computer to see what troubleshooting can be done from its end.

Many times, OEMs (Original Equipment Manufacturers) like Dell and Toshiba and Acer have special tools and files from Microsoft that you don't – even if you are a legitimate and registered Windows 10 user. So, having a tech support specialist remote into your machine and/or send a needed file can spare you this entire journey of resetting your computer. Try that first if your computer is having problems.

Only and only after first consulting with your PC manufacturer, try the "Reset This PC" option. This is a manual process from within Windows 10 that lets you choose specific files – to keep them or remove them – in hopes that this decision process will help to restore full Windows 10 functionality. Click "Get started" to initiate this process. **I recommend that only Windows 10 System Administrators actually carry out this operation.**

For those of you who have your Windows 10 Installation file (usually an ISO file) and who have ALREADY backed up your applications and data files, you can use the "Advanced Startup" option. Click on the "Restart now" button and follow Microsoft's lead throughout this process. **I recommend that only Windows 10 System Administrators actually carry out this operation.**

Section 91: Windows 10 Settings for License Activation

Go to Start Menu > Settings > Updates and Security > Activation.

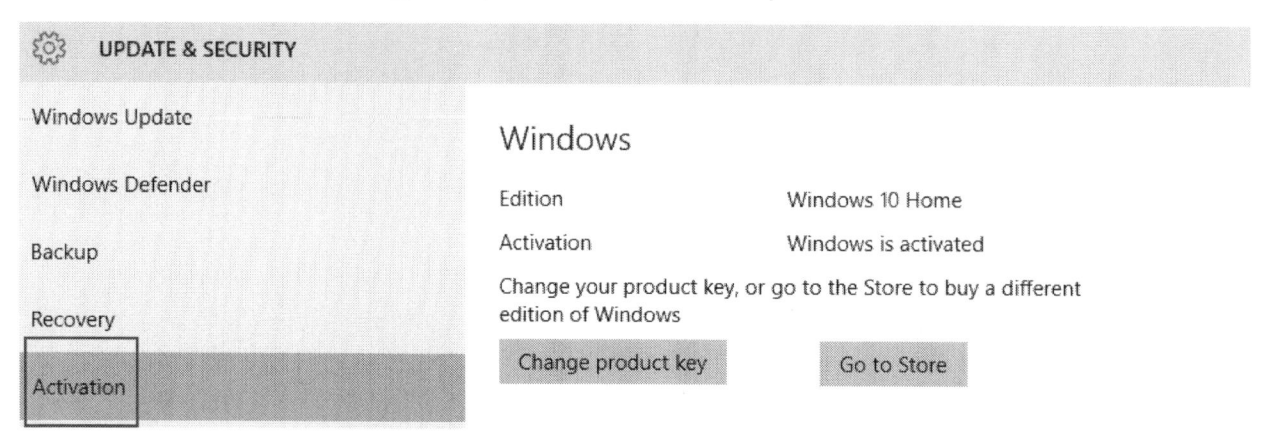

The Activation Settings option is here for two purposes.

First, if you have installed Windows 10 and only have a temporary key or a key given to you through the Windows Insider program, clicking on the "change product key" button will allow you to send Microsoft a new and permanent key that will get you out of key-limbo and into permanent product registration status with Microsoft. This will help to legitimize and establish the Update process for your machine. *Second,* let us imagine that you have Windows 10 Home but want to upgrade to Windows 10 Pro, you can do this through the "Go to Store" button. At the Microsoft Store you will find Windows 10 Pro and can make your upgrade there. Follow Microsoft's lead for this upgrade process.

Section 92: Windows 10 Action Center

Last but not least we have the Windows 10 Action Center! At your Windows 10 Home Screen, *on the far right side of your taskbar*, you will see an icon that looks like a "quotations emoticon". This is the icon and one-click shortcut to your Windows 10 Action Center. Single click on this icon.

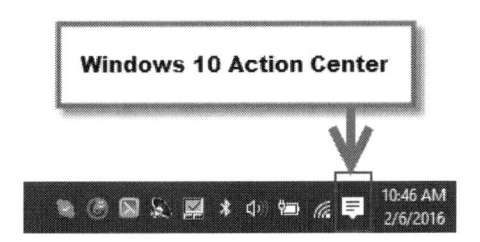

Windows 10 opens your Action Center as follows (The normal display is totally vertical: Action center ... then Mail ... then Action Tiles. But to optimize the space of this book and keep it under 250 pages, I have had to show several screen shots like this one in "pieces" across an available horizontal space):

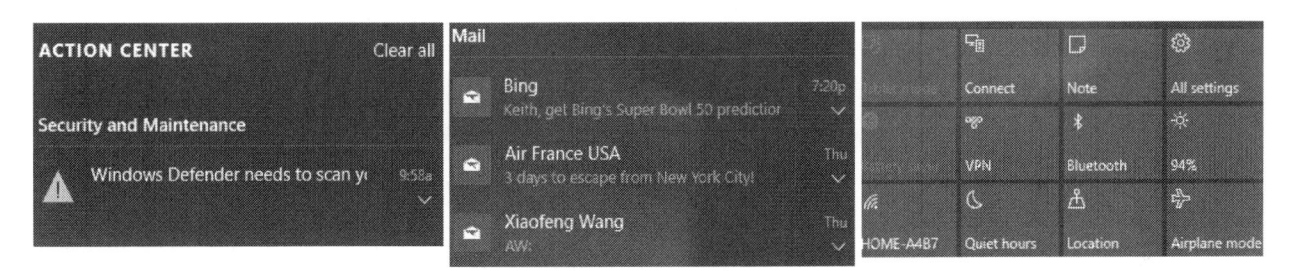

Action Center shows immediate tasks that Windows 10 recommends for you. There are different icons displayed next to the task to indicate its importance. Yellow icons are warning versus red icons are serious and should be taken care of immediately. Mail is incorporated into the Action Center as a convenience. You can attend to emails as you have time. Finally, the last section is Action Tiles that are essentially shortcuts to Settings options that govern your overall Windows 10 experience: Mode of display (tablet mode does not apply here because I have a laptop and not a Surface Pro or actual tablet), Connect (this helps you connect to other devices like an iPad or Android tablet or Windows tablet), Note (this is a shortcut to OneNote if you have Microsoft Office on your computer), All settings (this takes you to the Parent Window for all Settings options), Battery saver (this option must be on for you to access the Battery Saver Setting), VPN (this is to help you manage a Virtual Private Network connection if you have one), Bluetooth (this helps you to manage connections with tablets, computers, and more that are engaged via Bluetooth devices), Monitor or Screen Display Brightness Percentage, Wi-Fi Sense (shows your current Wi-Fi connection), Quiet Time – is when you choose *not* to display notifications on your computer, Location Setting (if you right click on any of these tiles, this one too, then you are directed to the respective Settings Option where you can set the customized value or ON/OFF setting that is best for you), and Airplane Mode (this is when you need to disengage from Wi-Fi, VPN, and Network connections like when you are on an airplane and it is either taking off or landing and Federal Aviation mandates require you to set your device(s) to Airplane Mode for about 15 minutes).

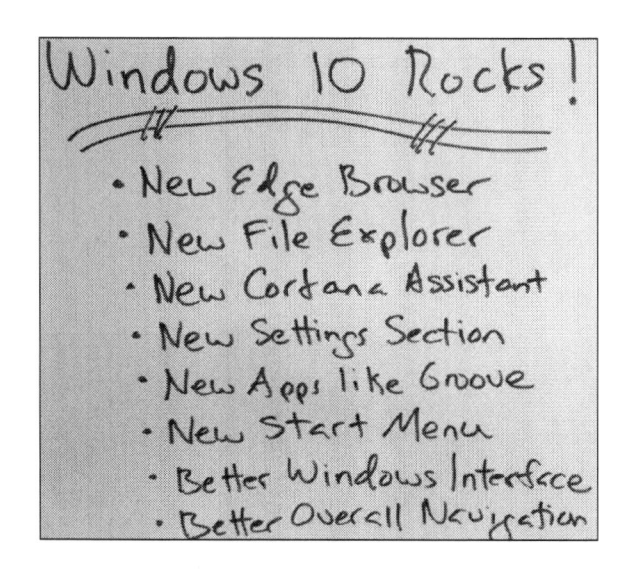

> **Windows 10 Rocks!**
> - New Edge Browser
> - New File Explorer
> - New Cortana Assistant
> - New Settings Section
> - New Apps like Groove
> - New Start Menu
> - Better Windows Interface
> - Better Overall Navigation

Section 93: Thank You for Reading

Dear Reader ... Thank you for your time amidst your busy day-to-day schedule and life in general. Not only is it hard to find time to write a book, but sometimes it is even more difficult to find time to read a book – because this requires attention to what has been written and taking on new ideas that challenge your current level of understanding. This is never easy. So, I say KUDOS to you. Over the years, Microsoft products like Windows and Office have enabled me to accomplish many great things in my Technical Writing career. I believe that Windows 10 is a great release of the Windows Operating System.

I sincerely hope this book helps you to get the most out of Windows 10.

Best Regards to you and yours.

Keith Johnson, Senior Technical Writer
www.techwriterguy.com
www.lulu.com/techwriterguy
www.amazon.com/author/techwriterguy

Section 94: References (by Section)

About

Words of author only.

The Windows Saga: Windows 1 to Windows 10

https://en.wikipedia.org/wiki/Windows_1.0

https://en.wikipedia.org/wiki/Windows_2.0

https://en.wikipedia.org/wiki/Windows_3.0

https://en.wikipedia.org/wiki/Windows_3.1x

https://en.wikipedia.org/wiki/Windows_NT_3.5

https://en.wikipedia.org/wiki/Windows_95

https://en.wikipedia.org/wiki/Windows_98

https://en.wikipedia.org/wiki/Windows_2000

https://en.wikipedia.org/wiki/Windows_ME

https://en.wikipedia.org/wiki/Windows_XP

https://en.wikipedia.org/wiki/Windows_Server_2003

https://en.wikipedia.org/wiki/Windows_Vista

https://en.wikipedia.org/wiki/Windows_Server_2008

https://en.wikipedia.org/wiki/Windows_7

https://en.wikipedia.org/wiki/Windows_8

https://en.wikipedia.org/wiki/Windows_10

Windows 10 Welcomes You

https://blogs.windows.com/windowsexperience/2015/07/30/windows-10-the-first-24-hours/

Windows 10 Best New Features

Improved Start Menu

http://windows.microsoft.com/en-us/windows-10/getstarted-see-whats-on-the-menu

OneDrive

http://windows.microsoft.com/en-us/onedrive/skydrive-to-onedrive

Groove Music

https://www.microsoft.com/en-US/store/apps/Groove-Music/9WZDNCRFJ3PT

WiFi Sense

http://windows.microsoft.com/en-us/windows-10/wi-fi-sense-faq

Microsoft Edge

http://windows.microsoft.com/en-us/windows-10/edge-privacy-faq

Settings in Windows 10

http://windows.microsoft.com/en-us/windows-10/getstarted-a-new-look-for-settings

Windows 10 Hello Secure Login

http://windows.microsoft.com/en-us/windows-10/getstarted-what-is-hello

Windows 10 Cortana

http://windows.microsoft.com/en-us/windows-10/getstarted-what-is-cortana

File Explorer

http://windows.microsoft.com/en-us/windows-10/windows-explorer-has-a-new-name

Windows 10 Editions Released by Microsoft

http://windowsreport.com/windows-10-retail-packaging

https://www.microsoft.com/en-us/windows

Windows 10 Installation & Activation

http://windows.microsoft.com/en-us/windows-10/upgrade-to-windows-10-faq

Windows 10 Logging On Steps

http://windows.microsoft.com/en-us/windows/accounts

Section 06: Windows 10 User Interface

http://windows.microsoft.com/en-us/windows-10/keyboard-shortcuts

Windows 10 User Navigation

http://windows.microsoft.com/en-us/windows-10/getstarted-see-whats-on-the-menu

http://windows.microsoft.com/en-us/windows-10/keyboard-shortcuts

Windows 10 "Cortana"

http://windows.microsoft.com/en-us/windows-10/getstarted-what-is-cortana

Windows 10 File Search

http://windows.microsoft.com/en-us/windows-10/getstarted-search-for-anything-cortana

Windows 10 "Edge" Web Browser

http://windows.microsoft.com/en-ph/windows-10/getstarted-get-to-know-microsoft-edge

Windows 10 Skype App

http://blogs.skype.com/2015/01/22/skype-in-windows-10-preview-built-into-windows-10-so-you-can-do-more-with-friends-across-devices/

https://support.skype.com/en/skype/windows-desktop

Windows 10 Entertainment & OneDrive

http://windows.microsoft.com/en-us/windows-10/what-is-the-microsoft-groove-music-app

http://windows.microsoft.com/en-us/windows-10/getstarted-onedrive

Windows 10 Accessing Apps

http://windows.microsoft.com/en-us/windows/taskbar-overview#1TC=windows-7

Windows 10 Accessories

http://www.techwriterguy.com/2016/01/windows-10-accessory-apps.html

Windows 10 Administration

http://www.techwriterguy.com/2016/01/windows-10-administrative-tools.html

Windows 10 Ease of Access

http://windows.microsoft.com/en-us/windows-10/getstarted-make-your-pc-easier-to-use

http://www.techwriterguy.com/2016/02/windows-10-ease-of-access-apps.html

https://commons.wikimedia.org/wiki/File:Magnifying_Glass_Photo.jpg

https://en.wikipedia.org/wiki/Microsoft_Narrator

Windows 10 Powershell

https://en.wikipedia.org/wiki/Windows_PowerShell

http://www.techwriterguy.com/2016/02/windows-10-powershell-apps.html

Windows 10 System Apps

http://www.techwriterguy.com/2016/02/windows-10-system-apps-folder.html

https://en.wikipedia.org/wiki/List_of_DOS_commands

https://en.wikipedia.org/wiki/Run_command

http://www.symantec.com/connect/articles/list-run-commands-windows-7-and-8

Windows 10 Total Apps – Listing

http://www.techwriterguy.com/2016/02/total-apps-listing-for-windows-10-home.html

Windows 10 Settings – Overview

http://www.techwriterguy.com/2016/02/total-apps-listing-for-windows-10-home.html

Windows 10 Settings for System – Overview

http://www.cnet.com/how-to/windows-10-settings-menu-the-system-tab/

Windows 10 System Display

http://www.tenforums.com/tutorials/4910-screen-resolution-display-change-windows-10-a.html

Windows 10 System Notification

http://www.keithjohnson.us/2016/02/windows-10-notifications-and-actions.html

Windows 10 System Apps and Features
http://www.keithjohnson.us/2016/02/windows-10-apps-and-features.html

Windows 10 System Multitasking
http://www.keithjohnson.us/2016/02/windows-10-multitasking-settings-option.html

Windows 10 System Tablet Mode
http://windows.microsoft.com/en-us/windows-10/getstarted-like-a-tablet

Windows 10 System Battery Saver
http://www.makeuseof.com/tag/can-extend-battery-life-windows-10-battery-saver/

Windows 10 Power and Sleep
http://www.techwriterguy.com/2016/02/windows-10-power-and-sleep-settings.html

Windows 10 Storage
http://www.techwriterguy.com/2016/02/windows-10-storage-system-settings.html

Windows 10 Offline Maps
http://www.techwriterguy.com/2016/02/windows-10-offline-maps-system-settings.html

Windows 10 Default Apps
http://www.techwriterguy.com/2016/02/windows-10-default-apps-system-settings.html

Windows 10 "About"
http://www.techwriterguy.com/2016/02/windows-10-about-system-settings-option.html

Windows 10 Settings for Devices – Overview
http://www.techwriterguy.com/2016/02/windows-10-devices-settings-options.html

Windows 10 Settings for Printing/Scanning
http://www.keithjohnson.us/2016/02/windows-10-printers-and-scanners.html

Windows 10 Settings for Connected Devices
http://www.keithjohnson.us/2016/02/windows-10-connected-devices.html

Windows 10 Settings for Bluetooth
http://www.techwriterguy.com/2016/02/windows-10-bluetooth-settings-option.html

Windows 10 Settings for Mouse/Touchpad
http://www.techwriterguy.com/2016/02/windows-10-mouse-and-touch-pad-settings.html

Windows 10 Settings for Typing
http://www.techwriterguy.com/2016/02/windows-10-typing-settings-option.html

Windows 10 Settings for Autoplay
http://www.techwriterguy.com/2016/02/windows-10-autoplay-settings-option.html

Windows 10 Settings for Network and Internet

http://www.techwriterguy.com/2016/02/windows-10-settings-options-for-network.html

Windows 10 Settings for WiFi (Sense)

http://www.techwriterguy.com/2016/02/windows-10-wifi-sense-settings-option.html

Windows 10 Settings for Airplane Mode

https://en.wikipedia.org/wiki/Airplane_mode

http://windows.microsoft.com/en-us/windows-10/turn-on-airplane-mode

Windows 10 Settings for Data Usage

http://windows.microsoft.com/en-us/windows-10/set-your-data-limit

https://en.wikipedia.org/wiki/Data

Windows 10 Settings for VPN

https://en.wikipedia.org/wiki/Virtual_private_network

http://windows.microsoft.com/en-us/windows/set-workplace-remote-connection-vpn#1TC=windows-7

Windows 10 Settings for Dialup

https://en.wikipedia.org/wiki/Dial-up_Internet_access

http://windows.microsoft.com/en-us/windows-vista/advanced-dial-up-settings

Windows 10 Settings for Ethernet

https://en.wikipedia.org/wiki/Ethernet

http://windows.microsoft.com/en-us/windows/setting-home-network#1TC=windows-7

Windows 10 Settings for Proxy

https://en.wikipedia.org/wiki/Proxy_server

http://www.cnet.com/how-to/windows-10-settings-menu-the-network-internet-tab/

Windows 10 Settings for Personalization – Overview

http://www.techwriterguy.com/2016/02/windows-10-personalization-settings.html

Windows 10 Settings for Background

http://www.techwriterguy.com/2016/02/windows-10-background-personalization.html

Windows 10 Settings for Colors

http://windows.microsoft.com/en-us/windows-10/getstarted-change-desktop-background

Windows 10 Settings for Lock Screen

http://windows.microsoft.com/en-us/windows-10/getstarted-lock-screen

Windows 10 Settings for Themes

http://windows.microsoft.com/en-us/windows-10/getstarted-get-started-with-themes

Windows 10 Settings for Start

http://www.pcworld.com/article/2960788/windows/how-to-customize-windows-10s-start-menu.html

http://www.techwriterguy.com/2016/02/windows-10-start-personalization.html

Windows 10 Settings for Accounts – Overview

http://www.techwriterguy.com/2016/02/windows-10-account-settings-option.html

Windows 10 Settings for Your Account

http://www.techwriterguy.com/2016/02/windows-10-your-account-settings-option.html

Windows 10 Settings for Sign-In Options

http://www.techwriterguy.com/2016/02/windows-10-sign-in-settings-option.html

Windows 10 Settings for Work Access

http://www.windowscentral.com/manage-user-accounts-windows-10

Windows 10 Settings for Family

Same as above.

Windows 10 Settings to Sync Devices

Same as above.

Windows 10 Settings for Time/Language – Overview

http://www.techwriterguy.com/2016/02/windows-10-time-and-language-settings.html

Windows 10 Settings for Date/Time

http://www.cnet.com/how-to/windows-10-settings-menu-the-time-language-tab/

Windows 10 Settings for Region/Language

Same as above.

Windows 10 Settings for Speech

Same as above.

Windows 10 Settings for Ease of Access

http://www.techwriterguy.com/2016/02/windows-10-ease-of-access-settings.html

Windows 10 Settings for Narrator

http://windows.microsoft.com/en-us/windows-10/getstarted-make-your-pc-easier-to-use

Windows 10 Settings for Magnifier

Same as above.

Windows 10 Settings for High Contrast

Same as above.

Windows 10 Settings for Closed Captions

Same as above.

Windows 10 Settings for Keyboard

Same as above.

Windows 10 Settings for Mouse

Same as above.

Windows 10 Settings for Other Devices

Same as above.

Windows 10 Settings for Privacy

http://www.techwriterguy.com/2016/02/windows-10-privacy-settings-options.html

Windows 10 Settings for General Privacy

http://www.keithjohnson.us/2016/02/windows-10-general-privacy-settings.html

Windows 10 Settings for Location

http://www.keithjohnson.us/2016/02/windows-10-location-privacy-settings.html

Windows 10 Settings for Camera

http://windows.microsoft.com/en-us/windows-10/camera-privacy-faq

Windows 10 Settings for Microphone

http://www.techwriterguy.com/2016/02/windows-10-privacy-settings-option-for.html

Windows 10 Settings for Speech/Inking/Typing

http://windows.microsoft.com/en-us/windows-10/speech-inking-typing-privacy-faq

Windows 10 Settings for Account Information

http://www.techwriterguy.com/2016/02/windows-10-privacy-settings-option-for_7.html

Windows 10 Settings for Contacts

http://www.techwriterguy.com/2016/02/windows-10-contacts-privacy-setting.html

Windows 10 Settings for Calendar

http://www.techwriterguy.com/2016/02/windows-10-privacy-setting-for-calendar.html

Windows 10 Settings for Messaging

http://www.techwriterguy.com/2016/02/windows-10-messaging-privacy-setting.html

Windows 10 Settings for Radios

http://www.techwriterguy.com/2016/02/windows-10-privacy-setting-for-radios.html

Windows 10 Settings for Other Devices

http://www.techwriterguy.com/2016/02/windows-10-other-devices-privacy-setting.html

Windows 10 Settings for Feedback & Diagnostics

http://windows.microsoft.com/en-us/windows-10/feedback-diagnostics-privacy-faq

Windows 10 Settings for Background Apps

http://www.tenforums.com/tutorials/7225-background-apps-turn-off-windows-10-a.html

Windows 10 Settings for Update/Security

http://www.techwriterguy.com/2016/02/this-is-microsoft-windows-10-settings.html

Windows 10 Settings for Windows Update

http://www.cnet.com/how-to/windows-10-settings-menu-the-update-recovery-tab/

Windows 10 Settings for Windows Defender

Same as above.

https://en.wikipedia.org/wiki/Windows_Defender

Windows 10 Settings for Computer Backup

Same as Windows Update.

https://en.wikipedia.org/wiki/Backup

Windows 10 Settings for Recovery

Same as Windows Update.

Windows 10 Settings for License Activation

Same as Windows Update.

Windows 10 Action Center

https://en.wikipedia.org/wiki/Action_Center

Thank You for Reading

Words of author only.

Printed in Great Britain
by Amazon